First Strike

Preemptive warfare is the practice of attempting to avoid an enemy's seemingly imminent attack by taking military action against them first. It is undertaken in self-defense. Preemptive war is often confused with *preventive war*, which is an attack launched to defeat a potential opponent and is an act of aggression. Preemptive war is thought to be justified and honorable, while preventive war violates international law. In reality, the distinction between the two is often blurred and highly contested.

In *First Strike*, author Matthew J. Flynn examines case studies of preemptive war throughout history, from Napoleonic France to the American Civil War, and from Hitler's Germany to the recent US invasion of Iraq. Flynn takes an analytical look at the international uses of this military and political tactic throughout the last two hundred years of western history, to show how George W. Bush's recent use of this dubiously "honorable" way of making war is really just the latest in a long line of previously failed attempts.

Balanced and historically grounded, *First Strike* provides a comprehensive study of one of the most controversial military strategies in the history of international foreign policy.

Matthew J. Flynn is Assistant Professor of twentieth-century military and US diplomatic history at Arizona State University's Department of Language, Cultures, and History. He is the author of *China Contested: Western Powers in East Asia*.

"In *First Strike*, Matthew Flynn draws on a rich set of historical case studies to advance a powerful case against preventive and pre-emptive war. A timely and important contribution to one of the key military issues of the post-9/11 era."

—Robert Singh, co-editor of *The Bush Doctrine and the War on Terrorism: Global Reactions, Global Consequences* (Routledge)

"Matthew Flynn's *First Strike* presents a hard-hitting, provocative assessment of the Bush administration's doctrine of preemptive warfare and its application to Saddam Hussein's Iraqi regime in 2003. By reviewing earlier instances of preemptive war, from Napoleon's campaign of 1805 to Israel's Six Day War of 1967, he demonstrates that the temptation to 'strike while the iron is hot' motivated the instigators of most of the major conflicts of the past two centuries. He shows how national leaders frequently exaggerated the threat posed by the intended victim in order to win public support and establish the moral justification for preemption."

—William Keylor, author of *A World of Nations: The International Order since 1945*

"Matthew Flynn engages with current events by placing the invasion of Iraq in an historical perspective. The difficulties of preemptive war are clearly indicated. This provocative book will not convince all, but it is an important contribution to the literature."

—Jeremy Black, author of *Rethinking Military History* (Routledge)

First Strike

Preemptive War in Modern History

Matthew J. Flynn

Routledge
Taylor & Francis Group

NEW YORK AND LONDON

First published 2008
by Routledge
270 Madison Ave, New York, NY 10016

Simultaneously published in the UK
by Routledge
2 Park Square, Milton Park, Abingdon, Oxon OX14 4RN

Routledge is an imprint of the Taylor & Francis Group, an informa business

© 2008 Taylor & Francis

Typeset in Minion by
Florence Production Ltd, Stoodleigh, Devon

Printed and bound in the United States of America on acid-free paper
by Edwards Brothers, Inc.

Library of Congress Cataloging in Publication Data
Flynn, Matthew J.
    First strike: preemptive warfare in modern history/Matthew J. Flynn.
        p. cm.
    Includes bibliographical references and index.
    1. Preemptive attack (Military science) – Case studies.   2. Just war
    doctrine.   3. Military history, Modern.   I. Title.
    U163.F59 2008
    355.4'22 – dc22   2007038276

ISBN10: 0–415–95844–X (hbk)
ISBN10: 0–415–95845–8 (pbk)
ISBN10: 0–203–92926–8 (ebk)

ISBN13: 978–0–415–95844–8 (hbk)
ISBN13: 978–0–415–95845–5 (pbk)
ISBN13: 978–0–203–92926–1 (ebk)

To my wife, family, friends, and students.

Contents

Introduction

Today, the United States finds itself involved in an ugly guerrilla war in Iraq, one draining its manpower, its resources, and its national will. The fight in Iraq also raises questions of the usefulness of this war in the American effort to protect itself from further terrorist attacks in the post-9/11 era. To some, victory appears far off, to others, it seems unattainable. Most agree that it is not clear what will constitute victory. These are troubling times and Americans are looking for answers as to why the United States may have to settle for less than total victory on the battlefield. A key reason is the Bush preemptive doctrine. Here lies the source of the problems in Iraq. An explanation of American woes of facing, if not defeat in Iraq, an outcome certainly falling short of American aspirations of victory, must begin with the policy leading this nation into war in Iraq in the first place.

Preemptive Warfare

Nations covet preemption as a rationale for going to war. Preemption is when one nation launches a military strike against another after concluding that the other nation was threatening to attack it and do it great harm. This attack may or may not be preceded by a formal declaration of war. Because attacking first—or attacking before any additional attacks occur—preserves one's national integrity and can be thought of as an act of self-defense, a preemptive war is considered a just or moral war. By acting preemptively, the attacking nation can *start a war* and still claim the moral high ground of self-defense, avoiding the odious label of aggressor. Other nations may then join with that nation in waging a "just" war. International approbation of a preemptive attack also means the attacking nation has an increased likelihood of isolating the enemy, since few nations will come to the aid of the nation "deserving" such an attack. Theoretically then, when this international isolation is teamed with the crushing military blow envisioned by those launching the preemptive strike, the reason for acting preemptively is clear—the promise of winning a war in rapid fashion.

George W. Bush and Preemptive War

Preemption is seldom achieved, however, if at all. President George W. Bush's invasion of Iraq in March 2003 is the latest effort by a nation to attempt to act preemptively to attain the moral high ground in war, and the latest effort to fail. Bush's definition of preemption is confused, his administration's application of the preemptive doctrine flawed, and the goals of preemption contradictory. The consequences of this policy failure are profound for the United States. Not only is its security poorly served, but the moral purpose of US foreign policy is jeopardized as well. In striving for the moral high ground of preemption, Bush has put his nation on a path to follow in the footsteps of some of the most notorious aggressors in modern history.

First Strike puts the Bush administration's preemptive doctrine in historical perspective by placing it alongside an analysis of modern warfare. The origins of major, conventional wars of the past 200 years are examined through historical case studies that emphasize the preemptive nature of these conflicts. The preemptive characteristics of several regional conflicts that clearly contributed to the evolution of modern war have also been considered. The result is a look at a wide range of conflicts that allows a thorough analysis of preemption since 1800. These historical examples are then compared to the Bush preemptive rationale for war in Iraq in 2003. The final chapter assesses the uniqueness of Bush's preemptive doctrine and the value to the attacking nation of having acted preemptively.

The Historical Case Studies

By confining preemption to the dynamic of major or regional conventional wars, the definitional problem has again imposed limits on the study. A conventional war is but one type of war. Do guerrilla wars also start with preemptive attacks? What of limited wars or colonial wars? These considerations have been weighed and a focus on what many would consider unconventional war dismissed in favor of a focus on conventional war because it best matches Bush's use of preemptive doctrine. This is an irony of some significance given that the Bush doctrine of preemption is in response to a terrorist attack that was itself an act of unconventional war. Bush's reply with preemption is an effort to employ conventional force at the forefront of his response to the terror threat. The incongruity of this approach underscores the confusion endemic to the Bush policy of preemption. A look at preemption throughout history helps us to better understand how this confusion arose.

It is helpful to the examples that follow to restate the definition of preemption offered above. First, a country can wage a preemptive war and therefore cling to the moral high ground of self-defense. This understanding of preemption holds to the narrowest definition of the term: attacking to meet an imminent threat to preserve one's national security. For this reason, most military experts agree that true preemption is a rare occurrence. Second, Bush's preemptive doctrine does not meet this strict definition because the American use of preemption against Iraq has expanded US power to the point where it has moved the country away from self-preservation. Preemption in this broader sense suddenly becomes much more frequent. It also becomes a justification for aggression.

The historical case studies make this distinction clear as well as outlining the consequences of this line of argument. Many of the most infamous aggressors of the past, as well as a few nations with less odious or even favorable reputations, can be said to have launched preemptive strikes in the name of self-defense under Bush's expanded definition of preemption. Are some of the great offenders in history to be given a reprieve and declared to be acting preemptively—that is, morally—or is the Bush policy of preemption to be condemned for pushing the United States in the direction of acting as an aggressor state? The choice is stark, but the historical context provided in the case studies here offers a compelling answer.

The first case study in Chapter 1 focuses on the emerging state of total war as defined in Europe at the turn of the nineteenth century. The foremost practitioner of this style of warfare was Napoleon Bonaparte, emperor of the French. Napoleon rose from obscurity to wield a powerful military apparatus that he unleashed on Europe, ostensibly to export the benefits of the French Revolution. Opposed by England and its coalition partners on the Continent, Bonaparte soon believed himself involved in a war of survival that justified preemptive strikes against what he termed "England's puppets" on the borders of France. This chapter captures his most spectacular success in preemptive war as he launched his seasoned army against the nations of Austria and Russia in the autumn of 1805.

Chapter 2 shifts to a case study examining an important regional war. The American Civil War added many facets to our understanding of modern war and the Southern belief that it had to fight a preemptive war is one of these contributions. The cultural fissures between the northern and southern geographical sections of the United States had reached such a point by the mid-1800s that Southerners could talk of a Northern oppression threatening their cherished way of life. Reduced to colony status, facing a belligerent North of growing power, the South had to act to blunt the aggression of its openly hostile neighbor. This chapter follows Southern resolve to launch a preemptive strike against the Union by initiating the "war between the states" at Fort Sumter in April 1861.

The third case study in Chapter 3 looks at a regional war in Asia at the turn of the twentieth century. The newly created Japanese state positioned itself against a flourishing background of European imperialism in Asia in the late 1800s. To defend itself and survive, Japan quickly learned to imitate its western competitors in the region. However, its own imperialism soon drew Japan into conflict with Russia over both Korea and Manchuria. Despite Japan's rapid modernization, it still contemplated war with Russia in foreboding terms. A preemptive strike at sea eased Japanese fears of not being able to successfully engage the Russian Empire, and it resolved to begin hostilities with a surprise attack on Russia's Asian fleet. Japan's preemptive strike at Port Arthur initiated the Russo-Japanese War in 1904. When it ended twenty months later, Japan had humbled Russia and established itself as a power in Asia.

Chapter 4 returns the focus to Europe and a case study involving Germany on the eve of World War I. Germany's own struggles with modern statehood propelled it on a collision course with the great powers of Europe. Determined to free itself from "encirclement" at the hands of the Russians in the east and due to French intransigence in the west, Germany searched for a successful military proscription that would allow it to wage war and establish itself as the dominant power in Europe. It decided on a preemptive strike, one directed at France alone, but sure to lead to war with not only France, but England and Russia as well. However, confident in the military advantage of acting preemptively, Germany reassured itself that it could overwhelm France in a matter of weeks, and then turn east to face the Russians. It was an incredible amount of reliance to place on the formula of preemption. Germany was willing to take the risk, and it set out on this road initiating World War I in August 1914.

The case studies in Chapters 5 and 6 have the unenviable task of comparing the two most infamous examples of aggression in modern warfare prior to US policy in the post-9/11 era. Regrettably, when following the logic of preemptive war as defined by the Bush administration, strong parallels can be established between the United States and both Nazi Germany and militarized Japan.

Germany is considered first in Chapter 5. Adolf Hitler succeeded in convincing the German people that war was necessary for the survival of a greater Germany. Germany's weakened power in the aftermath of World War I left it vulnerable to attack. Whether attack came from the west and the capitalist nations of France and England, or from the east and the Bolshevik state of Russia, Germany was surrounded by enemies seeking its destruction. To survive, Germany had to strike first and in a preemptive fashion to forestall the inevitable attacks of its enemies, singling out countries for destruction one at a time to ensure terms of war favorable to Germany. This chapter follows Hitler's success in first swaying the German people to this end and then in initiating a series of "preemptive" conquests up to June 1941 and the invasion of Russia.

Chapter 6 looks at Japan. Like Germany, the Empire of Japan embraced military might to serve the national good. And like Germany, the leadership of Japan argued that the nation had little choice but to act preemptively. Bent on war, the question for Japan was, which power posed the greatest threat to its survival: the USSR or the United States? Either way, war would be the option to deal with this threat, but it would have to be a preemptive war. Since both potential enemies refused to acquiesce to Japan's expansion in the Pacific, Japan had little choice but to launch a preemptive strike to cripple the military might of one of its enemies, which would allow it to then secure the natural resources it needed to fuel its industry and face the other threat. For Japan, this quest for economic enrichment and therefore national self-sufficiency meant a preemptive strike at the United States at Pearl Harbor on December 7, 1941.

One other key participant in World War II is also addressed in this study in Chapter 7. Stalin's determination to subjugate Finland in the early stages of World War II appeared to add another instance of aggression to a conflict already marred by the violence of German acts that brought about the war. Fearing attack from the west by either Germany or France and England, Stalin looked to carve out a buffer zone protecting the USSR. This "forward defense," as he termed it, stretched from Poland in the west to Finland in the north. When the Finns refused to come into the Soviet orbit, Stalin believed he had no choice but to act preemptively to assert Russian control over Finland, denying this country as a base for other powers inimical to the USSR. Facing uncertain times that posed unacceptable risks to the USSR, Stalin ordered his armies onto Finnish soil and started the "Winter War" in November 1939.

The case study in Chapter 8 addresses one of the numerous flash points of the Cold War where that conflict threatened to escalate to a general state of hostilities on a global level. The Korean War that erupted in 1950 was probably the most volatile of these situations. This conflict between North and South Korea quickly developed into a larger struggle, as first the United States and then Communist China entered the fray. The People's Republic of China (PRC) sent an army into North Korea to blunt a possible American drive from Korea into China to unseat the newly established Communist government. PRC leader Mao Zedong reasoned that it was better to act preemptively and fight in Korea than to allow an American thrust into China. This would be a preemptive war on ground ideally suited for defense and therefore favorable to the Chinese military. By exercising this right of self-defense in the last few months of 1950, the PRC placed itself in the midst of the Cold War by sending large numbers of its soldiers into Korea to confront American units advancing into the far reaches of North Korea.

Chapter 9 presents a case study at the crossroads of the Cold War conflict and the new struggle emerging involving terrorism. Israel's hard-fought for existence as a nation left it with sovereignty but also an unenviable defensive position. Surrounded by hostile enemies, the small state chose preemptive war as a national policy. This preference for preemptive strikes as a means of self-defense paid off spectacularly in 1967. Taking Arab propaganda at its word, the state of Israel looked to forestall the impending aggression of its neighbors against itself by launching a surprise attack using air power and rapid armored thrusts aimed at crippling Arab military might. In June of 1967, Israel achieved a remarkable victory made possible by a close adherence to a preemptive war policy that allowed for offensive operations in the name of self-defense.

The last case study in Chapter 10 examines the American assault on Iraq in March 2003, which formally initiated the preemptive war doctrine of the Bush administration. This chapter follows the evolution of the US policy of preemption in the wake of 9/11, and then tracks the push within the Bush administration for war in Iraq as a necessary first application of this policy. Stressing the unprecedented threat of weapons of mass destruction in the hands of Iraq's president Saddam Hussein, Bush believed he had no choice but to act preemptively and deter another 9/11-type attack on the United States. Confident that he was protecting both the United States and civilization, Bush ordered the US military to disarm Iraq and establish that country as a bulwark of democracy in the Middle East. The moral purpose that characterized American foreign policy now tested the merit of preemptive war.

These case studies cover the full range of preemptive war. Both the Confederacy's attack on Fort Sumter to start the Civil War and the Israeli attack opening the Six Day War reveal how a nation can act morally when using preemption to start a war. The seven other historical case studies demonstrate how preemption has been more commonly used as a shield for countries acting as aggressors against their neighbors than as a true moral right of self-defense. The final chapter illustrates how the United States now operates under a policy of preemption similar to the reasons for using military force offered by Napoleonic France, militarized Germany and Japan, Communist Russia, and the People's Republic of China, putting it squarely in the company of aggressors. This broad comparative historical analysis is needed to help determine the true measure of the shift of American policy from deterrence to preemption.

Preemption in the Literature

One of the more remarkable features of a study of preemption is that there are relatively few articles and books dedicated to the topic. Many of these, like Russ Howard's chapter, "Pre-emptive Military Doctrine: No Other Choice," in *The Changing Face of Terrorism*, and Robert J. Pauly Jr. and Tom Lansford's book, *Strategic Preemption: US Foreign Policy and the Second Iraq War*, endorse preemption as necessary given the unprecedented threat posed by terrorism. John Lewis Gaddis captures this alarm in *Surprise, Security, and the American Experience*, a book that offers his personal reflections on the significance of 9/11 and on what he sees as the bold policy initiative of President Bush. Betty Glad and Chris J. Dolan, in *Striking First: The Preventive War Doctrine and the Reshaping of US Foreign Policy*, and Erick Labara and James L. Clark, in *Preemptive War*, are more cautious. These authors and those included in their texts urge a more comprehensive understanding of the meaning and implications of preemption before supporting it as policy. My efforts in *First Strike* follow this lead of seeking a more complete analysis of preemption, in particular determining the significance of elevating this military tactic to the level of policy.

Most of this literature is dated post-2002, after Bush announced his policy. Prior to this development, little was said about preemption even among military historians. When it did receive attention, it came from an unlikely source. Those analyzing the concept of a "just war" naturally had to consider the morality of preemption. Michael Walzer's 1977 book, *Just and Unjust Wars: A Moral Argument with Historical Illustrations*, is probably the most widely read account of assigning morality in conflict. He narrows the use of preemption to only cases of imminent threat, and stresses the amorphous quality of the term "imminent." Therefore, a justified preemptive attack seldom occurs. Rejoinders are hard to find for two reasons. First, observers of interstate conflict believed preemption to be infrequent. So there were few examples to study. Second, when it did occur, experts considered it merely a tactic starting a war, not a policy unto itself. Therefore, it fell in the domain of military history, and given the diminished importance academia ascribed to that field, preemption as a topic suffered further neglect since professors at universities shunned the study of military history in general and military tactics specifically.

In the wake of the US invasion of Iraq, the literature on preemption has grown and now enjoys coverage by a variety of disciplines. Recently, James Turner Johnson returns to the just war theory typified by Walzer in *The War to Oust Saddam Hussein: Just War and the New Face of Conflict.* He concedes the difficulty of justifying preemption on the basis of imminent threat and instead drops preemption as a valid reason to go to war in Iraq and looks to other concerns that he believes make the war in Iraq a just war. Policy experts also weigh in on the topic. For example, Lyle J. Goldstein's book, *Preventive Attack and Weapons of Mass Destruction,* upholds preemption—he prefers the label preventive war—as a matter of law-abiding states protecting themselves from terrorist attacks of unfathomable dimensions given the proliferation of weapons of mass destruction. D. Robert Worley of the Strategic Studies Institute, in *Waging Ancient War: Limits on Preemptive Force,* argues that preemption is but a tactic and therefore must not play too large a role in balancing the military and nonmilitary aspects of policy, or what he labels "grand strategy." According to Worley, Goldstein's emphasis on preemption is misplaced. Legal experts have recently focused their attention on the topic as well. By and large they dispute the legal grounds for Bush's preemptive policy in Iraq as deviating too much from the concept of self-defense. Alan M. Dershowitz, in *Preemption: A Knife that Cuts Both Ways,* affirms this point but does not disallow the use of preemption in circumstances other than Iraq, a categorical rejection that Helen Duffy does make in her book, *The "War on Terror" and the Framework of International Law.*

The new and growing literature on preemption makes it clear that the topic lends itself to interdisciplinary study, perhaps requires it, and *First Strike* tries this approach by seeking to marry the fields of history and international relations. As mentioned, the first nine chapters of the book present historical examples of preemption. Given how Bush defined his policy of preemption, there are more examples to consider than one might expect. In each case, I rely on the rich secondary literature on the origins of the selected conflicts to craft a narrative of the preemptive act under consideration. The origins and articulation of the Bush doctrine are covered in Chapter 10. This analysis rests on primary sources. These are surprisingly available, in spite of the now famous secrecy of the Bush administration. So this contemporary subject, normally reserved for political scientists or those specializing in international relations, is treated in historical fashion and benefits from this approach. The conclusions in this chapter rest on a body of evidence that includes intelligence reports, leaked memoranda, government documents, and public statements by administration officials, sources more authoritative than the usual prevalence of news outlet citations so common in these contemporary studies.

History of this nature is still limited by a lack of sources. However, there is enough evidence to prove that the Bush administration confused its definition of preemption. It is unlikely additional source-work in archives opened twenty or more years from now will countermand this finding. Researchers may ask other questions, such as who most shaped the policy, or to what extent did Bush rely on his "gut" in embracing this policy. Most importantly, more research may reveal that behind the scenes powerful members of the administration gave much careful thought to the policy, that those weighing in on the policy did understand the confused terminology they employed and had some reason for doing so, perhaps a valid reason. Such a finding still does not weaken the conclusion offered here: that the public statements of officials of the Bush administration registered a confused policy and that despite this inaccuracy those making the comments insisted that this was the best course of action for the United States.

When the Bush policy of preemption is placed in historical context, the failure endemic in not clearly defining the policy becomes clear. Here lies the chief lesson of the book. Terms comprising an official policy connote great import, and these terms have to be defined carefully for the policy to work. A lack of clarity is dangerous since it leads to ambiguities that grow out of generalized language inherent in bad policy. Bad policy forfeits lives, wastes money, and, in a democracy, fragments the body politic into such diverse wings that the public's will to fight and meet real dangers is damaged to a perilous degree. This dissension means that implementation of a good policy is all the more difficult for a government to accomplish, and that the challenges it faces go unmet. In the security realm, this failure leaves a nation vulnerable to attack. When it came to preemption in Iraq, the Bush administration failed to understand that the language it used to define its preemptive policy compromised its duty to defend the United States from terrorism. This failure was never more harmful to US interests.

A Note on the References

The first nine chapters of this book offer an analytical synthesis of some famous history. The most important books utilized in writing these chapters are listed in the Select Bibliography. Additionally, in each of these chapters, all direct quotations are referenced with an asterisk (*) indicating the presence of a footnote at the bottom of the page. The final chapter, Chapter 10, "A Dangerous Simplicity," departs from this format since it is based on primary research. The documents and other reference material are cited in numeric endnotes appearing at the end of the chapter. A list of much of this primary source information appears in the Select Bibliography after Chapter 10.

CHAPTER 1

The Seven Streams: Napoleon Moves on Vienna, 1805

Introduction

In the late afternoon, Napoleon Bonaparte, Emperor of France for a year and a day, reviewed the field of Austerlitz. The battle was over and he was pleased. On this day, December 2, 1805, the French army had seized 12,000 prisoners, captured 180 cannon, and taken 50 standards. A further 15,000 Russians and Austrians lay dead on the field of battle. Napoleon had achieved a phenomenal success. His outnumbered forces had successfully defeated the combined strength of Austria and Russia deep in enemy territory and at the cost of not even 9,000 French casualties. The Austrians, having previously lost their capital of Vienna to the French and now having lost the major battle of the campaign, quickly sued for peace. The Russians fled back east whence they had come. In a swift, preemptive campaign, Napoleon had crushed two of the allied armies of the Third Coalition. Still, Napoleon's main enemy, England, remained unbeaten so no matter this victory, the war continued. To Napoleon, it was clear that just as this war had been forced upon him, so too would another. This reality dampened an otherwise glorious campaign.

Austerlitz established a Napoleonic presence in Europe in dramatic fashion. It would last another ten years, until Bonaparte met final defeat at the famous Battle of Waterloo in Belgium in June 1815. In this ten-year interval, he would march his armies into every capital on the European continent waging a series of "Napoleonic" wars. Before this point, the emperor's rise to power had been just as dramatic but on lesser playing fields. Trained as an artillery officer in the French Royal Army, the convulsions of the French Revolution handed the ambitious Bonaparte several opportunities for rapid advancement. First he expelled the English fleet from the port of Toulon. He then protected the revolutionary government, the Directory, when his cannon fired on a Paris mob. More significant commands followed. In 1797, Bonaparte's outnumbered and ill-supplied army overran the Austrians in Italy. The rising general next served as the expeditionary commander of a French army in Egypt. Returning to France in 1799, Napoleon had won enough acclaim through his military exploits to profit the most from a coup. He again won a victory over the Austrians in Italy in 1800, this time serving at the head of the French government as First Consul. Humbling France's military foes won converts at home, as did his efforts at healing France's revolutionary wounds. He rode this combination to absolute power, proclaiming himself emperor on December 2, 1804.

Given his expansion of French territory, it is hard to see Napoleon as anything other than an aggressor. The following pages reshape this outlook by analyzing the Napoleonic campaign of 1805 as an example of preemptive warfare. This view of Napoleon offers a much more sympathetic picture of him than that of an aggressor. He had always had his admirers but these writers had to confront the awful consequences of their hero's actions. It is estimated that 1.2 million Frenchmen died during the Napoleonic wars and countless other Europeans died as well. These horrible losses detracted from his genius tenfold. Surely only a man serving his own interests could pay such a price. To admire the man and his deeds meant condoning this loss of life. Most writers lauded his generalship and his military victories but not the aggression inherent in both. Now, from the gaze of preemption, the moral stain on Napoleon can be lifted and his military accomplishments and feats of generalship can stand unblemished and therefore supreme. Yet the pardon preemption offers Napoleon is not total since determining the morality of his actions remains a chief part of any analysis of his life. Aggression proves a hard stain to remove, as this chapter makes clear.

The Case for Preemption

Before 1805, Napoleon's preferred target had been England. How did the French army end up fighting on the Moravia plains northeast of Vienna in 1805? In the answer to this question lies the value of preemption. The latest round of English and French rivalry stretched back over a decade.

Already France had rebuffed two coalitions raised by England that tried to use military force to invade France, restore the Bourbon dynasty, and end the revolution. The first allied effort met defeat at the hands of a French revolutionary army at the battle of Valmy on September 20, 1792. This victory made it clear to Europe that France had unleashed a powerful movement within its borders. The second coalition floundered in 1800 in Italy when French armies led by Bonaparte pounced on Austrian forces and defeated them in June at Marengo, an achievement that announced to Europe that the Corsican upstart possessed more talent than previously believed. After another French military victory over the Austrians, this time in Germany at the battle of Hohenlinden in December 1800, Austria made peace with France in February 1801. With England fighting alone and France exhausted, both sides agreed to a tentative peace in March 1802.

Napoleon had done well to broker this treaty. Having helped engineer the *coup d'état* of Brumaire in 1799, he now ruled France as First Consul. His success as a warrior had got him to this point. But France had grown tired of its constant struggles and looked to its latest savior to end hostilities abroad and to heal fissures at home. While Napoleon relished his position of prominence, he understood he had to produce results in other than the martial arena to keep his seat. The general was going to have to exhibit some statesmanship.

This deed he soon achieved to the satisfaction of the French people. The Peace of Amiens won France a reprieve from war and the country enjoyed peace for the first time in ten years. It was badly needed given the devastation brought about by the internal upheaval and wars fought in the name of defending or advancing the revolution. French problems were legion in the countryside, including burned crops and farms, poisoned wells, and dead livestock. The situation was hardly better in the cities. Political convulsions had resulted in a suspension of basic functions, meaning sanitation problems had become acute and amassing enough food to feed the inhabitants there problematic. There was no shortage of security, but it was arbitrary in the extreme and dependent upon whatever political front held the ascendancy. Its measure of justice was equally extreme and executions were frequent, often for the most trivial reasons. The Terror had claimed thousands of victims. Now only uncertainty reigned throughout France. These problems needed to be addressed and the tension within France eased. The newfound peace gave Napoleon the opportunity to do just that.

The peace with England was short-lived, however. French military victories had merely won the nation a truce, nothing more. With no sea change in the disposition of the two principal antagonists, hostilities loomed once again. They came in May 1803, the peace having lasted only thirteen months. Malta proved the main sticking point of the treaty. This key island in the Mediterranean Sea had come under English control after Britain crushed French naval power in Egypt in 1798 at the Battle of the Nile. England refused to evacuate the island as it had agreed to do in the Peace of Amiens, fearing renewed French military adventures in the region. England thereby saddled itself with having started a new war with France. Much as had been the case with the revolutionary governments that had preceded him, Napoleon had war forced upon him by a recalcitrant England.

Once the Peace of Amiens collapsed in May 1803, Napoleon engaged in elaborate preparations for an invasion of the island nation. He would settle this war with England once and for all. To do so, he chose the most direct route available, a cross-Channel assault to occupy the British Isles. Napoleon assembled 180,000 soldiers in seven camps along the French coast facing Britain. Perhaps sheer numbers might unnerve England and bring it to its senses so it would make a permanent peace with France. If no peace came, then he would go forward with the invasion. To make the threat of such an attack a reality, the First Consul committed France to achieving naval parity, if not superiority, vis-à-vis England. In the coastal town of Boulogne and nine other ports, his troops and sailors readied barges in great numbers. Training on these craft assumed a regularity to further give evidence of France's commitment to invasion and to its feasibility.

He stuck by his goal no matter the glaring failures in the execution of his plans and the surfacing of near insurmountable obstacles. His admirals plagued him the most. They suffered from a universal unwillingness to engage English warships in battle. Understanding this limitation, Napoleon devised several schemes to bring superior numbers of French ships to bear on England's navy that was guarding against a Channel crossing. The most elaborate operational plan was to be put into practice. Multiple French fleets acting in unison would emerge from the safety of their ports, break the English blockade, and race to the Caribbean. After reinforcing the garrisons of French colonies, these fleets would unite and return to the Channel. On paper at least, close to sixty French men-of-war could be assembled at one time. Surely this was enough to prompt his admirals to fight and disperse the English ships protecting the British Isles.

His hoped-for fleet never materialized as his plans went awry for a number of reasons. French admirals insisted Napoleon understood little of war at sea. Ships could not be moved around as one directed a land army. Indeed, the far-ranging maneuvers stretching from Europe to the Americas could hardly be considered sound planning. That Napoleon created a navy of barges as well as ordering the construction of additional warships also spoke to the unworkable nature of his plans. He pursued two endeavors at once and this duplication of effort with already scarce resources doomed the entire enterprise. Yet, this error spoke to Napoleon's desperation to at least try an invasion, a stand that separated him from his admirals. To the amazement of all except possibly Napoleon, the assembling of a grand French fleet almost came to pass on several occasions, but these brief opportunities were lost by his dithering admirals, especially Vice Admiral Pierre de Villeneuve.

No matter these disappointments, Napoleon remained steadfast in his purpose to finish the war with England. If Napoleon had had his way, the war would involve only France and England and its duration would be short. Either French forces would perish when crossing the Channel and Napoleon would fall from power, or a French army would land on English soil and conquer the nation. Napoleon believed only 15,000 men would be necessary to complete a march from the coast of Kent to the city of London. He prodded his reluctant admirals by boasting, "Let us be masters of the [Dover] Straits for six hours and we shall be masters of the world." He later upped the total needed to three days.* If boastful and relying on the dubious expectation of a spontaneous revolt of the English people in sympathy with their French liberators, it was clear he was willing to gamble everything on a war with England. The last thing he wanted was a war on the Continent that would only take him away from his purpose of invading Britain by undoing his elaborate invasion plans, thereby forfeiting the time and expense levied to make this attack possible.

Doggedly for over two years Napoleon kept his cross-Channel invasion hopes alive. In the meantime, he looked for other ways to hurt England. French troops seized territory on the Continent allied to or dependent on England. This step meant that Hanover in Germany, Naples in Italy, and Holland and Belgium to the north of France all came under Napoleon's control. Soon he formed satellite states in each region and added their military forces to the French order of battle. Then in a sweeping mandate, the First Consul prohibited trade with England in all areas allied to France. Additionally, Napoleon ordered the arrest of English citizens in French territory. He could do nothing other than this and his frustration grew as England raided French merchant ships and seized French colonies. Anticipating his impotence before English sea power, Napoleon had relinquished control of French territory in North America and sold Louisiana to the United States in 1803. This retreat of French power he dismissed as no more than a minor setback, convinced as he was that the

---

* Robert B. Asprey, *The Rise of Napoleon Bonaparte* (New York: Basic Books, 2000), 483. Alan Schom offers Napoleon's revised schedule of three days. See Schom, *Napoleon Bonaparte* (New York: HarperCollins, 1997), 362.

United States would prove a maritime rival to England. This development lingered in the indefinite future, and at present Napoleon remained focused on an invasion of England. It was an odd war, the two sides steadfast in opposition to one another but unable to land blows that would push the conflict to a point of resolution. The standoff appeared as complete as the intransigence driving the antagonists to make war on one another.

England possessed one more card that promised to break the deadlock. Britain decided that if it could not directly strike effectively at France, then it would spend money bolstering continental allies who could. It was an old formula but maybe it would work this time around. When William Pitt the Younger became prime minister a second time in May 1804, he worked diligently to assemble a Third Coalition consisting of England, Sweden, Austria, and Russia. Prussia maintained its uneasy neutrality. It very well might decide to enter the war against France should England's partners enjoy an early military success at Napoleon's expense.

The Third Coalition was already strong and it threatened to grow stronger should Prussia enter the war on the side of England. By 1805, Napoleon could no longer ignore the fact that England's allies on the Continent posed an immediate threat to France. Napoleon knew they had to be neutralized, but how? Only a swift, devastating attack into central Europe could cripple these allies of England before they united and invaded France. A preemptive strike by the emperor's armies could catch the Austrian and Russian forces separated from one another and initiate a battle favorable to France. A quick victory promised to ensure Prussian neutrality. Once Napoleon eliminated this primary danger, the other threats along the periphery of France, such as English activity in Naples and Sweden's menacing of northern Germany, would recede. A preemptive campaign would deprive England of its mercenary armies on the continent and he could again focus his attention on England. For Napoleon, the advantages were too great not to act preemptively and the necessity equally plain.

Another military necessity demanded the French employ a preemptive strike. Even should the preferred invasion of England prove successful, Napoleon's position was untenable. Once on English soil, what of the powers allied to that island nation? A now unprotected France lay vulnerable to assault. To strike England with the continental members of the Third Coalition at his back would be folly but to head east to meet this threat meant giving up an attack on France's chief foe and passing on an opportunity that might never come again. To do nothing meant France faced defeat at the hands of invading armies of superior numbers. In a very real sense, Napoleon's great army of 180,000 men lay impotent on the Channel coast.

The creation of this strategic dilemma is a great tribute to the diplomacy of Pitt who worked very hard to create the new coalition. In this way, in

1805, Pitt ensured that war would not come across the Channel and to England but gravitate toward central Germany. But England's diplomatic success also underscored the limited choices available to France and therefore made preemption a preferred choice almost by default. As scholar David Chandler wrote in his great treatment of the military history of the Napoleonic era, *The Campaigns of Napoleon*, "By striking for the Danube, the Emperor hoped to forestall his continental enemies, crush them in detail and thus deliver a telling blow against his inveterate insular opponent."* Even a hostile biographer of Napoleon like Alan Schom recognized this imperative, writing in *Napoleon Bonaparte* that because of his inferiority in numbers, the emperor "had to act swiftly to divide and crush the Allies before they could unite and attack him en masse."** France would fight its way out of this seemingly intractable problem and it would do so in preemptive fashion. First Napoleon would crush the Austrians with a rapid French attack, this before the Russians arrived to lend a hand. Then Napoleon could focus on defeating the Russians. While Pitt's new coalition had earned a reprieve for England, in the process of securing this end he helped to launch a whirlwind of military activity upon the rest of Western Europe directed by a master tactician, Napoleon Bonaparte. The results would be as monumental as they would be unpredictable.

A larger imperative prompted Napoleon to act in preemptive fashion. England's war against France singled out the revolution as its primary enemy. The convulsions that had gripped France since 1789, indeed, that had made Napoleon's rise to power possible, made France Britain's target long before 1805. No matter the divisions within the English home front as to the virtues and sins of the French Revolution, all parties could agree that Napoleon at the helm of the most populous state in Europe, and now one possessing a revolutionary dogma, could not be countenanced. The balance of power in Europe, so long treasured by England as a necessary staple of its foreign policy, faced upheaval should France export its newfound faith in equality and liberty and rally the Continent against Britain. Eventually, all political factions in England came to this conclusion. They recognized that the talented Bonaparte could use such a creed to advance the territorial interests of France to the detriment of England. England never ceased waging this struggle after 1802 until it had defeated and incarcerated Napoleon. It would take over a decade but the fight would be worth it from Great Britain's perspective.

An English victory at the expense of the revolution was an end Napoleon could ill afford since he posed as the savior of the revolution, as the man

---

* David G. Chandler, *The Campaigns of Napoleon* (New York: Macmillan, 1966), 327.

** Schom, *Napoleon Bonaparte*, 399.

best able to procure the fruits of this frightening period of recent French history. Napoleon's ability to negotiate the Peace of Amiens had been one of his early accomplishments as First Consul. The French people welcomed a steady hand to restore order and sanity to their daily lives. In gratitude they voted to extend his term as First Consul to life.

In broad terms, Bonaparte used his government to offer stability to France. Tranquility on the home front meant guaranteeing private property, something forfeited during the revolution, providing favorable conditions for commerce, and increasing agricultural development. Once the government set these economic goals, the immediate result was that hard currency emerged from hiding and sparked investment funds. Soon new industries developed. Enjoying this air of confidence, the small Paris stock exchange returned to operation. As an added calming mechanism, Bonaparte backed freedom of worship and to this end he made peace with the Catholic Church on July 15, 1801. More importantly, this concordat meant the church no longer served as an ally of Bourbon restoration. This act only partly squelched royalist dissent, however. To meet the lingering and at times violent uprisings in the west of France on behalf of this sentiment, Napoleon sent in the army and ordered extreme measures to be taken. Much bloodshed ensued but the revolts ended. Civil war no longer plagued France and this step brought more stability to the country.

Individual liberty also became more viable once Napoleon turned his attention to legislating on behalf of his new country. He regularized civil legal codes, a time-consuming process only completed and implemented in January 1804. And it was largely his doing, since he presided over every change in the articles of the code. Education received much special attention with notable achievements, such as the reopening of the National University and the offering of thousands of national scholarships to deserving students. The benefits of education reached further than ever before since Napoleon opened these intuitions at all levels of instruction to anyone showing merit. Talent would decide a person's opportunities, not birth. Even women enjoyed greatly expanded opportunities in the educational system. The Legion of Honor fully exemplified the defense of individual liberty since this institution again guaranteed that persons of merit and not merely of noble blood would receive the honors of state. If this antagonized émigrés by elevating inferiors to positions of equality, Napoleon assuaged this group as well by welcoming them back to France and promising to restore to them their property confiscated during the revolution, if at all possible.

Napoleon had gone a long way to securing the gains of the revolution and his acts in this regard were numerous, achieved their purpose, and left France stronger than before. The benefits were self-evident even if a more prosperous France had to overlook a glaring contradiction in relation to the revolution. Napoleon was at once its savior and its destroyer. At the same time that he declared that the revolution was over, he had clearly preserved many of its tumultuous changes. Napoleon was an enigma and his achievements hard to categorize. What was clear was that should England prevail in this great struggle, all that France had endured over the past twelve years would be trauma suffered in vain. Somehow the nation must triumph and preemption offered Napoleon a viable and necessary recourse to achieve this end of self-preservation on behalf of France.

Military necessity and the larger imperative of preserving the revolution compelled Napoleon to attack before England's allies were ready to advance into French territory. A third reason guided this preemptive strike and that was to protect the person of the emperor. For 1805 was a very different time than 1792 and 1800, the dates of the first two anti-French coalitions. Bonaparte now ran France as Emperor Napoleon, having successfully held a national plebiscite deciding this issue on November 6, 1804. The coronation took place on December 2. The title of emperor, however, signaled to all of France that the revolution remained in play, that Napoleon represented only much-needed law and order, not an end to the movement that had deposed the hated Bourbon dynasty. He was not a king but an emperor in the tradition of the leaders of the Roman republic.

Such an outcome worried and appalled the English. Newspaper caricature of France's newfound savior was frequent and increasingly profane. One depicted Napoleon as the devil, arranging his name as NAPOLE ON BUON APARTE, this to mirror the 666 synonymous with the Antichrist. Another hinted at Napoleon's incestuous love affair with his stepdaughter, Hortense Beauharnais. While these barbs could be dismissed as only so many words and rumors, the very real plots against Napoleon's life escalated the stakes. A bomb nearly killed Bonaparte on Christmas Eve in 1800, then serving as First Consul. What of other possible attacks?, he asked himself. To forestall these, Napoleon ordered some heavy-handed acts to intimidate the opposition, such as the killing of Louis Antoine, duc d'Enghien, a possible heir to a restored Bourbon throne. Napoleon ordered his capture and execution to stem a royalist plot to kill Bonaparte discovered in February 1804. The man's involvement was uncertain but after this execution, it seemed clear that Napoleon would stop at nothing to preserve his newly won crown, and his person. This had been the point. He put it plainly, remarking while in exile on St. Helena that, "When they attack my person, I return blow for blow."* He justified such measures since he was convinced that on the safety of his person rested the safety of France.

---

* Schom, *Napoleon Bonaparte*, 346.

Not convinced that sheer intimidation could protect his rule, Bonaparte sought power for life and a title exuding royalty to establish himself in the company of European kings. Such monarchical legitimacy might at last force the enemies of France both at home and abroad to accept Napoleon as the product of the revolution. France could then enjoy peace and prosperity. Yet even after he had secured these trappings of royalty, England continued to encourage intrigues against him and it remained committed to war with France. Its implacable hostility was a reminder to France that English designs extended beyond ending Napoleon's reign. A preemptive strike in 1805 was necessary if for no other reason than to preserve the person of the emperor and so preserve the revolutionary beacon that was France.

The Attack

The time of decision came in 1805. Napoleon watched the actions of his enemies closely and formulated his plans accordingly. Austria assembled its armies in forward positions to carry the fight into France rather than risk war on Austrian soil. In September 1805, an Austrian army of 70,000 troops under General Baron Karl Lieberich Mack and Archduke Ferdinand entered Bavaria and occupied the city of Ulm. Three Russian armies totaling nearly 100,000 soldiers were moving west to join the Austrians in Germany. None had arrived as of yet to aid Mack. In Italy, Austria's ablest commander, Archduke Charles, massed an army of 95,000 men. England, in conjunction with Sweden, the Kingdom of Naples, and small Austrian contingents, hoped to accumulate a further 50,000 men and strike in northern Europe into Hanover from Pomerania and in the Mediterranean into Italy via Naples.

Perhaps this was a sound strategy on the part of the allies, given Austria's previous defeats at the hands of France. This time the initiative would lie with Austrian forces. This fact alone could ensure that superior numbers would make it very difficult for France, even with Napoleon in command, to defeat the invasion forces scheduled to come from multiple directions, first from Italy and then from Germany once Mack, reinforced by the Russians, pushed past Strasbourg into France itself. With Austria dictating the course of events, Napoleon would not be able to transfer his smaller forces from one front to another to defeat one army at a time. Instead, he would be too busy fending off the advancing Austrian and Russian forces. But timing and coordination of forces were paramount in such a plan and the Austrians had proven deficient in both areas in the past.

Given these shortcomings and therefore the unrealistic expectation of keeping France on the defensive, a certain desperation clouded the preparations for war of the Third Coalition. Strategically, when the numbers were counted and the dispositions of the armies considered, Napoleon's situation looked hopeless. Hemmed in on all sides, facing superior numbers in every theater of action, bereft of major allies, the new state of imperial France appeared doomed. Tactically, however, the situation was not so bright for the allied nations. Napoleon's ability to wage war in rapid and unpredictable fashion had already served him well in two campaigns against the Austrians. Understanding these risks, at least one Austrian dignitary strongly urged his government to ensure that all war preparations be conducted in secret as far as was possible. Why risk a preemptive attack, he reasoned? His cautions were ignored and quite the opposite ensued with Austria making plain its alliance with Russia and England on August 9, 1805. The Third Coalition stood poised to bring France to heel.

Napoleon responded on August 13, 1805, when he ordered his army to break camp on the Channel coast and head south. This it did, the many corps of the *Grande Armée* advancing so smoothly and efficiently, that Napoleon proudly referred to his army's movements as "my seven streams."* In a matter of weeks the French had the new enemy in sight and Napoleon was ready to execute his preemptive strike. Mack's exposed army at Ulm was quickly encircled by the corps of the *Grande Armée* and he surrendered over 30,000 men on October 20, 1805. It was a first, great success. French armies now moved forward down the Danube heading for Vienna, the Austrian capital. Austrian forces retreated in the same direction, carrying a few scattered Russian forces with them. The initiative clearly lay with Napoleon, and the benefits accrued quickly. The Austrian capital fell without a fight, French forces entering the city on November 14. Napoleon, however, considered this a hollow triumph since the remaining Austrian forces had escaped and joined forces with the now present Russian armies. The campaign had started well but was not over.

In many ways, Napoleon's preemptive attack left France in a more precarious position than was the case before the outbreak of hostilities. This was the situation no matter that his offensive had gone according to plan. In Italy, a French army of limited strength checked the much larger Austrian army under Archduke Charles. Here was a strategic victory. In Germany, Napoleon had decimated the Austrian armies before him, and forced the Russians into a humiliating retreat back from whence they had come. This was the good news. But the bad news was more plentiful. Napoleon's main force was now weak in numbers after its dash to Vienna. Worse, the *Grande Armée* found itself exposed in hostile territory since the one shattered enemy, the Austrians, had found refuge with a yet undefeated Russian army.

---

* Richard Holmes, "Austerlitz, 1805," in *Two Centuries of Warfare* (London: Octopus Books, 1978), 65.

Together these allies outnumbered the French forces Napoleon could assemble in and around Vienna. Worse, scattered and bypassed Austrian forces under Archduke Charles far to the French rear in the mountainous region of the Tyrol threatened Bonaparte's lines of communications stretching from Paris to Vienna. In Italy, Austrian generals were no longer deceived into believing that this would be the main theater of action, as had been the case in 1800. Charles could now detach significant forces to aid in the defense of Vienna. In sum, Napoleon's enemies were getting stronger while his own forces were getting weaker. Preemptive war had gained the emperor only a temporary advantage at best.

What the French needed was yet another stupendous military victory like that at Ulm, and Napoleon plotted to achieve just that. If Bonaparte utilized a superior number of men and cannon to achieve victory in his later battles, and this reliance on brute force commented unfavorably on his generalship, this was not the case here. In shaping the battle to come, he demonstrated great subtlety and daring, two hallmarks of outstanding military leadership. First, he advertised the French weakness in numbers to feed the growing confidence of his enemies. He correctly judged that their self-assurance would entice his opponents into risking battle. His next step was to ensure that such a battle would occur on ground of his own choosing. This task he accomplished with equal skill. He reconnoitered the terrain that lay between the opposing armies and deployed his French soldiers along a plain dominated by a commanding plateau. But he left the Pratzen Plateau unoccupied. His hope was that the allied armies would be so emboldened as to advance and meet the French army in the field. Once recognizing his weakness and concluding that Napoleon had no choice but to risk his army and his throne on a battle, they would be just as overjoyed to learn that he was not smart enough to pick terrain best suited for defense. It would be a simple matter of advancing and defeating the French army. But their thoughtlessness would undo them. Certain of victory, the Austro-Russian army would strike an apparently vulnerable French flank. To do so, they would leave their center unprotected, counting on the high terrain to shield their advance. Understanding the inadequacy of this defense, Napoleon would send his reserves into this gap in the center of the allied line, split the enemy in half, and defeat them in detail. It was a clever plan, if it worked.

It worked brilliantly and the battle of Austerlitz proved a great French victory. Once the allied armies moved to the attack, Napoleon struck their exposed center and occupied the all important heights. Having divided the enemy, Napoleon enveloped their left flank, winning the decisive battle that he needed to win. Russian losses were particularly heavy, including the repulse of the elite Guard Cavalry. The reality of defeat on the ground reverberated psychologically. The unbelievable, the unthinkable, had happened. The upstart emperor and his revolutionary army stood victorious on the field of battle, a bright, shining sun warming French hearts on this cold December day. The sun of Austerlitz reminded many a Frenchmen of the coronation of their emperor a year ago, an event also graced by sunshine on a winter's day. The significance did not escape either the Austrian monarch Emperor Francis II or the Russian ruler Czar Alexander I as they fled the field of battle. Far from vanquishing their enemy, they understood that this battle solidified Napoleon's control of France and gave new life to the surging French Revolution. In its wake the Third Coalition was dead. Seldom had a battle so badly needed to be so convincingly won.

Success

Scholars consider Austerlitz Napoleon's finest battle. The emperor concurred. To a stricken Russian officer lamenting his disgrace in the aftermath of defeat, the emperor remarked, "Calm yourself, young man. It is no dishonor to be defeated by my army."* Still, the victory had its limits. Napoleon wrote to his brother Joseph shortly after the battle that, "Peace is a word devoid of meaning. It is glorious peace that we need."** His quest for this satisfaction meant he shunned English overtures of peace after Austerlitz, a gesture made possible on the part of Britain largely because of the death of Pitt, Bonaparte's obdurate enemy. This opportunity passed and Napoleon again focused on defeating England. It was the all-important task. The Third Coalition had indeed been given a rebuke at Austerlitz that caused its collapse, but the war did not end since England continued the struggle. New enemies on the Continent were likely, even looming, and Napoleon understood that the defeat of Austria meant more battles, not less, in the future. Could he duplicate the martial feat of Austerlitz again? Outwardly he voiced nothing but confidence. But he also knew that battles were never without risk; he had just proved this point to Austria and Russia in dramatic fashion. It was likely that France would find itself on the losing side of one of these battles sooner or later.

The old enemy remained and England, though just as stunned as was Europe with the results of Austerlitz, took heart in its own tremendous victory, a naval triumph. Several months prior to Napoleon's success in Moravia, the English navy had decimated a combined French and Spanish

---

* Henry Lachouque, *The Anatomy of Glory*, trans. Anne S.K. Brown (New York: Hippocrene Books, Inc., 1978), 65.

** Steven Englund, *Napoleon: A Political Life* (New York: Scribner, 2004), 281.

fleet off Cape Trafalgar near the Spanish city of Cadiz. The Battle of Trafalgar, fought on October 21, 1805, cost Napoleon at least eighteen warships. The significance of the defeat was more than a material one. With English naval supremacy assured, the war would go on. Napoleon faced the same problem he had encountered before the campaign of 1805, an obdurate England massing Continental allies to challenge French supremacy in Europe. The war was just beginning against the emperor and ongoing against France.

Napoleon accepted the challenge, and the wars did indeed continue. French armies turned on Prussia in 1806, swiftly crushing this state. The following year, another Russian army, this time making common cause with Prussian soldiers, met defeat in East Prussia as Napoleon won another large, set-piece battle at Friedland. French forces stood on the doorstep of Russia, and Alexander sued for peace. After 1807, Napoleon's wars ranged widely. French armies invaded Spain in 1808, and Austria renewed the struggle against France in 1809. Austria again sued for peace but the war in Spain degenerated into a costly struggle that even large numbers of French troops could not force to resolution. The strain of empire was taking its toll, French forces stretched thin and tiring of the fighting. But far from curbing his military ambitions, Napoleon raised his largest army to date and sent it against Russia in 1812. This enterprise ended disastrously, broke French strength, and a quick fall from power ensued. Napoleon was forced to abdicate his throne in March 1814. Unbridled expansion had cost him everything.

Such a track record is generally considered the cost of aggression. But in the context of preemption, this tale takes on a different light. In a very real sense, Napoleon's expansion of French power was in pursuit of a duplication of his effort in 1805. France could not be safe so long as England remained an enemy free to galvanize Continental opponents to make war on France, nations that once having licked their wounds were willing enough to take English money and continue the fight, as did Austria in 1809. Others could be bribed to fight given their fear of growing French power. The French offensive against Prussia in 1806 was a case in point. English gold backed Prussia and pushed that state to action. In any of these instances, Napoleon could ask himself why he should wait until Austrian, Prussian, or Russian armies united their forces and attacked France. More preemptive strikes clearly were necessary, just as had been the case in 1805. The source of trouble for France was not the Continental armies of its neighboring states. These nations could be defeated, as Napoleon proved time after time. No, the true enemy was England, safely ensconced across the Channel plotting the downfall of France with blood money harvested from its domination of the sea that allowed its commerce to grow unchecked. The true task remained, how to defeat England?

Napoleon's response was an economic war. England would be denied access to trade in any area under French control. Obviously, if France could control Western Europe, England could be brought to its knees all the more quickly. It is no coincidence that Napoleon's decree announcing this aim of his Continental System came while he occupied Berlin in 1806. European states were put on notice that cooperation with England would make them an enemy of France. Napoleon pursued offensives in Spain and Russia due to this reasoning. Portugal's refusal to join his Continental System led directly to Napoleon's debilitating war in Spain starting in 1808. Russia's ingenuousness in this regard meant a French invasion of that country in 1812. Each attack was preemptive, undertaken in the hope of humbling the power of British sterling, thereby bringing peace to Europe. It was a vain hope. Military rule of Europe was beyond French power and this limitation meant Napoleon's ability to choke off trade with England remained imperfect. Also, a trade embargo hurt Europe as much as it did England. Nations allied with France or even under French control evaded the Berlin Decree as much as possible, as did France itself. The unworkable nature of this economic plan soon proved its futility, and doomed Napoleon's bid for victory through preemptive war.

Conclusion

The war Napoleon fought in 1805 was one he did not wish to fight. But he had no choice. England kept raising Europe against him. A new anti-French coalition grew out of the Peace of Amiens that Napoleon had worked so hard to achieve. This erosion of the peace fell on the shoulders of England. It refused to evacuate Malta, a breach of the accords that indicated the deep-set nature of English hostility to France. England's goal was world domination, its empire seeking that goal via commercial success. Napoleon had to stop this from occurring before France fell to the status of a second-rate power.

Facing an implacable foe in England, the question quickly became how best to prosecute this war. A cross-Channel invasion was risky but Napoleon was willing to undertake the task. He dedicated enormous resources to the enterprise. He assembled a large army on the coast, built transport vessels, and prepared a plan for the French navy to seize control of the Channel. He also urged his admirals to attack, and after a two-year period his efforts had given shape to a viable threat. Moreover, the massing of his army along the northern coast of France made it clear to Europe that Napoleon's target was England. The rest of the Continent had no reason to fear French arms.

When he made war on the Continent in 1805, he did so only when forced to because England raised a formidable alliance that arrayed numerous armies against him. Surrounded on all sides, facing superior numbers, Napoleon had little choice but to attack preemptively and try to defeat his enemies one at a time. After all, given this situation, a strike at England suffered from tremendous complications. Even to successfully cross the Channel and land on English soil risked too much. France could face a devastating assault on land from England's Continental allies. Should this attack develop, Napoleon could fall from power even should he overcome English defenses. The French had to win a great battle against the Austrians before Austria received help from the Russians. This meant a swift attack to catch the Austrian armies in Bavaria. Only this success could make an Austerlitz-type battle possible. For these reasons, Napoleon's 1805 campaign made sound military sense.

Nevertheless, the stakes were high and served to make Bonaparte a reluctant warrior. He wished to remain focused on strengthening France. In fact, he had done much along these lines. Civil unrest and strife within France had ended. Bonaparte had made peace with the church. Commerce flourished once given adequate government protection and encouragement. The same could be said for the French citizenry now benefiting from the Napoleonic Code. Individual liberty already was paying handsome dividends by offering greater educational opportunities to all French citizens and by ending the grip of the nobility on entitlements, in favor of merit deciding career advancement. France had come very far under Napoleon's hand in a short period of time.

These gains were too valuable for France to forfeit. They also relied heavily on Napoleon serving as protector of France and of the revolution. His newly won title of emperor symbolized the connection. It also raised the ire of England, and its determination to stop what they considered an abomination. This was made clear in its hostility and in the barbs its people directed Napoleon's way. More than mere rhetoric, on too many occasions Napoleon had had to survive assassination attempts that he believed found backing in England. Such terrorism had to stop and Napoleon intended to protect his person and his crown with force. Even so, he desired more than his individual survival. Personal defeat meant nothing compared to the sorry fate France would have to endure should he fail to protect her. War and civil unrest would again decimate the country, endangering the gains of the revolution. Agreeing with this sentiment, the French people backed their new leader's call for a preemptive war in 1805, and would do so in the future, time and time again.

The specter of new wars threatened to push France to the edge and possibly lead to that nation turning on its savior, Napoleon. The question is, why did he take the risk with these wars? To better understand this imperative, one must realize that Napoleon believed his cause to be that of defending French civilization at the fore of a revolutionary movement that put that country at odds with England and all of Europe. Napoleon convinced himself that French hegemony was superior to English domination of the Continent. Here was a civilizational conflict and French civilization must triumph. This end would break English power and benefit France, Europe, and the world. France, with liberty, equality, and fraternity, offered a higher ideal than did England's money-centered system of economic exploitation at home and abroad. This war had to be fought. Should nations be foolish enough to back England, then the emperor would unleash his armies and impose the revolution on those nations. A preemptive policy would serve France well, crippling the threat posed by England's lackeys on the Continent and serving the interests of all of Europe in the process.

Well might the powers opposing him single out Napoleon as the source of their troubles, but ultimately they knew this to be a profound simplification. Revolutionary France had threatened the authority of every European monarch. Napoleon's self-created status of Emperor only heightened their fears of a militarized France actively seeking to destroy or replace the monarchs of Europe. The irony here was that even as Napoleon acted to preserve his own throne, and in this way lend standing to his enemies' claims of royal authority, he led a revolutionary movement that undermined imperial legitimacy. France had weathered this storm, allowing Napoleon to act as both a product of and a deliverer from the revolution. Other European rulers had no wish to experience such turbulence, unsure of their ability to handle such upheaval with as much adroitness or as much luck as had the French emperor. By 1805, Napoleon had to be defeated to ensure their survival. Overwhelming numbers, they hoped, would offset the unsettling groundswell of support that lent him credibility and at the same time weakened the authority of the powers of the Third Coalition. For Napoleon, this allied imperative meant his cause was that of self-defense, his method, preemption.

To suggest Napoleon acted preemptively in the name of self-defense is to ignore that, in many ways, the emperor earned the negative caricatures thrown his way. There can be no disputing his personal ambition in pushing France to war in 1805. The war with England exemplified this fact. How seriously he contemplated invading England was always in doubt given his vulnerability to a land attack should he even reach the British Isles, and given the difficulty of challenging English sea power. There could be no French victory over England. There could be some form of coexistence along the lines of the Peace of Amiens. Napoleon rejected this option, however. Instead, he treated England's push for a balance of power as a personal affront. This reaction explains why he blamed England for the émigré plots on his life, forgetting or refusing to acknowledge the obvious motives, independent of England, which these refugees had for wanting him out of power. His response, especially the murder of duc d'Enghien, revealed him to be a petty thug. His pretense of defending the revolution in this instance and others meant that he forced upon France a bitter war for national survival that primarily served Napoleon's interest in preserving his rule.

His actions helped to break the peace with England and also gave cause to other nations to join the Third Coalition and try their luck in battle against the French. For example, Bonaparte did nothing to assure an Austria smarting under previous defeats at the hands of France that he intended this nation no further harm. In fact, his actions in Italy conveyed the opposite message. In 1805, Napoleon first annexed Piedmont into the French empire. He then proclaimed himself king of Italy. Both of these steps alarmed Emperor Francis, as Napoleon must have known they would. Bonaparte gave Russia equal cause for concern by his aggressive posturing in the Mediterranean, an area of great strategic interest to Czar Alexander. In this context, French control of Belgium and Holland no longer appeared actions threatening only England. Napoleon was seizing upon the momentum of the revolution to serve his expansionist desires. In the process, he was eroding security on the Continent. Now two forces had to be stopped, the revolution and its monster, Napoleon.

Not surprisingly, the members of the Third Coalition readied themselves to resist Napoleon's drive for Continental domination. The constant training of the army for use against England testified to the formidable nature of this force should France's new emperor turn away from a cross-Channel invasion and seek out the Continental enemies of France. Austria and Russia both took notice of the army Napoleon had assembled on the coast to threaten England, and decided that the threat it posed was multi-faceted. Already, in 1797 and 1800, Austria had witnessed a demonstration of the rapidity of Napoleonic warfare and had lost wars decisively in each case. If England were to be defeated, a strong counter-weight to France would disappear. The monarchs of Europe agreed that this development would threaten their own existence. The problem was not quelling popular discontent within their own countries due to sentiment awakened by the French Revolution, but fending off an aggressor serving his own interests. With this in mind, England was a valued ally, not a bully using blood money to raise a coalition.

The Third Coalition stood justified in its aim of bringing France to heel, England validated in its obdurate resistance to France. Napoleon would be contained, his contagion stamped out, and the natural order of things restored. The Russian and English treaty in 1805 stated this plainly, since it called for "the establishment of an order of things in Europe which effectively guaranteed the security and independence of the diverse states and establishes a firm barrier against future usurpations."* If general and therefore vague in meaning, the target was clear: France and Napoleon. The purpose was equally clear, protecting the status quo in Europe. The alternative was highly undesirable. Under Napoleon, the threat of French domination of the Continent had come to pass, and all of Europe would suffer.

Europe rejected French hegemony as much as England did and Napoleon's Continental System had a lot to do with this result. Burdened by French control, one seeking to isolate Europe from England, the chief provider of dearly needed and desired commodities, the European states made a choice and that was to support England's drive to establish a balance of power. That this end served England's needs best did not lessen the fact that this choice meant a rebuke of Napoleon's goal of a unified European nation under the benevolent hand of France. The ruthlessness with which the "liberator" used nations and peoples to further French war aims underscored the legitimacy of this resistance. He failed to rally the Continent to a French standard of culture. The impossibility of this aim should have been clear to him by December 1805, when he defeated the Third Coalition but realized peace was still beyond his grasp and more fighting lay in the future. Austerlitz should have demonstrated the futility of a strategy of preemption and not served as a validation of the feasibility of the goal of defeating England through European domination.

That Napoleon plunged ahead anyway with more preemptive war points to the self-serving nature of his rule. Creating enemies abroad served Napoleonic ambitions at home. The *Grande Armée* that Napoleon used to threaten England kept France on a war footing and allowed Bonaparte to consolidate his power. But his aim was tyranny. If his reforms of state power had assured citizens that the excesses of the revolution were over, some additional controls were put in place alongside those enacted in the name of stability. For instance, education and commerce faced government regulation. Freedom of speech disappeared. A police state ensured tranquility throughout the nation based on intimidation and fear. Violent upheaval may have ended, but a different terror remained. Legislative

---

* Frederick C. Schneid, *Napoleon's Conquest of Europe: The War of the Third Coalition* (Westport, CT: Praeger, 2005), 84.

bodies existed but held no authority as power became centralized in the hands of Bonaparte. Worse, the authoritarian rule meant the revolution had ended. Republicanism faded in the Napoleonic state. This outcome registered plainly with Bonaparte's monarchical ambitions, evidenced in his creation of a new nobility answerable to him, the Legion of Honor, and the elevation of members of his family to fiefdoms and principalities. Such personal rule underscored that the war with England had turned into a narrow contest between that nation and one man, Bonaparte. To defend his person and newly won crown, he set the resources of France in a death struggle against the island nation.

Clearly Napoleon capitalized on circumstance to advance his personal ambition. This motive spoke to aggression more than any need to act preemptively in the name of self-defense. However, preemption offers Napoleon a reprieve in two respects. First, under Napoleon, France would never be secure. The problem was not Napoleon so much as it was the threat of the expansion of the French Revolution. In this sense, Napoleon faced an imminent threat. Would England and the European powers have left him alone had he stayed within the natural borders of France? Or would England have remained at war, determined to undermine the revolution and to do so by raising allies on the Continent to reduce French power? Napoleon could not be sure and so he weighed his plans accordingly. He would attack and not take any chances. Second, Napoleon's 1805 campaign was also preemptive in purpose, and that purpose was civilizational with a hegemonic consequence. Napoleon convinced himself that Europe welcomed French hegemony, sparking as it did a cultural renaissance enjoyed by all nations, not just France. The Code Napoleon would liberate millions of Europeans. A single standard of commerce would benefit all Europeans. A peace ushered in by French force of arms would bring peace to the Continent. Prosperity would follow. True, Europe would be bound together by a single power emanating from France, but it was more than military power and in its totality its benevolence was unquestioned.

Given these slender grounds for war, Napoleon launched a series of military campaigns in the name of preemption. But this justification for war is not enough to place Napoleon's 1805 campaign in the category of preemption, or any of his campaigns after this date for that matter. His cause was not preemption to stave off an imminent threat, but a war of choice to preserve his throne. His was a personal empire and it was a crucial weakness. The greater good of France—or Europe for that matter—came second to the purpose of humbling English power, an end that sustained Napoleon's rule. Ultimately, the needs of the aggressor outweighed the benefits of preemption. Even these benefits were limited since his strategy of preemption was unsuccessful. England survived, not Napoleonic France.

England grew stronger and France grew weaker. Classifying the Napoleonic Wars as preemptive obfuscates these failures and acts to pardon Bonaparte's self-indulgent motives. But his self-interest remained paramount. France suffered as Bonaparte looked for "security" by fighting wars in foreign lands, a goal that earned him the label of aggressor.

Preserving a Way of Life: The War Between the States, 1861

Introduction

On April 9, 1861, General Pierre Gustave T. Beauregard of the newly created Confederate States of America demanded the surrender of the Union's Fort Sumter in Charleston Harbor, South Carolina. The garrison commander, Major Robert Anderson, refused. Anticipating a Southern attack, he already had put his troops on alert to defend the position no matter some glaring handicaps. His force mustered but 80 men; Sumter required 650 to properly defend it. Because of a shortage of ammunition, he prepared only a few cannon to return fire in response to any Southern attack; the stronghold could situate over 146 pieces. Given the paucity of his defense, he did not believe the fort posed a threat to any Southern interests, but he realized he was on the front line of a possible shooting war. Secession already had taken place, South Carolina being the first state to leave the Union on December 20, 1860. As the states arrayed against the Union grew in number, why give the South a cause to turn secession into war? Anderson would defend his position but try not to stumble into a war. His counterpart, Beauregard, also understood that the fort could not defend itself and that he had enough cannon to force its surrender and to start a civil war. At 4:30 am on April 12, 1861, the rebel batteries opened fire on Fort Sumter. This first act of violence declared the South's desire to wage war against the North, and Anderson's return of fire the North's resolve to meet this challenge. The opening salvos in Charlestown also signaled the South's determination to launch a war against an intransigent Northern foe. This war was overdue and the time had come to settle the issue with a preemptive strike.

The Southern attack on Fort Sumter initiated a four-year war within the United States between the Northern states remaining loyal to the Union and the eleven Southern states forming a new nation, the Confederate States of America. The fighting would not stop until April 1865. By that time, close to 600,000 Americans would be dead, a testimony to the extent of the violence this conflict produced. The eastern theater was the center-stage of the war, a duel of two opposing armies, Abraham Lincoln's Army of the Potomac, and the Confederacy's—really Robert E. Lee's—Army of Northern Virginia. From the outset of the war to its end, the fighting here raged incessantly in places like Bull Run, Antietam, Chancellorsville, Gettysburg, the Wilderness, and Petersburg, just to name a few. On these now-famous battlefields hung the balance of the war. But the broader parameters of the conflict determined the result in the east. From the west came the North's strategic victory that signaled the end of the Confederacy's chances of withstanding the Northern onslaught, despite the successful generalship of Lee. Once the Union split the Confederacy in half by winning control of the Mississippi River in 1863, the South's chances of even a stalemated end to the war rapidly diminished. The North's ability to fight on more than one front meant a slow strangulation of its enemy. Moreover, by this point in the conflict, Lincoln had discovered a number of capable commanders who now presided over the Union war effort, Ulysses S. Grant being the most important. Grant's unbroken string of successes in the western theater was the chief reason for the Union victory there. His ability to duel Lee on equal terms in the east during an extended period of conflict in 1864–1865 demonstrated Northern resolve to restore the Union, and the South's inability to prevent this from occurring. The war ended in a testimonial to military power. Union armies forced a settlement, but the extent of the fighting also cast a larger shadow in that it spared no one the horrors of war. Lincoln's assassination a week after the end of hostilities emphasized this price of "total" war. Whether one person or many thousands, whether an important individual or a nameless bystander, the uneasy feeling left by the Civil War was that the reach of total war had been just that: total. This new reality meant a troubled reckoning of the conflict in terms of declaring a winning side, and in assessing the future of warfare itself.

The American Civil War would traumatize the United States, but this is the extent to which most scholars pass moral judgment on the war. In the vast writings on the conflict, the tone and import are one of tragedy, that the war could have been avoided if only one thing or another had happened or had not happened. When authors examine the origins of the war, there is little blame assigned to one party or the other for starting this war. Instead, there seems a shared mutual responsibility. Yet James McPherson, an authority on the period, in his book, *Battle Cry of Freedom*, wrote of the South's desire to strike preemptively at the North, that Southerners convinced themselves of this necessity. McPherson does not address the moral dimensions of this conclusion. But his statement alone gives reason to reexamine the causes of the war in the context of preemption if for no other reason than to assign blame to one party or the other. If the South acted preemptively, did it act in self-defense and therefore act justly by starting a conflict that was coming anyway? Conversely, should the call to preemption prove false, did the South act as an aggressor nation when waging war on its neighbor? An analysis of preemption on the part of the Confederacy stands to add much to a discussion of the origins of the Civil War. One way or the other, the morality that under-girds this conflict again becomes a question of right and wrong in starting the war, not just a tragedy in fighting it.

The Case for Preemption

By any measure of military strength, the South should not have gone to war against the North in 1861. The odds were too heavily stacked against it. Military armaments were one key measure and certainly one that spoke to the disparity of strength between the two regions. The North manufactured over 90 percent of all firearms produced in the United States. The rail lines intersecting the nation lay mostly in the North in almost as one-sided a proportion, 75 percent. This capacity spoke to the advantages of industrial development in the North that far exceeded that of the South. Add in the vastly superior textile production of the North, and it was clear that this part of the United States could equip more soldiers with uniforms, arms, and provisions, than the South could hope to do. Since the North also had three times the population of the South, translating into a manpower advantage of at least three to one, the North would be able to field an army that far outnumbered the South. Additionally, the South would possess virtually no navy, conceding a significant military advantage to the North. Given the odds, the South was foolish, reckless, and perhaps unbalanced to contemplate a war against its neighbor.

The military imbalance grew out of a larger economic disparity. Canals in the South, much like rail lines, accounted for a pitifully small number of the nation's total, just 14 percent. Transportation was not in high demand given that, by 1842, the South was home to less than 18 percent of the nation's manufacturing capacity. This number helped explain Northern population growth, a 20 percent advantage over the South in the 1840s alone, much of it from Southerners moving north looking for employment. A concerted effort in the South to increase industry there took hold in the 1850s. Manufacturing doubled as capital investment rose by 75 percent, and labor in the industrial sector climbed by 25 percent. But the South made little progress in comparison to Northern gains. The disparity remained.

The South could point to the cotton boom as proof of its economic vitality, and this certainly was true since the boom reached its height in the decade before the Civil War. However, a dependence on agriculture meant more economic disadvantages. Southern staples, cotton, tobacco, and sugar, overwhelmingly went for export. These commodities traveled on Northern rails and boats. Starved of capital, the slave owner turned to Northern banks for money. This financing then went to purchasing more slaves and land. It was a cycle that held the slave owner in financial bondage to Yankee interests to the amount of $100 million annually. Still, plantation owners did better than the rest of the South since a large majority of whites enjoyed no access to monetary resources at all. This rebounded with another economic negative. Southerners had no money to buy consumer goods, so no industry rose in the South to meet this demand because there was no such demand. A small Southern elite imported its finished goods. In sum, Yankee economic strangulation of the South was complete, and it imposed a binding constraint on the entire South, not just the upper class. Preemption was needed to break these bonds and achieve economic self-sufficiency to recoup funds totaling millions of dollars.

Many Southerners believed that more land would cure these ills by allowing a greater number of whites to enjoy the fruits of the cotton boom. But Northerners refused this courtesy. Restricted in acquiring new slave lands, the South saw only conspiracy. The Wilmot Proviso in 1846 was one important example where indignant Yankees refused to allow slavery in any land seized from the war with Mexico. Yet, these same detractors sought to admit California to the Union as a free state four years later. The South fought in vain to head off this disaster. In Congress, the House already did the North's bidding, given that the North enjoyed much more representation. The Proviso was stopped in the Senate. To lose control of the Senate with the admittance of both California and New Mexico as free states would be disastrous for the South. Defeat in territorial expansion meant only more tyranny in the absence of political representation. The increasing number of free states would ensure a defeat of Southern interests in Congress, no matter how these interests were defined. Clearly the South could not stay within the democratic process to secure its welfare because that right of representation had been eliminated by Yankee control of Congress, or soon would be.

A few brave souls tried to get past the barriers imposed on the South by the North. These intrepid adventurers looked to Latin America as a means to expand slave lands. William Walker is one very good example, given that his exploits in the mid-1850s carried him first into Mexico and then Nicaragua. In each locale he and his "army" of not quite one hundred men established free republics. In Nicaragua, he also openly declared in favor of slavery. Here was an invitation to the South to join him in turning Central America into a fertile ground for Southern expansion. There were many other such men advocating the expansion of slavery into Central America; the favored target was Cuba. Due to their actions, Manifest Destiny became a Southern burden, one Southerners believed they carried nobly. Yet the schemes came to nothing. Mexican authorities forced Walker from that country and the Nicaraguans eventually did the same. Honduran authorities finally executed this hated *gringo*. In other instances, the Northern-dominated US government interfered and stopped these endeavors, branding them unlawful. However, Southerners watched as Northern vigilance relaxed when it came to enforcing the Fugitive Slave Act, the key concession the North granted to the South in the Compromise of 1850. Numerous instances of slaves escaping into Canada due to aid from sympathetic Northerners, or of slaves continuing to hide in the North and not facing the legal sanctions of the fugitive slave law, enraged Southern sensibilities. Better to leave the Union and make laws for the betterment of the South than to bow before an arbitrary enforcement of laws that reflected an abusive Northern rule.

The abolitionist drive in the North to end slavery struck at the core of Southern existence, both monetary and cultural. Deprived of its labor force, the Southern economy would collapse. With such an economic downturn, how would the South incorporate some four million ex-slaves into its society? This problem included the practical aspect of labor and the cultural bomb of assimilation, since emancipation necessitated some accommodation with former slaves. What the North was asking for was a revolution. The South turned to preemption as a means of counter-revolution. The South believed that it must strike first to protect the status quo before the destructive forces of revolution arose. Slavery would remain in place to ensure economic vitality, of course, but also to stop the prospect of racial barbarity. Southerners would thwart the Northern perversion of their lifestyle. Waiting invited disaster.

Slavery boiled down to a question of defining freedom, not for slaves, but for Southerners. The very essence of democracy was at stake. The South needed slave labor to ensure its economic vitality that in turn ensured upward mobility. The "Southern gentleman" was a goal all Southerners aspired to. Land made this happen. As much as landed wealth was an ideal,

Southerners believed that toiling the soil necessitated a debasing of the human condition. Should whites have to conduct this labor, the great ill of democracy would soon become apparent; a labor class would emerge to challenge the social order. Slavery avoided this pitfall by assigning one race to the role of day worker, and in turn raising the condition of the entire white race. In the South, slavery meant a certain stability of the social class, and therefore of democracy. By acknowledging the fate of some group having to inevitably exist at the bottom of society, Southern introspection rationalized slavery and therefore saved democracy.

Other considerations substantiated Southern claims of the "good" of slavery. Northern exaggerations of the abuses of slavery, perhaps best captured in Harriet Beecher Stowe's novel, *Uncle Tom's Cabin*, hid the supposed inferiority of the Negro race that justified its subservient role in Southern society. In the view of Southerners, slavery was a humanitarian gesture they bestowed unto a race of people struggling to survive when forced to live on their own. In the South, slaves enjoyed security for life. This Southern success contrasted mightily with the perversion of democracy unfolding in the North. There, industry relied on a labor force clearly suffering abuse at the hands of manufacturers. A business elite ruled Northern industry in tyrannical fashion, certainly in undemocratic fashion, and these men pointed to the South as a means to deflect criticism from their own exploitative practices. These were undemocratic in the extreme, a limited number of cartels colluding with one another to dominate the proceeds of business. The South had achieved a true democracy, one the North looked to destroy since the Southern model had embraced a Jeffersonian ideal that reflected the true virtues of democracy.

These facts were obscured by a Northern cultural domination of the South. The many Northern books and magazines in the South were there because of successful business tactics that crowded out the numerous and outstanding Southern periodicals, not because of a conscious choice by the Southern reader. This cultural reach extended into the classroom, where textbooks represented abolitionist views willingly emphasized by teachers from the North. Nor did the South enjoy a reprieve when it came to higher education since so many of its youths went north to gain a college education. A homegrown education at all levels, a faculty that came from the South, a body of literature written by men from the South that spoke of Southern ideals such as the agrarian livelihood, all of these steps would ensure the intellectual independence of the South from the North. Ending this cultural oppression by separating from the North gave the South as much cause to act preemptively as did reasserting its economic and political freedom.

Even a firm conviction in the necessity of acting preemptively could do little to offset the glaring realities of the military disadvantages the South faced in comparison with the North. However, as it considered a preemptive strike, Northern material superiority barely upset the calculations of Southerners pushing for secession. These "fire-eaters" were confident of victory because they believed that a number of intangibles mitigated the unfavorable military circumstances. In the first place, the South would be defending its homeland and gain two advantages from this circumstance. One, they would enjoy a boost in morale. Two, they would know the terrain. Both factors bolstered defense, the posture the South assumed it would adopt in the event of hostilities. In related fashion, those Southerners demanding war could tell themselves that for the South to be defeated, the North would have to occupy the entire South, an enormously difficult thing to do given the expansive land mass. At the very least the onus of winning the war fell on the North. This reality again favored defense. In the second place, the Southerners counted on the indomitable Southern spirit, a warlike quality normally muted within a gentlemanly ease, but once called into battle it was a fearsome quality to reckon with. Such militarism would translate into outstanding leadership, worthy of leading the dedicated Southern soldier in battle. The combination of these factors was thought to more than offset Northern material advantages and for this reason a great many Southerners welcomed a conflict with the North.

By 1861, the South was ready to fight. Some scholars argue that tensions had built up to such a point by this time that strife was inevitable, something Bruce Levine called "the inexorable logic of events."* They make a persuasive case that this was so. In the wake of the Compromise of 1850, political failings and economic and social strains became frequent and numerous. In 1854, Senator Stephen A. Douglas reopened the issue of slavery in western lands when he pushed for popular sovereignty in the Kansas–Nebraska territory to try and ensure that a rail line passed through there to his home state of Illinois. In attempting to please both Southerners and Northerners by allowing a popular mandate to settle the question of slavery in this volatile territory, he inflamed this hot spot. John Brown spread the fire in 1856, leading a band of anti-slavery advocates on a murderous expedition to avenge a Southern insult, the destruction of an anti-slavery press in the town of Lawrence, Kansas. Brown's party killed and mutilated five people, but he escaped prosecution and reemerged in the east to direct the infamous raid at Harpers Ferry in 1859. Brown's goal this time was to lead slaves in rebellion against their Southern masters; the federal armory

---

* See Bruce Levine's chapter by that title in, *Half Slave and Half Free: The Roots of the Civil War*, rev. edn. (New York: Hill and Wang, 2005), 225–242.

at Harpers Ferry was to supply the weapons. His grand aim faltered and this time he was arrested by US authorities. His subsequent execution, however, only made him a martyr for the abolitionist cause, and therefore a hero in the North. To Southerners, he was a villain, an example of crusading Northerners unlawfully interfering in Southern affairs.

John Brown was more a victim of economic downturn than he was a proponent of abolitionism. The financial turbulence of the early 1850s claimed Brown as a casualty, bankrupted him once again, and gave him more reason to pursue the "holy" cause of abolitionism. The Dred Scott case soon placed the legal question of slavery in a moral context that outraged the North and lent credence to the actions of a man like John Brown. Scott, a slave who sued for his freedom once he reached free territory, lost his bid for emancipation before the Supreme Court in 1857, and in language that framed the black man's subservience to whites in stark racial terms. Brown's martyrdom was possible only given the obvious failure of the Scott case to use a legal avenue to address slavery, since right and wrong vanished from the equation. Only race mattered, a fact that Brown realized all too well. That a man like Brown could spread terror in one part of the United States, then spread revolution in another, and still symbolize the tensions between the North and South, can only attest to the myriad twists and turns of the moral debate about slavery. Perhaps the meaning of the immorality of slavery had been lost by this point, to Brown's disgust. Dispensing with the immorality of waging war would be an easy step to take after that.

Of course, denying the "wrong" of slavery only called attention to the failure of political leadership in bringing this crisis to a suitable resolution before 1861. In fact, the opposite was the case—"blundering" politicians used the slavery issue to advance their careers and incite the push toward civil war.* Douglas' effort to secure a railroad through the Kansas–Nebraska territory only stresses a more glaring instance of this abuse than was Lincoln's use of slavery to position himself as a national candidate for the presidency. In the famous debates between these two men as they vied for the Senate in 1858, Lincoln fixed morality at the center of the slave issue. It was wrong to be a slave owner, he said. Douglas pursued the tactic of focusing on stopping the spread of slavery and not its right to exist in a free nation. Douglas won this battle and kept his Senate seat. But Lincoln won the political war by asserting that slavery must come to an end some day. His clear opposition to the South won him much popular support in the North. Lincoln's political triumph was complete when he emerged as

---

* See Kenneth M. Stampp's examination of this issue in *The Imperiled Union: Essays on the Background of the Civil War* (New York: Oxford University Press, 1980), 207–208.

the Republican candidate for president in 1860, and then won the election. However, in making plain the chasm between the two Northern approaches to slavery, ending it altogether or simply limiting its growth, Lincoln and Douglas had provided the South with a *causus belli* for preemption because the Northern endorsement of Lincoln as president clearly meant the Northern validation of the end of slavery. Therefore, Lincoln's triumph was marred by the prospect of war since his election sparked secession.

Through a combination of human error and circumstance, the country sped to civil war in understandable if tragic terms. This evaluation is not complete, however. Preemption adds one more factor to the analysis. The South's willingness to fight in 1861 revealed that the cultural neurosis of the North–South division had reached a boiling point, though more so in the South than in the North. Preemption released that tension in the South. The war would finally come and the tension would be resolved. Still, the South would be unique in clinging to a preemptive strategy without believing that a first strike would actually give them a sufficient military advantage to prevail in the war that followed. Instead, the larger context of preemption drew the South to attacking the federal position at Fort Sumter and starting the Civil War. Without taking a stand, Southern culture would face destruction at the hands of the North anyway. Even if the odds were too great to make success likely, most, though by no means all, Southerners deemed the fight worthwhile. Either way, the South faced destruction. Since it had no choice but to act, why not ensure an honorable fate and fight?

Many Southerners did express great confidence in their unique attributes that could enable them to win a struggle against the North. But the prospect of war still weighed heavily on their minds. One reason was the obvious reluctance to take the step to war and invite its terrible consequences: loss of life, destruction of property, etc. This fear was dismissed by a cavalier attitude that no matter what came, the fallout would be minimal. Very little blood would be spilled. Confidence in a limited clash allayed concerns arising from the second reason why the South hesitated to wage war against the North, the inability to predict the course of such a war with certainty and therefore to be sure of the consequences of war. The bloodshed might be great. Even a quick "victory" with limited loss of life might produce unwelcome change. The hazards of war clearly stared Southerners in the face since there was no telling what might come of a clash between North and South.

The South needed a reason to believe they could win this fight and preemption gave them this hope, though for surprising reasons. A sharp blow inflicted on Union forces would not redress the material imbalance between the two warring parties. The disparity was too great for a Southern attack to achieve this at the start of war. Rather, preemption was valued as a means to indicate Southern resolve. This came in two respects. First, an initial exchange of shots might stop a real shooting war from occurring. Northerners would shrink from the prospect of violence. Armed with this rationale of preemption, the South looked forward to waging war against the North and ending the tensions between the two regions with a show of military force that would defuse the possibility of a greater war.

Should this not occur and a longer, deadlier struggle result, the second benefit of acting preemptively came into play. With some bloodshed, there could be no going back. The South would have to fight. But what constituted the South, and the depths of its resolve, were still in doubt. Once South Carolina left the Union, six other states followed. This much had been expected and it was significant in getting things started. But seven states were not enough to realistically expect the South to fight a successful war against the North, and more states needed to join the Confederacy for the South to expect to win such a conflict. A preemptive strike overcame this problem since it added legitimacy to the Southern cause. Once some fighting erupted, other states would have to make the hard decision of whether to leave the Union and join the Confederacy. When important border states saw the North try to bully the South into submission with the threat of war, they would side with the Confederacy. More states made the Confederacy more powerful, and Union resolve would weaken when faced by such a formidable foe. With additional states in the Confederacy, a war might be averted altogether, and for the same reason as before: Southern resolve would discourage Yankee aggression. Should a fight occur, the South would be stronger and better able to defend itself if it consisted of more than seven states.

In using an act of preemption to avert a war, the South pushed the United States into civil war. Should war erupt, many Southerners expressed confidence in defeating Union arms. Others embraced a conflict in fatalistic terms: a war might end in defeat, but the current prospect of Northern domination was disgraceful and to fight redeemed Southern honor. The logic was at times painfully confused. A clash at Fort Sumter would both avert a war and produce a war that would rally additional states to the Southern banner. Ultimately, the South would take the plunge and risk war with the North because it deemed the Northern threat too great to ignore. The North would not let the South grow in size to free itself from commercial bondage at the hands of the North. When teamed with a political loss of power, the Southern way of life was in great jeopardy, as seen in the already significant inroads of Northern culture. Hemmed in in every way, the South had no choice but to act preemptively and defend itself.

The Attack

Fort Sumter was one of several federal forts commanding the harbor of Charleston, outposts that were vulnerable to attack following South Carolina's secession from the Union. A state dominated by slavery and one with a preexisting record of favoring secession, that it left the Union first was no great surprise. Its leaders now contemplated how to bring the wavering border states into the Confederacy. A quick seizure of these forts in Charleston harbor would indicate Southern resolve and Northern weakness and so encourage these other states to join in the act of secession.

As would be the case with so many personal stories involved in the Civil War, conflicting allegiances impacted the decisions of the officers and men fighting at Charleston. Major Robert Anderson commanded the Northern defense in the harbor. Anderson was a Southerner from Kentucky, but he decided his loyalties lay with the army and therefore with the North. Aware that his vulnerable position could be the tinder that ignited civil war, he attempted to lessen this explosive potential by evacuating one fort, Fort Moultrie, and reinforcing the other, Sumter. Fort Moultrie was indefensible anyway. Fort Sumter was an island and therefore easier to hold. In thus strengthening his position, Anderson hoped to lessen the temptation of the Southern militia now on station in the city to batter the forts into submission. Rather than reducing tensions, Anderson unwittingly amplified them. His reinforcing of Sumter was a great act of defiance praised by Northerners since he had secretly evacuated the one fort in favor of the other at night and struck a blow by fooling the Southerners. Anderson's action was a great insult to Southerners, more evidence of Yankee treachery and aggression since Lincoln had promised not to strengthen Union defenses in Southern territory.

These military developments spurred the rush to war over Sumter, but not before Lincoln had tried one more act of diplomacy. He ordered the fort re-supplied, something the authorities in Charleston had warned him they would consider an act of war, and therefore result in the outbreak of civil war. Lincoln sidestepped this ultimatum deftly, publicly announcing the re-supply of the garrison with unarmed ships. If there was to be fighting, the South would have to push the nation over the edge. Lincoln had put the burden of starting a war on the Confederacy.

It willingly obliged. Southern militia opened fire at dawn, April 12, 1861, before any re-supply could occur. After two days, the fort surrendered and did so without the loss of a single man on either side. Even though it was a bloodless battle, the South had shown its fortitude. The North would surely not go to war now. Lincoln thought otherwise and ordered the call-up of a ninety-day militia totaling 75,000 men to put down an insurrection that, as he described it, was "too powerful to be suppressed by the ordinary course of judicial proceedings."* The Northern response to Lincoln's call to arms was overwhelmingly favorable and the machinery of war began to grind into action. Political unity visited the North as well. Lincoln's long-time opponent, Stephen Douglas, publicly told a crowd, "There are only two sides to the question. Every man must be for the United States or against it. There can be no neutrals in this war, only patriots—or traitors."** It was strong language, very different from the president's success in using subtlety to place the blame of the conflict on the South over the Sumter crisis.

The South accepted the challenge and prepared for war. Still, the South believed that there would be no fighting. If fighting came, it would be limited, a few lives lost. Sumter validated this wishful thinking. So too did the actions of four of the eight border states. In response to Lincoln's appeal to arms, Virginia, Arkansas, Tennessee, and North Carolina all seceded from the Union and joined the Confederacy. These were powerful states with significant populations and ones offering other military advantages. Southerners could take heart that the South was now too powerful to be defeated by the North. Secession, they thought, would go unchallenged. However, the Civil War had arrived. The South now had to confront the uncertain consequences of war.

Success

Fort Sumter turned out to be an aberration. There would be lots of bloodshed from the beginning of this conflict to its end. The first great battle came on July 21, 1861, a few months after the Confederate shelling of Fort Sumter. At the Battle of First Bull Run fought near the Union capital, a Southern army defeated its Union counterpart in a hard-fought struggle that lasted most of the day. The loss of life testified to the folly of hoping for a bloodless war: almost 2,000 killed and wounded on each side. Additionally, the spectators from Washington D.C. who turned out to watch the "contest" also highlighted the folly surrounding the war in its opening months; the war would not be a colorful display. Lincoln's call to arms of a ninety-day militia would be another reminder. He soon concluded that a more permanent standing army would be necessary to win the struggle. Both sides now prepared for a longer war. Taking this step at last

---

* Richard N. Current, *Lincoln and the First Shot* (Philadelphia: J.B. Lippincott Company, 1963), 157.

** James M. McPherson, *Battle Cry of Freedom: The Civil War Era* (New York: Ballantine Books, 1988), 274.

indicated that the state of disbelief that had in no small measure drove the South to arms had finally dissipated.

Repetition would eliminate any lingering hopes of a short, bloodless war. The Battle of Bull Run was fought again the following year, although the result was the same, a Southern victory. In this eastern theater of war, the opposing sides would face each other in a series of battles that revealed a grudge match taking shape that produced a slowly escalating conflict and mounting casualties. Early on, the South got the best of these battles and in no small part due to the fact that a number of brilliant leaders did surface to aid its cause. Foremost in this regard was Robert E. Lee. A trusted military advisor to Jefferson Davis, the president of the Confederacy, Davis named Lee commander of what would become the Army of Northern Virginia in 1862. His command came at a fortuitous time, for the North had again assumed the offensive and threatened Richmond, the Southern capital. Lee defeated General George B. McClellan's Army of the Potomac in a number of battles fought over seven days, eventually ending the threat to Richmond and sending the Union forces back to their defenses surrounding Washington D.C. The bloodshed had been acute, the Peninsula Campaign claiming 16,000 Union casualties, 20,000 Confederates. Lee's peers deemed his operations a success. Lee was less convinced that his "offensive-defensive" strategy had succeeded.* The peril to Richmond had ended, but the Union army had not been destroyed. This latter aim had been Lee's objective, massing military force to avoid a passive defense and so win a decisive victory.

Lee now assumed overall command of the Confederate armies in the east. It was in this capacity that Lee made a crucial decision. The South must assume the offensive and attack the North, he believed, rather than await another Union attack. Continued fighting would only wear down his forces, the North turning to its inexhaustible manpower to eventually force the Confederacy to submit. A Southern offensive into Union territory turned the tables. It brought the Union army to a battlefield of Lee's choosing, and with the destruction of that army, this defeat would bring the war home to the North. Northerners would then sue for peace. In assuming the offensive, Lee desired no permanent territorial objectives. The South was not expanding. Rather, the South was dictating a tempo that it hoped would produce a decisive battle to force the North to make peace. The South could then enjoy its status as a separate nation.

---

* Russell F. Weigley offers the best analysis of Lee's offensive-defensive strategy and of Grant's divergence from this approach in favor of a strategy of annihilation. See Weigley, *The American Way of War: A History of United States Military Strategy and Policy* (Bloomington, IN: Indiana University Press, 1973), 102, 144.

Lee's strategy was remarkable for many reasons. For one thing, it admitted what had been denied by Southerners in the rush to war: the great material advantage the North enjoyed could defeat the South. Additionally, his offensive plans transgressed on the hopes of fighting a successful defensive war. It must have been troubling to Southern partisans that Lee would stick with the strategy of invading the North despite winning two great defensive battles, Fredericksburg in December 1862, and Chancellorsville in early May 1863. A certain desperation influenced his determination to invade the North. At least the South would not be burdened with having to conquer the North, as did the North when it attacked the South. This great strategic principle remained intact, and it did somewhat bolster Lee's strategy. But Lee's decision eliminated the last shred of optimism that had accompanied the South into the war, since his offensive plans forfeited the assumed advantages of staying on the defensive that had preceded the conflict. Lee gambled that he could force the North into a negotiated peace before the North simply wore down the South and won the war on the basis of attrition alone. He needed a great battle to offset the prospect of a long, agonizing war that would cost many lives.

Lee soon adopted his strategy to try and end the war by invading the North and forcing a settlement. On two occasions, he led his army into Northern territory only to meet defeat both times. In September 1862, after a bloody struggle he held the battlefield of Antietam and won the day. It was ugly carnage, some 22,000 soldiers dead and wounded on both sides about equally distributed between the opponents. But Lee had failed to gain his decisive victory. Worse, he lost the edge he sought because he had to withdraw from Maryland back into Virginia, turning his battlefield victory into a strategic defeat. He had failed to win a battle that forced a peace. He tried again. The following year, 1863, saw a larger bloodbath, a clear Lee defeat, and an end to Lee's strategy. In three days in July, the opposing armies inflicted some 51,000 casualties on one another at Gettysburg, Pennsylvania. This time around Lee's army suffered more than did the Army of the Potomac, though the Northern army's losses of over 23,000 were great as well. But Lee again was forced to retreat, and his bid to take the fighting to the North ended.

The North now moved closer to waging a total war, its efforts a conscious attempt to conquer the South. This strategy came from U.S. Grant, a general fighting for the Union who possessed as much ability as Lee. Grant's talent, however, came in a specific form, a cold determination to see the war to an end no matter how great the cost in lives. This was less callous indifference on Grant's part to loss of life than it was a careful reading of the era of war he now found himself fighting in. He believed the time of the decisive battle had passed, and a new strategy was imperative. This involved coordinating multiple theaters of action, and waging war with an abandon that could not have been anticipated even by those fearing the scourge of war prior to the start of the fighting. The contrast to Lee was complete. Lee never coordinated the Confederacy's war effort on multiple fronts. His goal was seeking a decisive battle in the east that he believed offered a sort of remedy to the horrible nature of the conflict; the day-long battle could end the conflict and save lives by eliminating the need for further fighting. Even as the body counts rose with each battle, Lee clung to his belief in the decisive battle, at least up to Gettysburg. After this defeat, Lee only hoped to inflict enough losses on the North so that the war ended in stalemate. For this reason, Lee bore as much responsibility as did Grant for the horrendous causalities that characterized the last few years of the war.

Grant quickly turned Lee into a victim of total war. The Union general directed a series of offensives by the Army of the Potomac starting in 1864 that reduced Lee's army to a beleaguered rabble clinging to a chain of fortifications defending the town of Petersburg. In the western theater of the war, a trusted Grant lieutenant, William Tecumseh Sherman, marched on Atlanta, Georgia, and then to the coast on a deliberate mission to inflict harm on the Southern interior, more specifically to terrorize civilians. By December 1864, Sherman had reached Savannah and it was clear that the war had taken a horrible turn. The war in the west produced a swath of destruction seldom seen in North America. The campaign in the east had cost thousands of lives. Once Lee gave way at Petersburg, Richmond fell to Union forces in the first few days of April 1865, and Lee surrendered at Appomattox Courthouse on April 9. A few Southern generals tried to hold out, but Lee's capitulation essentially ended the war.

Lee may have got much wrong, but other factors were also significant in explaining his defeat. Most importantly, the South's bid for a preemptive war had failed completely. The Northern material edge in military resources had proved the deciding factor, no matter the indomitable Southern spirit or the brilliant Southern generalship. To uphold its culture the South had turned to preemptive warfare as a means of self-preservation. It ended this war a conquered state. By fighting, the South had achieved its preemptive purpose, that it would be destroyed one way or the other: either a Northern ascendancy would eclipse the Southern lifestyle sooner or later, or the South would fight a heroic war and lose, and thereby forfeit its culture as well. Never had preemption served such a forlorn hope.

The futility was all the more apparent given the aftermath of the war. A Southern identity tied to slavery did survive the war in the form of Jim Crow. The triumph of white supremacy in the South after 1865 testified to the cultural resilience of the Southern way of life. Since it did not face cultural eclipse at the hands of a Northern presence even after total military defeat, how could it have been so before the war? But this Southern "victory" of maintaining white supremacy after the war also testified to the moral limits of Southern culture. The cause of defending itself may have been valid and glorious, achieving a morality in this preemptive purpose, but the Southern aim of cultural freedom still victimized a group of people. This victimization of African-Americans indeed persisted after the war, undoing any claims to the moral necessity of preemptive warfare at the time of the Civil War.

Conclusion

The potential of a Northern military juggernaut held Southern independence hostage since the threat of Northern aggression allowed the North to take a hostile stand on the issue of slavery. Deemed a wrong by the North, Yankees looked to dictate economic realities to the South that could only end the freedom that region enjoyed. Southern disadvantages in infrastructure, rail lines and canals in particular, signaled, not a shortcoming of the slave system, but an effort of subjugation of the South by the North. Exports of Southern agricultural goods went north and abroad, finished products came south. Needing capital, the slave owner turned to Southern banks, but these answered to Northern firms. No matter where he turned, the slave owner faced Northern aggression in the economic arena. Preemption was the only recourse to ending this Northern strangulation of the Southern economy.

Economic persecution rebounded in social disaster. Ending slavery meant crippling the entire construct of Southern society founded on a labor-intensive agricultural model and a culture of gentility that spoke to the best traditions of the American nation. The founding fathers made the Southern case for them, declining to eliminate slavery at the founding of the nation. Their lack of action endorsed the agrarian paradise the South had constructed. What it had achieved by 1861 was the very dream of the founders. Americans lived on land that ensured a self-sufficiency that then produced the truest form of democracy. The realization of Southern culture meant the realization of the American dream. Its destruction meant the perverse notion of ending what had been forged in the blood of the Revolution. The South would not let this treason stand. Secession was a counter-revolutionary act, an act of patriotism, a symbol of what was best for the nation.

By 1861, the South believed it faced too great a threat from the North not to act. This oppression took other forms than that of attacking slavery. Western expansion had worked to Southern disadvantage. By denying slavery in the new lands, the North restricted the political representation of the South in Congress, despite great sacrifices of Southern blood in acquiring the new land. Northerners then abused their power in that governmental body, seeking restrictions that curbed Southern interests. When brave Southerners looked to Latin America to expand slavery and secure the interests of the South, they met opposition from the US government, answering to Northern calls of stopping the spread of slavery. Here again the North tampered with a cherished America tradition, Manifest Destiny, fostering it when it served Northern interests in western expansion, declaring it unlawful when it aided Southern aspirations in spreading slavery south.

Most importantly, the North stymied Southern culture by denying it the opportunity to achieve the ideal of the Southern gentleman. The Southern gentleman required both land and slaves. That this ideal could not gain any traction at all after 1820 came from a Northern dominance of Southern affairs. This Northern influence seeped into culture in unacceptable ways beyond mere economics. A college education usually came in the North. Opinion makers in the South had Northern roots; too many teachers and newspapermen had trained in the north or were Northerners living in the South. The conspiracy of Northern cultural aggression did not appear far-fetched given the actions of abolitionists in the north. Crusaders such as John Brown were allowed to go unchecked in the north, galvanizing Northern resistance to Southern culture. The popularity of *Uncle Tom's Cabin* added fuel to the fire. Condoning the exaggeration of Southern sins against humanity as portrayed in this novel revealed a Northern determination to remold Southern culture in its entirety.

No matter the tremendous advantages industry provided the North, many Southerners questioned the military viability of the Northern threat. The North might enjoy a great material advantage, but Southern spirit and the benefits of fighting defensively would offset this advantage. There was good hope that secession would pass without the outbreak of war should Southerners show some resolve. But should war come, Southerners were ready for a simple reason, that of desperation. Facing a grave threat, Southerners concluded that they had no choice but to fight. Armed with this determination, the South looked to preemptive warfare. This only furthered the moral aims of the South in resisting Union oppression. The morality did not come from striking preemptively. Rather, the morality came from fighting a preemptive war to preserve Southern culture. They reasoned they had little choice. Not to fight allowed the North to end their dream. To fight might in fact result in the South's destruction, but it would be an honorable fate. This preemptive purpose guided Southern leaders to war in 1861.

A mix of exaggeration and reality inundated the South and clearly influenced the calculations for preemptive war. The Southern spirit and leadership coupled with defensive warfare were to defeat Union force of arms, no matter the great material advantages the North enjoyed. To understand the extent of this exaggeration one need only consider the extensive list of Southern disadvantages. With no navy, the South was vulnerable to blockade, a fact that would accelerate the already pronounced Southern disadvantage in industry. Nor would financial capital allow the South to offset this economic disadvantage to any great extent by looking outside its borders. The ability to purchase sustenance, and during war, war materials, from abroad was limited due to the hold of the Northern capital on Southern business affairs. Material deficiency extended beyond counting soldiers in the field to the South's inability to sustain itself financially during a military encounter with the North. The South faced such a disparity that to contemplate a war did appear madness, the hope for mitigating circumstances merely wishful thinking.

Only by suspending disbelief could the South move to war since the agricultural paradise Southerners clung to contained many shortcomings. The economic disparities were the most recognizable. The South was too focused on agriculture to diversify its economy, to escape a dependence on Northern capital and infrastructure. This reliance was not bondage but a crutch keeping the Southern dream alive. How was separation to solve this problem? Without help from the North, the economics of the Southern ideal could not sustain itself despite more land or more slaves. Southerners knew this to be true, but clung to the Jeffersonian ideal that could not produce economic self-sufficiency no matter if it did produce the desired cultural norm of self-reliance. Southerners insisted on separation that had cultural appeal but lacked any business sense. In this way, the Southern call for secession certainly grew out of an economic disparity that was self-inflicted.

This problem of exaggeration was acute when it came time for Southerners to assess the "revolution" imposed on the South by the North. Historian James McPherson, in *Battle Cry of Freedom*, his famed treatment of the entire Civil War, described the Southern rationale of preemption as follows: "They exaggerated the Republican threat and urged pre-emptive action to forestall the danger they conjured up."* His was a negative view of preemption. In the name of counter-revolution, Southerners exaggerated Northern malice in seeking to dominate the South in terms of limiting slave territory and the political and economic plots to hold the South in

---

* McPherson, *Battle Cry of Freedom*, 245.

bondage to the North. The arguments of cultural domination were the most far-fetched, such as blaming Northern business practices for the widespread appeal of Northern literature. A homegrown Southern movement reflected a worry on the part of the planter elite over how best to ensure the loyalty of the more than two-thirds of whites in the South who did not own any slaves at all. This element of society combined with a restive slave population not convinced of its "good" treatment. The unity and survival of the South, in or out of the Union, became a huge problem. The Southern gentleman needed to exaggerate the Northern threat to meet the crisis he faced on the home front. In this sense, one has to agree with McPherson, theirs was a counter-revolution.

Nor did the model of the Southern gentleman necessarily mean a model for democracy. Many critics in the North derided this ideal as anti-democratic because once a landed aristocracy had been established, it remained in place largely because of the slave system of labor. The ideal was certainly a lure, but the reality a seldom-seen occurrence; only a very small percentage of Southern society resided in the plantation-style mansions that embodied the ultimate Southern lifestyle. The class system was rigidly in place, and there was little social mobility. The ideal of the Southern gentleman was just that, an ideal that fractured in reality. Instead of democracy, an aristocracy reigned supreme in the South. Pushing for more land to create additional planters merely allowed Southerners not to face this reality.

Southern defense of slavery fell short due to similar denial. Most citizens North and South tolerated slavery as an ill that Providence would some day eliminate. In the meantime, in other words indefinitely, they would merely bear the hypocrisy of living in a free country embracing slavery. Lincoln simply made this point plain in his debates with Douglas. Yet, in the eyes of Southerners, he became an enemy of the South. The extent of the exaggeration of Lincoln's intended harm to the South can be measured by placing Robert E. Lee's hope that Providence would end slavery next to Lincoln's. Though appealing to the same rationale, Lincoln remained a villain to the South, while Lee remained its chief defender.

The fact was that slavery as a "good" was a recent argument. Before 1820, Southern planters referred to slavery as a necessary evil. Not until after 1820 did the South feel compelled to embrace the logic of slavery as a good. What changed after 1820 was that Southerners asserted that states' rights should decide the issue of slavery. Congress was to decline to hear any mention of petition on the issue. The willingness of Southerners to rescind constitutional rights to advance slavery shifted Northern opinion behind the abolitionists. Even then, marked exaggeration carried the day for Southerners. Abolitionists certainly led the charge of accusing Southerners of committing the moral wrong of slavery. But this small group hardly spoke to the mood of the entire North. The planter elite's inclination to demonize the North as a land of madmen made for a good rallying point at home. What better way to control a Southern population than to keep it in fear of an imminent attack from more John Browns or something worse?

The South quickly identified Northern villains but turned a blind eye to its own. These individuals were numerous since the South fielded its own radicals in the form of the filibusters pushing Southern interests into Latin America. Defined as heroes championing the Southern cause, the reality was more base. These men did in fact commit unlawful acts, invading foreign countries or the colonies of other nations. For Southerners to call this aggression freedom, and then to propose slavery in these lands, made little sense. The South always took its basic contradiction with it: a free society resting upon slavery. The same irrationality plagued its ability to deal successfully with western expansion in the United States. Incensed over a lack of fair treatment, the South threatened secession repeatedly. How it was to gain redress for the wrongs the North had committed once it left the Union was not just unclear, but something Southerners never raised. The fugitive slave law is a key example making this point clear. A separate South meant a large bastion to the north to which slaves could escape. Southern interests were better served by remaining in the Union and preventing the creation of an enormous slave refuge adjacent to their new country, no matter the obstacles hostile Northerners might throw their way. At least while in the Union, Southerners could head north and reclaim runaway slaves. Of course the South could tell itself that it could address these problems more successfully as an independent state. But it is hard to see how it could have sealed its borders. To deal with this problem, the South never asked the question.

Denial, willful ignorance, and exaggeration proved a powerful combination and spurred the South to act preemptively. Southerners had their limits in facing the potential ugly realities of war, however. A show of force from the very beginning might convince the North not to fight. This belief did not stress Southern confidence in martial victory but the unease over the consequences of war. Loss of life and the destruction of property, as well as simply the unpredictable consequences from even a short war, naturally cooled the rush to war. This sobering perspective deflated the cavalier attitude Southerners held toward the military odds so heavily stacked against the South. However, this picture suffers when closely scrutinized, the best example coming from Southern lament of losing the war after being overwhelmed by Northern material weight. In the case of manpower, the South was indeed greatly outnumbered, but not due to a demographic disadvantage, rather because it never mobilized its manpower base satis-factorily. Malingerers, generous deferments to the wealthy, security forces needed to prevent slave uprisings, a government that could not administrate successfully, defection of non-slave holders from the Southern cause, all of these factors depleted Southern strength on the field of battle. The failure of the South to make the maximum effort on its own behalf provided a final staple of denial: the Southern soldier joining with leadership that did a remarkable job in the face of overwhelming odds. Should all of the South have been committed to the struggle and produced more soldiers, the outcome might have been different, given the superior Southern commanders early in the war.

The point is that the Northern threat was not that great. Nor was it imminent either. But at the end of the litany of exaggeration, the push to go to war in the South was too great to resist. Preemption put a name on this irrational act. It confirmed the belief that the Northern threat must be met and the sooner the better. Also, it solidified Southern resolve by promising action. To delay meant an intolerable threat to Southern society. To fight meant self-preservation since the South initiated a war designed to solidify its borders. The shelling of Fort Sumter made this clear. After compelling the fort to submit, it then awaited attack. It did not strike into the North until a few years into the war, and this only as a way to end the war. In sum, the South had no intention of converting the North to Southern democracy. It merely wished to be free of Northern influence when deciding its own affairs.

Of course, the Southern attempt to acquire land in Latin America before the war, and even the internal disputes over the fate of the land the United States had taken from Mexico, indicated some desire of Southerners to expand the South beyond its borders. But increasing the size of the Confederacy was certainly not a war aim. In 1861, the South went to war in preemptive fashion and, by not seeking to expand, it managed to uphold the moral principle of preemption—self-defense—even if the act was unnecessary given its exaggeration of the Northern threat. It was also an act of folly, as the Northern war against the South soon proved.

CHAPTER 3

Imperial Hegemony:
The Russo–Japanese War,
1904–1905

Introduction

Lights illuminated the outlines of the ships, making them good targets. The lights also revealed the gravity of the situation. Who would have believed such a scene? Eleven Japanese torpedo boats approached the mighty Russian fleet stationed at Port Arthur on the Chinese coast. The bold move unfolded as planned. Not having issued a declaration of war, the Japanese enjoyed the element of surprise and the small Japanese force crept closer to the Russian ships before launching their torpedoes and then rapidly withdrawing completely unscathed. Three hits on three different ships left the Russian fleet shaken but now alert and preparing for battle. It was a battle that never came, given Russian reluctance to fight. Their nerves shattered, the Russian ships took shelter behind the harbor's guns. The Japanese also took stock of the situation and recoiled from further attacks due to the limited return on their preemptive strike. The Imperial Japanese Navy confronted a wounded but still intact Russian fleet. The Japanese high command understood that the preemptive strike at Port Arthur had initiated a war, but the larger task remained—that of winning the war. Just how preemption contributed to this end was as unclear to the Japanese as their plans to end the war altogether. Preemption appeared to have served a very limited purpose indeed.

The Japanese surprise attack on the Russian fleet at Port Arthur on February 8, 1904, started the Russo–Japanese War. Once assured of naval supremacy, the Japanese invaded Korea and China. Three Japanese armies sought out the Russian ground forces there and found them at several battlefields, one at Mukden in Manchuria where a Japanese force defeated a Russian army and ensured Japanese control of Korea. The other significant ground-clash came at Port Arthur, the city falling to a Japanese army after a lengthy siege. The loss was important because Port Arthur fell before a new Russian fleet approached the area of operations. This reinforcement met the Japanese navy in the straits between Korea and Japan. The subsequent Battle of Tsushima in May 1905 resulted in a total Japanese victory. Astounding in its own right, this battle did not end the war. The Japanese still found themselves engaging Russian armies on the Asian mainland in Manchuria, with no clear sense of how to win peace. This was the case even after winning the key battles on land. Fortunately for Japan, the international community took an interest in this war and sought to impose a settlement. In this regard, the United States did the most and a lengthy peace process brokered by the American president Theodore Roosevelt officially ended the conflict in September 1905. Japan emerged victorious, the Russians humiliated, and the balance of power in Asia drastically changed. For these reasons, this regional conflict in Asia offered its own contribution to the world wars coming in 1914 and 1939.

The literature addressing this oftentimes neglected war mentions the Japanese preemptive strike at Port Arthur in heroic terms: the nighttime strike in cold waters, the small Japanese vessels edging close to the huge Russian ships. Such flattery contrasts with the larger picture of Japanese leaders deliberately using preemption to launch a surprise attack on the port before a declaration of war. Here was villainy. The reason most often given for this breach of protocol is that the Japanese used preemption to secure a military advantage. However, the limited success the Japanese achieved with this preemptive strike receives little comment from scholars. Did the attack need to be launched? Did the violation of international norms outweigh any advantage gained? Scholars also neglect the moral implications of the attack. In sum, they confine the Japanese use of preemption to a battlefield tactic, in this case a naval ruse. This analysis fails to draw out the full measure of the significance of this preemptive strike. The irony of the omission is pronounced given that scholars do call attention to the lessons of this war. The use of new weapons to prolong the fighting and increase the cost of war in human life and war materials, and the strain this sacrifice put on the home front of the warring nations, all of these developments foreshadowed the carnage of World War I. Writers commented that these lessons were significant in that they went unlearned. The catastrophe of World War I would surprise all nations, but it should not have, given the experience of the Russo–Japanese War of 1904–1905.

Another important lesson that went unlearned was that this regional conflict in Asia revealed a great deal about the difficulty of using preemption to claim the moral high ground for waging war, something Germany repeated in World War I but would not have done, if it had taken a close look at the Japanese attack on Port Arthur.

The Case for Preemption

Much of the trouble Japan faced at the turn of the twentieth century stemmed from the fact that it took the European model of statecraft too much to heart. This imitation was particularly true of its foreign policy. A desire to be a great power propelled it to action and to seize Taiwan, Korea, and make large inroads into Manchuria. Japan's ambition meant a clash with the Europeans present in these locations and elsewhere in Asia. The question facing Japan was which power to engage and when. Russia served as the answer to both of these questions in 1904. Its belligerence toward Japan in matters related to Japanese security established the Russian Empire as the chief foe of Japan. For this reason Japan turned its newly modernized armed forces against this country in the winter of 1904.

The battlefield would be Korea, a country that served as the crossroads of northeast Asia. Given this geography, for Japan to achieve security, a compliant Korea was a necessity. This imperative challenged a long-established pattern in the region of Chinese dominance over Korea. With the decline of Chinese influence, however, European nations competed for supremacy in this area. The seizure of Korea by a western power meant not only the blunting of Japan's interest in securing its own protection, but also it meant an enemy was now dangerously close to Japan. The Japanese foreign minister Komura Jutaro codified this army sentiment in 1903 when he argued in a formal report that a foe positioned on the Korean peninsula could threaten the home islands since "Korea is like a dagger pointing at Japan's heart and she could never endure its possession by a foreign power."* Merely allowing Korea to fall into the sphere of influence of a European power was dangerous because Japan acknowledged its inferiority and inability to compete successfully in the struggle for the control of Asia. Should this weakness be manifest, Europeans would likely target Japan next. In this alarmist atmosphere grew a need to defend the home islands with a stand in Korea that ensured that the peninsula would come under Japanese control. National security demanded a preemptive war on the Asian mainland for this purpose.

---

* Ian Nish, *The Origins of the Russo–Japanese War* (London: Longman, 1985), 159.

That Korea could serve as a springboard for an invasion of Japan was an ancient fear most famously branded on the Japanese psyche by the effort of the Mongol ruler Kublai Khan to invade Japan from that very location in the late thirteenth century. The great Khan's armies were so formidable that should they have gained a foothold in Japan, Japanese defeat was certain. Only fortuitous circumstance had saved Japan from defeat at this time: a great wind destroyed the invading fleet. The Japanese were not sure they could rely on the divine intervention of a *kamikaze* again. They resolved not to do so. As the European presence grew in Asia, Japan plotted its course of action with self-reliance foremost in mind. A painful modernization period unfolded rapidly in the 1870s after much deliberation on the correct course to follow and after civil war. Overcoming this turmoil and healing Japan's internal wounds took next priority, and Japan could again look outside its borders and assess its role in the world two decades later.

Also established by this time was Japan's determination to engage the European powers in the region and establish itself as an equal. Korea served this purpose. In 1876, Japan imposed a treaty on Korea that opened up that nation to trade with Japan. When China did nothing to counter this move, it effectively yielded suzerainty of Korea to Japan. This Japanese success over rival China sent a clear message to the European powers. They would not find it easy to assert their dominance over Japan. Therefore, this early success in Korea at the expense of China had many long-term benefits, among them discouraging European inroads into Japan. It was a lesson that Japan learned perhaps too well. From this point on, military action would gain prominence as a policy, a reliance that was overblown since Japanese success in 1876 was characterized more by military intimidation of a weaker opponent than by any overt military triumph. Nevertheless, forcing China to back down inflated Japan's sense of its own strength and it resolved to further ready itself for a clash with a western power.

Once decided, Japan embarked on its policy to establish its hegemony in the region by using military force. It also acted in a familiar context, a clash with China over Korea. Religious factions at war in Korea drew the attention of both of these states and in mediating the internal dispute, war erupted between Japan and China in July 1894. In this conflict the Japanese came out the clear victor. China suffered military humiliation when it lost two battles in two days in September, the Japanese army defeating the Chinese forces defending Pyongyang in Korea, and the Imperial navy successfully engaging the Chinese fleet at the mouth of the Yalu River. In the flush of victory, Japan acted to secure its interests on the mainland by entrenching itself on the Liaodong Peninsula in the key region of Port

Arthur. Powerless, China agreed to make peace in April 1895 to avoid a Japanese assault on Beijing.

In the Sino-Japanese War, Japan's success was tempered, not by the Chinese, but by the European powers. From the Liaodong Peninsula, Japan sat at one end of an avenue of advance that led directly to the Chinese capital. It also could use this route to further its interests in Manchuria when it so desired in the future. The European powers recognized both motives and several of them, Germany, France, and Russia, warned Japan to give up its recent gains. Japan reluctantly did so and withdrew its forces from the Liaodong Peninsula in May 1895, but it took a number of lessons from the experience. One, a clash with the European powers was inevitable. Two, Japan needed to grow stronger militarily to meet this challenge. And three, even after building up its armed force, Japan would not be strong enough to face a combination of these powers and it had to look to divide its foes.

For these reasons and others, Japan spent the next ten years preparing for a war of national survival. It armed itself at great cost in money and at great sacrifice to its society. It also worked hard to forge an alliance with a European power, and did so when it allied with England in 1902. In so doing, England hoped to blunt the excessive ambitions of its rivals in the region, made clear in the recent Boxer Rebellion. In 1900, a combination of European states—and Japan—crushed a Chinese rebellion intended to expel Europeans from China. The prospect of the collapse of China as a state in the aftermath of the rebellion moved Britain to try and prevent what it considered a potential catastrophe by seeking out like-minded powers. It enjoyed little success. England found itself bereft of continental allies at a time it was fighting an unpopular war in South Africa, fearing a German naval build-up, and looking to contain Russian expansionist designs from Afghanistan to the Asian coastline. It welcomed Japan as a partner helping Britain balance power in Asia.

Japan relished the opportunity. China under complete European control could harm Japanese interests in two ways. One, Japan would be excluded from the mainland. And two, those very same European powers could next direct their energy toward Japan. The meeting of minds with Britain produced a limited accord with that country. The English agreed to stand aside in the event of a war between Japan and another western power. Should Japan face a coalition, England would side with Nippon. It was a great diplomatic triumph for Japan. A major western power, and a major sea power, had treated it as an equal. In so doing, the European powers could not coalesce against Japan as they had done in 1895. The French responded to this arrangement in part by forming an entente with England in 1904. France had no interest in possibly disrupting its new alliance with

Britain by antagonizing Japan, given that France wanted England's help on the Continent to restrain Germany. German goals in Asia remained limited in order to allow that nation to concentrate on Europe, much to the consternation of the French. In fact, Germany's monarch, Kaiser Wilhelm II, assured Russia's leader, Czar Nicholas II, that he would safeguard Russian interests in Europe in the event of hostilities in the east. This assurance offered little comfort to any party. Both France and Russia had reason to fear German motives in Europe, and they had allied with one another in 1894 to forestall German ambitions. Japan soon recognized the brittleness of any European coalition opposing its actions in Asia, particularly one consisting of Germany, France, and Russia. While this group might not act, another arrangement was possible that did promise action unless a major power openly recognized Japanese interests and power in the region. The alliance with England served that end.

Japan further readied itself for war and it told itself that this was a desirable end with England effectively on the sidelines. So the stage was set for a Japanese war against a European power. The aim was to engage only one power at a time and to confine this fighting to the Asian mainland, preferably Korea. This was the area of foremost interest to Japan and it was close enough to Japan that the fighting could be managed logistically. This military challenge had long dominated Japanese thinking, and for this reason its navy had received particular attention from the state. Over an extended period of time, Japan's leaders purchased from England six battleships and six armored cruisers as well as fifteen destroyers. Consequently, a few years into the twentieth century, Japan presented itself as a formidable foe at sea. Nor had the army been neglected. Japan had allowed German advisers to train its ground forces, and these had improved in firepower and tactics. As a result, Japan could defend itself, an obvious priority, but it also could look forward with confidence to prosecuting a war in Korea. In 1904, this looked like a necessary step to take, given the actions of Russia.

Russian interest in Manchuria and Korea had ebbed and flowed depending on a range of circumstances from Russia's internal woes to European rivalry in the Pacific. In the end, both motives centered on a matter of prestige as Russia looked to maintain itself as a great power. This ambition was in trouble long before the opening of the new century and one way Russia dealt with this problem was an aggressive policy in Asia. Its intransigence toward Japan's occupation of the Liaodong Peninsula has been noted. This was in 1895. By 1897, the Russians had completed the Trans-Siberian Railway that connected Vladivostok to the west. To do so, it had demanded this right and land concessions from the Chinese, which it got. This included the occupation of Port Arthur leading to Russian domination of the Liaodong Peninsula, the very territory it had been so adamant in denying Japan in 1895. Russia then planned to connect Port Arthur to the main rail-line. From Japan's point of view, this action meant that the limited Russian presence in Manchuria could now increase a hundred-fold. At a minimum, Russia would be better positioned militarily to contest Japanese moves on the mainland.

The prospect of a Russian rail-line through Manchuria made Japan nervous. Russia's overtures to Korea made Japan alarmed. Yet another disturbance within the political establishment of Korea occurred in 1895, when the Japanese facilitated the murder of the queen by Korean dissidents, an overt act of terror that so alarmed the Korean king that he sought Russian protection. This outcome enabled Russia to enjoy a great deal of influence exactly where Japan did not want it to have influence, in Korea. Next, even while talking of concessions to Japan in Korea, the Russians negotiated with the Chinese to allow the Czar's navy to occupy Port Arthur. Russian foreign minister Count Mikhail Muravev completed this deal in 1898. A few individuals close to Nicholas expressed caution, including the army and navy ministers who both questioned the military utility of the port. The Czar rejected their advice. He believed that Japan could not stop him in the immediate future, nor would that country dare to try. Russia could look forward to dominating Manchuria, including the Liaodong Peninsula. Over the next few years, Port Arthur grew to be a powerful naval base and the key outpost representing the Czar's ambitions in Asia.

In a short period of time, diplomacy, aided by Chinese weakness, had won for Russia a dominant position in East Asia. It now controlled a warm water port, and it could threaten Japanese interests in Korea any time it chose to. These gains meant a resurgence of a western arrogance that Japan found intolerable. The Russians did not appear to notice or seem concerned that Japan might object to its advances. Such behavior stood in marked contrast to other European powers that had acknowledged Japanese territorial integrity even if insisting on commercial agreements with Japan. England, for example, after pummeling China in the Second Opium War ending in 1858, stated it had no interest in colonizing Japan. No such guarantee came from Russia. In fact, that power pressured Japan on several fronts. In March 1861, a Russian warship arrived at the island of Tsushima located in the straits separating Korea and Japan. Japan asked England to negotiate a Russian withdrawal and this occurred in September. Still, here was a warning of Russian aggression close to home. They continued. To the north, Russia disputed Japanese control of the Sakhalin Island. Three times, in 1865, 1867, and 1872, the Japanese attempted to negotiate the Sakhalin issue without success. Only Japanese initiative settled this problem in 1875 with Japan relinquishing its claims to the island in exchange for

Russian recognition of Japanese control of the Kurile Island chain. By 1904, despite the aggressive actions of numerous European nations in Asia, Japan centered its attention on Russia. It alone appeared determined to challenge Japan's vital interests in Korea and possibly closer to the home islands.

Another source of tension was that Russia failed to live up to its agreements. The Czar appeared to submit to Japanese demands of a neutralization of Korea by signing an agreement with Japan in April 1898 that assured that both parties would not interfere with Korea's independence. This was good news for Japan and more followed. In April 1902, Russia agreed to withdraw from Manchuria. However, the Russians did not act on their promises. Russia then established a garrison at the mouth of the Yalu River in April 1903. This act appeared to threaten Japan's position in Korea despite the earlier neutralization treaty. A final Japanese peace offering came in January 1904. The opposing parties would agree to spheres of influence, Japan in Korea, Russia in Manchuria. Russia did not reply but it did reinforce its troops in the area. Japan took the rebuffs in its stride but prepared for war since it believed its national existence was at risk.

Not all Japanese agreed on this path to armed confrontation with the west. Within the elite that decided the issue, many voiced fears that the militarism so prevalent in Japanese policy could not be sustained economically at home, certainly not on a par with the European countries. The internal split was acute and frequently caustic, but eventually the hardliners favoring military force won out. They neutralized objections within the *genro*, the select advisory body to the Emperor that presided over such key decisions. In particular they overcame the political efforts of men like Ito Hirobumi, a member of the *genro* and a man opposed to a military solution to the Korean problem. The militarists prevailed thanks mostly to Russian intransigence during negotiations. Despite repeated Japanese diplomatic efforts, the Russians demonstrated no willingness to compromise with Japan and accept Japanese control of Korea in exchange for Russian domination of Manchuria. But another factor surfaced as well. Those favoring a clash with Russia did not believe in certain victory. Leaders in the army set Japanese chances of winning such a war at only 50 percent. The navy expected to lose half its ships, though it believed it would completely eliminate the Russian fleet. In the face of such pessimism, the deciding factor to go to war was the Japanese sense of honor. A struggle awaited and although Japan might lose that struggle, not to face this test was a greater humiliation than defeat. It was an emotional appeal to overcome questionable policy.

The problem was that even a Russia troubled at home, and one without European allies in the Pacific, still presented a formidable foe. For Japan, the question quickly became, how best to engage this enemy militarily? The answer was preemption. The Japanese must crush Russian military might in the opening stages of the war. The target was the Russian fleet moored at Port Arthur. This was an obvious target since the Japanese needed to prevent this naval force from interfering with Japan's ability to transfer an army to the Korean peninsula and to then support that army. Additional benefits would be gained by a successful attack on the Russian fleet. First, it would boost Japanese moral. The navy was confident of success, and so too its commander, the capable Admiral Togo Heihachiro. Still, Japan was to clash with an Occidental power for the first time, and the novelty of this experience resonated deeply. For too long, European powers had been dominant in the region. To overcome this psychological disadvantage, Japan would seize any advantage it could. An opening victory would ensure the Japanese naval superiority obviously required for a successful campaign, but it also would reverberate on the ground and boost the morale of the Japanese soldiers who would be locked in combat as well. Second, Port Arthur was a coveted target. The Russian fleet needed to be vanquished to make the subsequent assault on the city possible. Command of the sea meant the port could not be reinforced or supplied from the water side, and once isolated on land, the port was doomed.

By 1903, Japan believed itself ready for war with Russia. The six battleships and six armored cruisers comprised the heart of the Japanese fleet. All of these ships were of modern vintage and therefore of comparable performance. The crews were elite and expert, driven by a belief in their commander and in their training. On the ground the Japanese intended to employ three armies totaling over 300,000 men. Another 600,000 men could be raised if necessary. The size of the ground forces ensured parity with their Russian foes, although this balance would be lost if the war lengthened and Russia brought its superior numbers to bear. For this reason, the moment chosen for attack was February 1904, a time when weather adversely impacted Russia's tenuous Far East rail link. Even with these and other precautions, the numbers hardly favored Japan. At sea, Russia boasted three fleets, the one in the Pacific consisting of a formidable force of seven battleships and six cruisers. The Russians hoped to finish building more battleships and send them to Port Arthur in the near future. The ability to reinforce the Pacific fleet with ships from the Baltic Fleet also threatened to turn the numbers against Japan. On the ground, the Russians garrisoned their possessions in Manchuria and near Korea with over 100,000 men. This number could increase dramatically if necessary. In the case of both the Russian naval and land units, the morale of the troops was low, the quality of the equipment poor. These shortcomings would lessen the effectiveness of the Russian forces in battle, particularly at sea, but the numbers still remained roughly equal; more precisely, the Japanese were slightly outnumbered at sea and on land. That the Japanese should contemplate attacking without a numerical edge violated military wisdom. Preemption was to compensate for this asymmetry of forces.

The Attack

The final Japanese appeal for peace failed to gain any ground with the Russians. Ito's efforts met total failure as the Russians remained obstinate. Russia was confident of beating Japan in a military clash; more than that, it was confident that its great prestige would deter Japan from going to war against it at all. The Russian buildup at Port Arthur would not provoke war with Japan because of Russia's great stature. Foreign Minister Muravev told the Czar: "One flag and one sentry, the prestige of Russia will do the rest."* The mixed message of reinforcing Russian forces in Manchuria but well short of an army large enough to intimidate the Japanese seems to have escaped him. The Czar himself uttered a phrase laden with meaning that he could not have guessed, remarking to the Kaiser that "there would be no war because he did not wish it."** The Czar's expectation of waging a war against Japan entirely on his own terms, and really believing he would not have to wage war at all no matter his provocative actions, would be shattered by Japan's offensive. Japan already had decided on war and to use a preemptive attack to start the war.

The lack of naval superiority and the need for control of the sea to undertake the war at all meant a Japanese ploy at the outset of hostilities: it decided to present a late declaration of war. The attack at Port Arthur and elsewhere would be underway before the official notification of war. Admiral Togo had pressed his government for this approach to increase the chances of the success of his opening attacks. The Japanese government acted accordingly. It severed diplomatic relations with Russia on February 6, the Japanese ambassador telling his Russian counterpart that Japan "had decided to adopt such independent action as was deemed necessary to defend its established rights and legitimate interests."*** The same day the Japanese withdrew all of their civilians from Port Arthur in a British steamship. In response to both actions, the Russian commander of the fleet in

---

* David Walder, *The Short Victorious War: The Russo-Japanese Conflict, 1904–1905* (New York: Harper & Row, 1973), 53.

** Denis Warner and Peggy Warner, *The Tide at Sunrise: A History of the Russo–Japanese War, 1904-1905* (New York: Charterhouse, 1974), 171.

*** Richard Connaughton, *Rising Sun and Tumbling Bear: Russia's War with Japan* (London: Cassell, 2003), 23.

Port Arthur, Vice Admiral Stark, ordered his ships to assume a heightened state of readiness, orders that his subordinates ignored. Consequently, the Russian Pacific fleet was unprepared to defend itself when the Japanese approached.

Togo set sail for Port Arthur on February 6 and he approached the city at night on February 8. Eleven destroyers made the first attack, a swift assault on the unprepared Russian fleet. Moored outside the harbor because of the limited ability of large ships to move in and out of the entrance, they presented excellent targets. Two Russian ships patrolled the area and did warn the fleet of the attack, but they raised the alarm at the same time the first torpedo hit a Russian battleship. They were too late to enable the Russians to repel the assailants and the first Japanese ships made unmolested passes on the battle fleet while the trailing vessels sought to take advantage of the confusion that soon surfaced among the prospective targets. Given the great opportunity, it is a telling comment on the inaccuracy of the torpedo that the Japanese damaged only three Russian ships, two battleships and one cruiser. The attack ended quickly and the Japanese sped away without loss.

Another Japanese surprise attack actually preceded the more famous torpedo strike at Port Arthur. The Japanese also attacked the port of Chemulpo (Inchon) in Korea, targeting two Russian vessels. Obviously these ships needed to be destroyed for the Japanese to land soldiers in the city. Togo assigned a strong force of cruisers to this task, calculating that they could easily overwhelm an unarmored Russian cruiser and an obsolete gunboat. The more difficult part of the assignment was ensuring the destruction of the Russian ships without harming any other ship belonging to a neutral power. These crowded the harbor. To solve this problem, the Japanese commander, Rear Admiral Uriu, summoned the Russians to sea for an engagement. He warned all parties that the Japanese would enter the harbor and attack the Russian ships should his ultimatum be rejected. Neutral ships would be responsible for themselves should the Japanese have to take this step. Captain Stefanov, the senior Russian officer, accepted his fate and led his ships to battle. Hopelessly outmatched, he returned to the harbor an hour later, both ships badly damaged but still afloat. The Japanese closed in to finish him off, prompting the Russians to scuttle their ships. A short time later, Japanese infantry disembarked in Chemulpo.

With its initial plans underway, Japan declared war on Russia on February 10. Now came the more difficult task of blockading Port Arthur. Following up his advantage, Togo attacked the port with his fleet the day after the torpedo attack, but he achieved little. The Russians were alert and the fire from shore batteries was very effective. Togo then looked for a way to keep the damaged Russian fleet in the harbor. Japanese volunteers attempted to sink a number of merchant ships in the path of the harbor, but this hazardous effort to block the entrance failed on two occasions. In April when the Russians sallied from the port, mines claimed victims on both sides, something that worked to the Japanese advantage. Two Russian battleships were lost to mines as well as a new admiral, the capable Vice Admiral Makarov, killed on his flagship, the battleship *Petropavlovsk*. Makarov had replaced the disgraced Stark, and his death further reduced Russian morale; the fleet did not leave port again until August. The Japanese also lost two battleships to mines at this time, but Togo remained on station before the harbor.

This success would prove decisive since Port Arthur fell to ground assault in late December 1904. Before the city surrendered, Japanese guns positioned on land had destroyed the five remaining Russian battleships. In a very close contest, the Japanese had used a combination of arms to eliminate Russian naval power in the Pacific. Yet the war continued as the Russians committed additional resources to the fight. Japan now faced a fear present before the onset of war, and that was a long war, one that favored Russia. How best to deal with this difficulty occupied Japanese strategists as a new Russian fleet made its way to the war zone.

Success

The Japanese attack on Port Arthur that opened the Russo–Japanese War of 1904–1905 defied a material measure of success since only three Russian ships were damaged. One would expect the Japanese to have inflicted more damage, given that they had achieved complete surprise and the Russian fleet was vulnerable to attack. Additionally, while the three damaged ships did then sink, Russian workers repaired them and they all returned to action. What the attack did gain for Japan was the initiative. It never lost this advantage and it reaped much benefit from it.

The first benefit was the preservation of the Japanese fleet. Togo could not afford to risk his fleet in an action before Port Arthur that, if it went badly, meant Japan would lose the war in the opening moments of the conflict. But without control of the sea, there could be no Japanese offensive. The task became one of containing the Russian fleet. The Japanese soon turned their attention to making sure the Russian fleet would never emerge from Port Arthur, or if it did, it would face a battle of annihilation. Togo, however, expected the Russians to play it safe and remain in the harbor. The change in Russian naval commanders only temporarily altered this standoff. By this measure, the surprise attack of February 8 was a great strategic victory for Japan.

The second benefit was that naval supremacy allowed the ground war to unfold. The immediate aim of the offensive on land was to ensure the conquest of Korea, and this occurred rapidly. Chemulpo fell quickly and a Japanese army began to march north toward the Yalu River. Another Japanese army landed on Chinese territory at Pitzuwo and headed south to the Kwantung Peninsula to invade Port Arthur. A third army landed nearby at Takushan, near the top of the Liaodong Peninsula, and moved north to meet the Japanese army advancing from Korea. Altogether the Japanese armies sought out the Russians hoping to force them into a decisive battle.

This goal of decisive battle would cost the Japanese army dearly as two great battles sapped its strength. To the south, the struggle over Port Arthur became a lengthy siege, something the Japanese had hoped to avoid to minimize casualties. Things had started well enough when the Japanese won a key battle at the neck of the peninsula, isolating the city. The next task was taking Port Arthur itself, defended by 30,000 Russians. The Japanese formally laid siege to the city on August 7, 1904, with General Nogi's new Third Army. First Nogi tried to seize the fortress by storm. Several assaults failed, with very heavy Japanese losses. Nevertheless, the Japanese continued to besiege the city, and it fell five months later, the Russian garrison surrendering on January 2, 1905. But Japan lost close to 60,000 dead. Nevertheless, the sacrifice was worth it from Japan's point of view. In October 1904, Nicholas had sent his second fleet, the Baltic Fleet, to relieve Port Arthur. If that fleet had arrived in the Yellow Sea with Port Arthur still in Russian hands, Japan would have found itself pressed by two different fleets and outnumbered at sea. The loss of Port Arthur ended this less than desirable scenario.

Before looking to fight another sea battle, Japan faced some additional hard fighting on the ground. The Russian stand at Port Arthur created strategic problems for Japan since Japanese troops diverted to the siege of that city could not be used in battle against the remaining Russian forces in Manchuria. Additionally, the fall of Port Arthur was unlikely to end the war so the Japanese had to wage a campaign to the north and do so at reduced strength. Even the amalgamation of all Japanese armies in the area netted strength inferior to Russian arms, some 175,000 Japanese soldiers opposed by 200,000 Russians. Nevertheless, the Japanese commander, General Oyosama, expressed confidence in securing a major victory that would end the war. He believed that the great mobility of the Japanese army meant it had an opportunity to surround a major portion of the Russian troops and force a peace on Japanese terms. With this goal in mind, the two enemies fought a series of battles over the course of eight months that followed a pattern. The Japanese advanced on prepared Russian positions, attempted to turn the flank of these defenses, and won the battle. But each time the Japanese failed to destroy a large piece of the Russian forces as the bulk of that army retired north. The main reason for this failure was Japanese exhaustion; they lost too heavily in the attack to then pursue effectively. Nevertheless, a climatic three-week battle came in February 1905 as Japan pushed into Manchuria. This clash resulted in another Japanese victory at Mukden on March 10, though again the Russians defending the town escaped destruction. This battle consolidated Japanese control of Korea but cost the Japanese a staggering 70,000 casualties and therefore underscored Japanese weakness instead of strength. Japan could not win battles on land that would force the Russians to make peace.

Japan hoped to achieve this result at sea by winning a decisive naval battle. It had good reason to be optimistic. Russia's Second Pacific Fleet mirrored the one trapped in Port Arthur in terms of numbers but also in the poor quality of the ships and the training of the crews. The fatalism of the man in charge, Admiral Rozhdestvenski, ensured that a gloom accompanied the fleet on its long voyage from its home waters off St. Petersburg to the coast of China. While the fall of Port Arthur ended this fleet's relief mission, it sailed on to meet the Japanese in battle nonetheless. The Czar hoped a crushing victory at sea might yet undo Japanese successes and win the war for Russia.

Rozhdestvenski attempted to oblige his monarch by taking the most direct approach to Vladivostok, the new destination of the Russian fleet. He ordered the Russian fleet to pass through the straits of Korea. There, near the island of Tsushima, the fleets met in battle on May 27. At end of two days of fighting, the Japanese had sunk or captured thirty-four of thirty-seven Russian ships with minor losses to themselves. Almost 5,000 Russian sailors died, the Japanese losing only three torpedo boats and 110 men killed. The catastrophe stemmed from a number of factors, such as obsolete Russian ships manned by poorly trained sailors suffering from low morale. Russian leadership also contributed greatly to the disaster, such as Rozhdestvenski appointing a man who had died days before the battle as second in command. When Rozhdestvenski was himself injured early in the battle and no longer able to issue orders, the Russian fleet had no one to coordinate its action and it lost any semblance of order. Each Russian ship soon became a solitary target for multiple Japanese ships working in unison with one another to bring a tremendous amount of firepower to bear on the targets. Togo's fleet hunted down the Russian ships one after the other and destroyed them. It indeed was a battle of annihilation.

The Japanese preemptive strike at Port Arthur had contributed significantly to the success at Tsushima. By trapping the Russian fleet in Port Arthur where it was eventually destroyed, Togo ensured a struggle of equal numbers at Tsushima. This engagement favored Japan, given its superior ships and crews. The Russians did have a greater number of battleships at Tsushima, seven to four, but this advantage did them little good. However, a force of three times the battleships the Japanese could muster might have produced a different result. Without the ships from Port Arthur, the Russians could hope for only a slight numerical advantage that gave Japan a good chance to win the battle. In the end, preemption allowed Japan to snatch a victory from a potentially unfavorable military situation.

The peace that followed the Battle of Tsushima meant Japan was the victor of the Russo–Japanese War of 1905. Korea now became a Japanese protectorate and in this way Japan ended the threat of another country occupying the Korean peninsula and thereby satisfied the empire's concern for its national security. Russia also yielded Port Arthur and the Liaodong Peninsula to Japan. These concessions ended Russian penetration into Manchuria, but more gratifying to Japan was the effacement of the humiliation of 1895 when it was forced to surrender this territory after taking it during the war with China. It now had to endure no such embarrassment, having bested a European power in a war that made it clear to the world that Japan was a great power. Better still, Japanese success came at the expense of its chief western rival, and in the wake of its triumph at Tsushima, the Japanese invaded and occupied the Sakhalin Island to make this point. The loss of this Russian territory quickly brought Russia to the peace table.

Japan now had to contend with the problems that came with its new-found status of imperial power. These surfaced immediately and in a wholly unexpected manner. Japan's military successes did not end the war. This result came due to the effort of the American President, Theodore Roosevelt. He brokered a peace that satisfied Japan and saved Russian face, so it was accepted by both sides on September 5, 1905. The treaty also exposed two limitations to the Japanese success. First, should the Russians have continued to fight on land, the Japanese could not have sustained their war effort. The financial burden and the strain on its manpower would have had untold consequences at home. Second, having to rely on American auspices to mediate a peace underscored the fact that Japan was a power in the region, but not the only power. Competition now came from the peace-maker, the United States. With the destruction of Russian naval power, and the diminished influence of England in the region, the only counterbalance to Japan was that posed by the United States from its colony of the Philippine Islands and its naval base at Hawaii. Japan did not like its chances in a war versus its new rival. Japan's industrial capacity could not compare to that of the United States, and should this deficiency not be remedied, it was all too clear which nation would emerge as the victor from such a clash. Its military leaders now started thinking on how best to overcome this weakness. That one war should plant the seeds of another meant that success indeed became transitory, if not ephemeral, given the prospect of a new showdown between nations previously of minor importance in the Pacific.

Conclusion

The Japanese clash with Russia in 1904–1905 emphasized long-term fears on the part of Japan. Russian interference on mainland Asia proved consistent and incremental despite Japanese warnings and admonitions. Japan was most threatened by Russian intrigues in Korea. Russian support of a Korean king hostile to Japan fueled more political instability there, a situation Japan found completely unacceptable. Already it had had to clash with China in Korea over the issue of Korean stability. Japanese success in 1895 did not gain it the freedom of action it had hoped for, thanks to European interference, Russia acting in concert with Germany and France to deny Japan the proceeds of a war it had won. The result was that that war turned from a beneficial one for Japan to a war with a dangerous outcome. An unstable Korea invited European attention and perhaps occupation. From this position, a European power could threaten Japan directly. In the name of national security, Korea warranted Japan's interest including military action if necessary. That such a stand would bring it into conflict with a European power, Japan considered a likely and necessary result.

In the years leading up to 1904, it came as no surprise to Japan that this power would be Russia. Japanese efforts to balance the ambitions of the two nations on the mainland were rebuffed time after time by the over-confident and arrogant Russians. The Russians made it clear they would not be content with merely dominating Manchuria. The Trans-Siberian Railway fed the growth of Vladivostok and also that of Port Arthur, once the line was extended to this port. The increase in the Russian naval forces at Port Arthur also testified to the Czar's ambitions in the Far East. Korea now fell within a growing Russian sphere of influence in Asia, one that included possession of the island of Sakhalin and the Kurile Islands to the north of Japan. While it was true that, overall, Japan along with the rest of Asia, had been forced from a self-imposed isolation by many western nations, only one, Russia, continued to press the island nation. In the face of this aggression, Japan assumed the unenviable task of learning from its new enemies and doing so fast enough to prevent invasion and occupation while it overcame its marked inferiority in terms of military strength. Japan's leaders deemed this step complete by 1903 and the nation ready for war.

This engagement with the European powers now so prominent on Japan's doorstep could not have been possible without help from England. Japan's ministers abroad had been shrewd enough to realize early on that Britain posed the greatest threat in the region given its marked naval strength when compared to the other European powers and given England's insatiable demand for trade. However, England's ability to dominate economically left it bereft of allies and open to new alliances in the early 1900s. Japan filled this void in Asia and careful Japanese cultivation of this relationship netted a treaty with England in 1902. This agreement meant more to Japan than merely playing one "barbarian" nation off another. Japan also armed its navy with vessels built in England. This fast road to naval readiness left it with a first-rate navy that could do more than defend the home islands. Japan was ready to assume its place as an imperial power alongside the European nations. It was a role England accepted and obviously encouraged given its treaty arrangements and arms sales to Japan. Japan's newfound status as a great power had the opposite effect in St. Petersburg. Russia remained unconvinced of Japan's transformation and looked to gain ground in Asia at that nation's expense.

Another tangible gain grew out of the Japanese–English alliance. By standing with England, Japan stymied the actions of other European nations as a clash with Russia grew closer. The power balance in Europe concerned France, Germany, and even Russia more than did the dreams of these nations of expanding in Asia or more than did their fear of Japanese expansion in the Pacific. The result was that by 1904 Japan could strike Russia with reasonable assurance of limiting the war to a fight between these two nations. Delay meant problems that Japan believed worked to its disadvantage. The European powers might reshuffle themselves and suddenly stand united against Japan, or gather together a grouping of nations that included an England suddenly opposed to Japan. Russia clearly was strengthening its military forces in Asia. Waiting allowed them time to complete this build-up and to possibly take the offensive. Nevertheless, while confident of success, Japan realized that the weight of Russian manpower and material strength doomed their cause. The Russians simply had too many soldiers and ships for Japan to look forward to winning a long war. Rather, a short, impressive victory that promised to end the war quickly was essential to Japanese plans.

Here their reliance on preemption came to the fore. A first strike by Japan meant that the prospect of a swift victory was feasible. Preemption as a tactic for starting a war that was coming in any event was needed to ensure Japan's ability to wage that war. Its forces had to transfer to Korea and be sustained in Korea. The Imperial Navy would be entrusted with this task and could perform this duty only if it neutralized its rival combat arm, the Russian navy. A sudden blow at the Russian fleet in Port Arthur that destroyed or neutralized this threat obviously offered the best prospect of success in the campaign to follow. Nor did Japan concern itself with the obligation to inform its target of the opening of hostilities until after that attack had come. Diplomatic ties had ended, and Japan had reason to believe that the Russians planned an offensive of their own. In fact, the Russians had fired the first shot of the war off the Korean coast at Chemulpo. Since Togo unleashed his attack confident that military necessity trumped international law, preemption was stripped of its morality to gain a military advantage. The results of war would determine whether the preemptive attack was perceived as a success or failure. Victory would allow Japan to define its own morality in the conflict. By 1904, on the eve of the attack at Port Arthur, the imperialism practiced by Japan matched its western counterparts and even surpassed this standard by exceeding the norms of western warfare given Japan's willingness to launch an undeclared war.

Japan soon discovered it could not wage war preemptively in a moral vacuum. Its modeling of the aggressive militarism inherent in the foreign policy of European nations reached such a point that the arrogance and bullying so objected to by Japan now became a hallmark of its own policy. Korea and China became chief targets. Japan's insistence on the need to control Korea to protect itself meant a constant meddling in that nation's affairs. The Treaty of Kanghwa in 1876, forced open three Korean ports to Japan and shadowed European dealings with China in the most overt fashion. So too did the result of such treaties: war. The war Japan fought in 1894 against China was one it was confident of winning. China was merely the showcase for the audition of beefed up Japanese militarism. The Japanese performed well and most countries took note of their success.

The Russians did not. Always contemptuous of Japan, the Russians assumed the role of foremost antagonist in Japanese eyes. But here Japanese realism, another hallmark of studying European war-making, let them down. A closer look revealed the Russians to be a lesser threat than Japan portrayed them to be. Even should Japan acquiesce to all of Russia's ambitions, from railroads across China to trading posts near or on the Japanese home islands, the economic impact of the Russian presence would be minimal due to its weak economy. Japanese emissaries in Russia sent back to Japan shocking reports of Russian backwardness at home that translated into that country's economic impotence. This revelation meant that Russia was not the main enemy. That Japan understood the relationship between war and economic vitality is clear in its own success in this regard during the 1904–1905 war with Russia. It financed a billion dollars in loans largely from the United States and this feat allowed it to overcome its own economic limitations and fight the war. Russia suffered from a similar strain but with less commercial resources and financing options than Japan. Still, Russia remained the main threat because Japan believed it could beat that nation in a war and reap several benefits from this outcome. A war with Russia promised a fast success that secured the Japanese presence on the mainland and ensured its place as a great power in the region. Both results enhanced Japanese security.

Japanese negotiations with nations such as England merely acted as insurance. Japan understood that Britain's woes in the early 1900s left that nation open to a diplomatic agreement with Japan. Not wishing to challenge its military might, an alliance served Japanese ends almost as well as a military victory over that nation. Having one barbarian deflect the advances of another, as Japan asked England to do in relation to Russia on several occasions, spoke to Japanese understanding of its rivals. That it used the Chinese indemnity after the war of 1894–1895 to purchase warships from England was more evidence of benefiting from western-style imperialism. It also revealed that Japan looked to be nothing less than an imperial power. It is hard to assign preemption as a means of self-defense to a nation scrupulously using time to serve its goal of arming itself in order to fight larger wars in the future in the name of imperialism.

Perhaps Japan had learned from the west all too well. The cause of war would be "just" simply because of the threat posed by the "stronger" Russia. That the opposite was the case and Russia's bullying was no more than that, a fact recognized by Japan, meant that the war between the two nations was a welcome one because Japan could look forward to winning it. Should this circumstance be true, Japan's need for war became one of aggression, a desired war against a weaker foe in the hopes of establishing itself in Korea and elsewhere on the Asian mainland at the expense of that nation and of course at the expense of China. National security mattered less—the argument that whoever controlled Korea pointed an arrow at Japan—than did a Japanese push toward hegemony in Asia. This end may have been inchoate in 1904 and it did not mature until the 1930s, but the drive to achieve hegemonic status emerged at the turn of the century. It needs to be stressed that in each case, 1904 and 1941, the Japanese offensive opened with a preemptive strike. In this longer timeframe, a reliance on a preemptive strike spoke to continuity of Japanese purpose, a use of military force to achieve hegemonic status. In the context of 1904, the just cause of self-defense evaporates before the aura of aggression in the name of expansion.

As to be expected, Japan added its own flavor to the imperialism it first unleashed on the western powers in 1904. The attack on Port Arthur and the simultaneous attack on Chemulpo came with no declaration of war.

This "sneak" attack was designed to ensure a Japanese military victory at the outset of hostilities. This added element of treachery turned the Japanese attack starting the Russo–Japanese War of 1904 from preemption in the name of self-defense to preemption serving the cause of aggression. Certainly this was the case from Russia's point of view, the Czar writing in his diary the night of the attack on Port Arthur, "And this without a declaration of war."* This opinion was not universal. More than a few editorials in the American press sanctioned the Japanese tactic, the *New York Times* remarking that the charge of treachery could "find no countenance either in the writings of the authorities or in the practice of nations."** The irony of this American support is plain, given the Japanese attack on Pearl Harbor almost four decades later.

That Japan could be seen as unleashing preemption without blemish in one war but with condemnation in the next war speaks to more than adopting a specific belligerent's point of view. Hanging in the balance is the view of preemption as a justified tactic starting a war that already was coming, or as an illegitimate reason to start a hegemonic or civilizational conflict. It is remarkable that Japan embraced a hegemonic motive by acting preemptively all the while not invoking any moral high ground since Japan's naval commander, Togo, merely sought a military advantage that presupposed no moral implications from his point of view. He deluded himself. No matter his belief, the attack raised the issue of morality at the heart of preemption. Japan's military advantage served the interests of the state, these being fending off a looming threat and establishing Japanese hegemony in the Pacific. The purpose was clearly more the latter. Japan did not face a threat to its homeland islands. What it stood to lose to Russian expansion in Asia was Japan's drive toward dominance of Korea and China and parity with the European nations striving for this same territorial end. The war Japan fought against Russia in 1904–1905 was a war of one imperial power versus another. The victor would assume regional supremacy. This hegemonic purpose stripped Japan of any claim to morality in using preemption to fight a just war. The result was a war of aggression.

---

* David Schimmelpenninck Van Der Oye, *Toward the Rising Sun: Russian Ideologies of Empire and the Path to War with Japan* (DeKalb, IL: Northern Illinois University Press, 2001), 108.

** William H. Honan, "Port Author: the First Pearl Harbor," in *"Fire When Ready, Gridley!": Great Naval Stories from Manila Bay to Vietnam,* ed. William H. Honan (New York: St. Martin's Press, 1993), 42.

Trapped into War: Imperial Germany and the Great War in Europe, 1914

Introduction

German soldiers entered Belgian territory on August 4, 1914, but found no French troops there. It is doubtful they expected to find any. The lead elements of the German force, the cavalry, distributed a proclamation that announced German regret at having to go into Belgium, and demanded that the Belgians did not resist. Two days later, German General Eric Ludendorff, a man who would come to dominate the war for Germany, demanded the surrender of the Belgium town of Liège. The Belgian garrison refused and a German assault on the city and its network of forts began immediately. The town fell on August 16. World War I was not quite two weeks old, and several revelations had occurred, all of them reflecting unfavorably on German war plans. Belgium would resist the German invasion, no matter German protests that their attack targeted only France. The German government insisted that it had had no choice in striking Belgium. It had to defend itself. However, with no French soldiers to be found, the question became, defend itself from whom? And from the opening days of the war, Germany revealed its willingness to assume the role of aggressor to serve its morally just purpose of breaking free of the encirclement imposed on Germany by the great powers in Europe. While it may have committed a wrong in the attack it unleashed in the west, the assault served a greater good in making it possible for Germany to defend itself from its enemies. No matter this way of thinking, the war that was to grow out of this preemptive doctrine would quickly dispel any illusions of good or justice for all parties involved.

World War I began as an eagerly anticipated struggle among European nations and ended in a continental anguish perhaps unsurpassed in western history. In the late summer of 1914, Germany attacked France, an assault that carried German armies through Belgium, a neutral power. Britain entered the war in support of France in response to this German aggression. However, the German attack in the west stemmed from circumstances defined in the east. When Serbian radicals assassinated an Austrian crown prince, the Austria-Hungary Empire demanded redress from Serbia, but in terms so harsh that war between these two states erupted. This local conflict soon drew the attention of, first, Russia, and then Germany. Once these powers came to the defense of their allies, the Russians in support of Serbia, the Germans in support of Austria-Hungary, the war took a big step toward engulfing all of Europe in the violence. The German attack in the west ensured that the conflict escalated to include all of the great powers, Britain aligning with France and Russia just a few days after war officially began on August 1. Other countries slowly entered the fray at various points after 1914, making this struggle a world war. Turkey supported Germany and Austria-Hungary, and formally entered the war in 1915, creating the Central Powers. Italy joined the Allied powers that same year. More importantly, the United States entered the conflict in 1917 on the side of the Allies, just as the Russians bowed out of the conflagration. No matter the order of the entry into the war, Germany faced a strategic dilemma that preoccupied it well before the start of hostilities. To face an expansive array of enemies, the Germans would have to fight a two-front war. Hoping to limit this disadvantage, the Germans looked to break free of encirclement at the hands of their enemies by striking preemptively. The attack was a failure that ultimately led to German defeat in November 1918, but not before Europe so devastated itself that peace in 1919 laid the groundwork for a recovery that would lead to a larger and more costly war a generation later.

This ghastly conflict has been the focus of intense study and therefore enjoys an extensive literature. Many scholars lay the blame at the feet of numerous powers for starting the war, either due to the alliance system in place in Europe, the imperial rivalries abroad, or, less concretely, the general martial "mood" in Europe. Eventually, however, the focus comes back to Germany. James Joll wrote in *The Origins of the First World War*, that, "German and Austrian plans involved the highest danger of general war." In *The Long Fuse*, Laurence Lafore added that Germany "played the most conspicuous role." In so arguing, these scholars saddle Germany with the burden of starting the war.* But the discussion of German war guilt does not address the issue of preemption at length, despite those authors' stress that the German attack was a preemptive strike. Perhaps most significantly Holger Herwig, a dean in the field, labels the German attack preemptive in the essay, "Why Did it Happen?" published in a recent book he edited entitled, *The Origins of World War I.* John H. Maurer's, *The Outbreak of the First World War,* calls the German attack preemption as well. Joll, in his book on the origins of the war, states the issue clearly: "what would now be called a preemptive strike was the only way of [the Germans] defending themselves against encirclement by hostile powers or because they thought a war was the only way to achieve the world power [status]." So preemption stemmed from two motives.** This chapter examines Germany's key role in starting World War I with the emphasis on the primacy that German decision makers gave to preemption. It matters less that Germany can be blamed for starting the war than it does establishing the limited and bitter returns on its preemptive strategy.

The Case for Preemption

Germany's quest for great nation status came during an age of European imperialism that meant a keen competition among these states to achieve the distinction of world power. The logic that convinced Germany to seek out foreign trade and colonies to bolster its position on the European continent meant a clash with other powers striving to reach the same goal. In fact, Germany was far behind in this race but striving to catch up. Its infrastructure in terms of rail lines and a merchant fleet had received a committed effort from governmental authorities since the 1870s. While its industrial strength was starting to reach competitive levels, other European nations still outstripped Germany, Britain in particular. Great Britain served as a model for Germany, given its high state of industrial development, its numerous colonial possessions that fueled this growth, and a strong navy and merchant marine fleet ensuring the supply of the island homeland. In short, Britain had what Germany lacked. Germany promised to close the

* James Joll, *The Origins of the First World War,* 2nd ed. (London: Longman, 1992), 105; Laurence Lafore, *The Long Fuse: An Interpretation of the Origins of World War I,* 2nd ed. (New York: J.B. Lippincott Company, 1971), 110.

** Holger H. Herwig, "Why Did It Happen?" in *The Origins of World War I,* eds. Richard F. Hamilton and Holger H. Herwig (Cambridge, UK: Cambridge University, 2003), 444; John H. Maurer, *The Outbreak of the First World War: Strategic Planning, Crisis Decision Making, and Deterrence Failure* (Westport, CT: Praeger, 1995), 119; Joll, *The Origins of the First World War,* 235.

gap quickly, but the question soon became, could two powers share global prominence without clashing?

For Germany, the answer was no. Britain favored a balance of power on the Continent, so the natural evolution of Germany to dominate Europe meant Britain would ally against it. France and Britain were trying hard to overcome the history of animosity toward one another. Moreover, Britain had turned its back on the rich history of Anglo-German cooperation against France in past European conflicts, notably the Napoleonic Wars. Germany also recognized that a generational shift had come to pass within the British diplomatic corps and the new personnel openly favored France. Practicality underscored this love affair the British had with French culture. A weakened France raised the specter of German power to unacceptable levels. In the name of a balance of power, Britain would ally with France to resist Germany's assertion of itself as a great power. Given Britain's stand, Germany had come to accept the inevitability of war in Europe.

Other nations mattered to Germany just as much but for different reasons. Russia loomed as a threat in the east. However, recent internal troubles had called attention to the decay of monarchial authority emanating from the Czar. Clearly Russia was in decline. A military defeat, particularly naval humiliation, at the hands of Japan in 1905 reinforced this view. Of course, a Russian recovery meant that that nation could again menace Germany, a development that greatly worried the German leadership beholden to safeguard the future of the Reich. By 1914, there were signs that this was indeed the case. Chancellor Theobald von Bethmann Hollweg described the fear of Russia on the eve of war as one that "Grows and grows and hangs upon us ever more heavily like a nightmare." A conflict was inevitable. Its time had come and not a moment too soon. Further delay only strengthened Russia. Germany must strike now or, as the chief of the general staff at the outbreak of war, General Helmuth von Molke, stated, "the sooner [war] comes, the better for us." It was this reasoning that prompted historian James L. Stokesbury to write that, "For the Germans, 1914 was almost preemptive war."[*] As Germany crafted plans to fight this war, Stokesbury's qualification was clearly unnecessary. For Germany, the Russian threat made the war in 1914 a preemptive one.

France, the great enemy to the west, was another story. Here German contempt was complete for the same reason that Germany dismissed Russia:

---

[*] Bethmann Hollweg quoted in Gordon A. Craig, *Germany, 1866–1945* (New York: Oxford University, 1978), 334. Molke's statement appears in Fritz Fischer, *Germany's Aims in the First World War*, trans. (New York: WW Norton, 1967), 50. James L. Stokesbury, *A Short History of World War I* (New York: William Morrow and Company, 1981), 62.

recent history. The rapid Prussian defeat of France during the Franco-Prussian War in 1870–1871 had underscored French weakness and German superiority. Another war with this nation would produce the same result of a quick German victory. This was but the first step. The key to the next war would be the aftermath. This time France was to be defeated and then destroyed. Germany would not allow a resentful France to remain as a neighbor, plotting to attack Germany once it recovered its strength. The destruction of France would signal German ascendancy on the Continent. With this footing, greater things were in store for Germany, such as world-power status. From this position of strength, Germany could look east with confidence of repelling any Russian threat or of expanding German interests in this area as well. But it all began with France. Given this reasoning, France became the chief enemy of the Reich and its chief target.

In sum, all powers were in decline as Germany rose in stature. Russia and France faced a historical eclipse of power. Britain was as vulnerable as Russia and France, if for different reasons; Germany was a power that could challenge Britain's colonial empire. In sum, Germany was a newly created nation whose fortunes could only go in one direction: forward to greatness. Yet, as German leaders surveyed the European landscape, they saw a disturbing pattern. Nations were allying against Germany, seeking to contain her. The 1904 Anglo-French *rapprochement* was a development in the affairs of Europe that underscored this point. Germany assumed this newfound meeting of minds between two long-time enemies was an effort to curtail German power. The two nations could do this better by working together more than apart. Russia and France already had allied with one another. Now, France looked to Britain. Should the three powers align against Germany, that is, Russia in the east and France bolstered by Great Britain in the west, the danger to Germany was all too apparent. The Triple Entente formed in 1907 made this threat real. The encirclement to prevent any German rise to great power status was complete.

Given this German reasoning about the danger of encirclement, the established lines of power-politics propelled Europe to war as much as the new dimension of global competition for colonies. However, even before 1914, Germany should have been aware that to a great extent a general war in Europe would be driven by the actions of lesser powers, not the great nations. Two prior wars in the Balkans already had alerted the great powers to this danger of a larger war growing out of local conflagrations. Because of this context, the issue of timing requires more analysis. Why war in 1914 stemming from Serbian and Austria-Hungary rivalry, and not in 1905 or 1911 over the first and second Moroccan crises, or in 1908–1909 over the Bosnian annexation crisis? The answer lies in Germany's determination to win a preemptive war to break the encirclement it believed it faced in Europe.

This German military aim revolved around France, of course, since Germany desired the destruction of this state first and foremost. However, in the west as in the east, a smaller nation at the very least circumscribed the outcome. Belgium claimed a neutral status that greatly complicated German war aims. It sat alongside France in such a way that its neutrality by default aided the defense of France by shielding the flank of that nation. German planners back to Count Alfred von Schlieffen had weighed the options of a western offensive and concluded that to defeat France, a great stroke must be launched and it must include Belgium in the fray. The German armies were so large as to require room to maneuver. More importantly, French defenses guarded the likely axis of advance; Belgium offered a way around this frontier battle that, even should it go in Germany's favor, figured to be a long, costly struggle that left Germany vulnerable to an offensive from Russia in the east. A two-front war posed obvious dangers and if the solution was but the violation of Belgian territory, a power that mattered little, then so be it.

German leaders knew the issue was not so simple. The other complication was Belgium's ties to Britain. This relationship meant a German attack on Belgium would lead to war with Britain. From this step would come another, Britain's *de facto* alliance with France. The three nations would stand together against Germany, if for three different reasons: French survival, British balance of power concerns, and the Belgians' misfortune of standing in the middle of the conflict. Hence, this lesser power assumed a key role since it could prevent Germany from engaging only France and rapidly defeating her, the entire purpose of a war in the west in the first place. Diplomacy became the chief German weapon since a Belgium assured of Germany's benevolence would stand aside when the fighting came. Its neutrality, even as German armies marched across its land, would forestall British intervention in a war. It was but a simple step to take, an agreement with an adjacent nation that could do nothing to resist German might. Surely these Belgians would see reason and not fight.

Diplomacy netted Germany few returns anywhere in Europe, so despite its efforts over a number of years, the fear of encirclement remained alive. German diplomats worked hard to ally Germany with Turkey, but this came to nothing. Turkey lost ground and prestige in the Balkan wars. The actual curtailment of Turkish power meant little to Germany, except for the fact that the Turks had to look elsewhere for support since German efforts had been discredited; Germany simply could not meet its needs. This shortcoming was most evident financially, and when Turkey turned to France for financial aid and received this aid, German clout suffered. An effort to gain allies to ensure that Germany was not isolated clearly suffered in the process. The sense of isolation accentuated the fears of encirclement facing

Germany. As it turned out, Germany went to war in August 1914 without Turkey. Even when this state did enter the fray a few months later and sided with Germany to help create the Central Powers, how much it eased German encirclement remained a debatable point. For Germany, the appearance was always more telling than the reality, its fears always more pronounced than its ability to engage in sober analysis. Consequently, while Germany would not go to war alone in 1914, this fact hardly mattered. Its encirclement remained intact psychologically. It would prove an impossible handicap to overcome.

The other key German ally in central Europe was Austria-Hungary. Despite its troubles that led German planners to dismiss this power as a declining empire, it was an ally nonetheless. The most recent incident with Serbia presented Germany with a chance to back this state and tie it firmly to the Reich. In the wake of the assassination of Archduke Ferdinand, German diplomats pushed the Austrian crown into delivering a stern note to Serbia that all but promised war and this was the end in mind. This stand would mean the intervention of Russia, as Germany knew. Yet, this end was desired. Russia troubled Germany's military leaders most of all. Moltke believed a rapid recovery of its military strength meant an inevitable clash in Europe. Better to fight this war sooner than later, that is, before the Russians surpassed Germany in military strength. The mechanics of mobilization worked to Germany's advantage as well. The slow process to full mobilization of the Russian "steamroller" meant Germany would have the opportunity to attack west, to attack France, before Russia was ready to bring its full military weight to the battlefield. A few years' delay in fighting a war would defray the temporary German advantage. Last, there simply was great contempt for Slavic influence in Europe, an early racism foreshadowing Nazi Germany's rationale for preemptive war in 1939. Moltke put these sentiments plainly when making claims for war as a means of the advancement of European civilization under a German protectorate.* Kaiser Wilhelm II, the imperial leader of Germany, overtly considered it a race war, a question of "whether the Germanic race is to be or not to be in Europe."** Because of its great fear of Russia, Germany decided at this point to risk war in Europe over the "July crisis" involving Serbia and Austria-Hungary.

Focusing on Russia as the cause of war earned Bethmann Hollweg an additional advantage. Only in the context of fending off Russia with no other recourse than a preemptive attack against France, could Germany

---

* Herwig, "Why Did It Happen?" in *The Origins of World War I*, 186.
** Fischer, *Germany's Aims in the First World War*, 33.

attack in the west and violate Belgium's neutrality without worrying about provoking revolution at home. The most radical political party, the Social Democrats, could not oppose a war that had been forced upon Germany, even if Germany acted preemptively. A defensive war in Europe was needed to satisfy more than the Social Democrats, however. Germany's conservative elite worried about socialist gains in the Reichstag, the German parliament. Such a popular base accentuated their fears that socialism might infect the army once conscription inducted these undesirables into the armed forces. Yet they concluded that war abroad would promote internal harmony, rallying even these dissenters to the German cause of self-defense. For Bethmann Hollweg, this was a more palatable option than the forceful measures urged on him by the elite, such as outlawing the Social Democratic Party. Preemption offered him a chance to go to war without fear of significant political dissent at home that would upset the war effort and perhaps destabilize the German state. Otherwise, the chance to end the encirclement of Germany would certainly slip away should the newly formed German nation fracture in the midst of the conflict that could propel it to greatness.

While he found a war with Russia useful in easing his fears of dissension at home, Bethmann Hollweg attached a greater importance to Russia starting a European war. With the Russians "provoking" Germany into acting preemptively, he believed Great Britain would not intervene in the ensuing war. Such a war would not be painted as German aggression, a bid to control Europe, but German service to the Continent, an effort to defend western civilization from Russian conquest leading to western decay. For this reason, Britain would overlook its alarm at Germany upsetting the balance of power in Europe with an attack on France. He had no real basis for this belief, but he clung to it, ignoring Britain's alliance with France and Russia and the repeated warnings of British emissaries that Britain would honor its treaty commitments. For example, Lord Haldane impressed this point on the German ambassador when visiting Germany in February 1912. This was an important meeting to discuss naval armaments. These talks, like others before it, floundered, the British coming away convinced of the German intention to challenge British sea power. Nothing could push Britain more quickly toward France. Yet, Bethmann Hollweg believed otherwise, revealing that something amounting to a willful denial guided his thinking as he surveyed the European scene. It was a sign that German thinking was not clear or rational, a shortcoming afflicting more than the chancellor. This shared irrationality of the German leadership would contribute to Germany's decision for war in 1914, and it centered in part on the belief that a preemptive attack could overcome all difficulties.

If Bethmann Hollweg had moments of doubt, the military leadership helped him overcome them by emphasizing the value of preemption. Even should Germany be acting rashly and not weighing all the consequences of its actions, especially with regard to Britain's position and intentions, this oversight mattered little to the chancellor once Moltke assured him of German military superiority and Russian and French military weakness. A war in the west versus France would be over quickly, even if the British intervened. The British army would be too small and probably would be deployed too late to make a difference in the fighting in France. Even with Britain in the war, France would be defeated in six weeks and Germany could turn its attention east. On this front, the Austrians were to hold the Russians at bay until German military might arrived. The Germans could engage all enemies, even Britain, because of the favorable military circumstances at the moment. It was an opportunity that might be lost with delay; Germany's enemies were growing stronger. In 1914, the timing was right for a preemptive strike.

The divergence between German and Austria-Hungarian war aims was clear in this planning: Germany looking for a general war, Austria hoping to settle its Balkan troubles with Serbia. Either scenario served German interests. A larger war tied Austria to Germany. Should no general war erupt, Germany still would have thwarted the Triple Entente, and regained its prestige in the eyes of Austria. A stunning German success in the Balkans also meant that Italy and Romania would turn to Germany. Turkey would be reassured as well. By risking war, Germany could gain much, most importantly breaking out of its encirclement with its allies or by discrediting the allied coalition opposing it. The inaction of the great powers in the face of German resolve would be their undoing. Either the attack against France would go forward and Germany would emerge victorious, or the Russians or the French or both would back down and Germany would have ended the threat of encirclement. Such were the promises of acting preemptively.

In spite of the "good news" for Germany of a possible war in the east over Austrian and Serbian tensions, the picture did not brighten in the west. Belgium refused to clarify its stand should Germany cross Belgian territory to strike France. The Germans made repeated efforts to pin down Belgian intentions. German diplomacy reached a new low when the Kaiser directly appealed to the King of Belgium in 1904 and offered Leopold II two million pounds for Belgian neutrality. This bribery offer in exchange for Belgian neutrality came to naught. The offer hoped to capitalize on the famous avarice of the Belgian king, but when even he balked, the offer stood as an outrageous breach of international protocol. And there it remained with lasting damage since it probably contributed to subsequent German frustrations with Belgium. The Kaiser also failed to convince Leopold's successor, King Albert, of the just German cause in waging preemptive war versus France at the expense of Belgium. He apparently did not repeat his financial offer. When diplomacy failed, the military option came to the fore. It did so easily since Germany refused to be held "hostage" by a smaller nation.

By 1914, breaking free of encirclement had boiled down to a military problem for the Germans. European nations clearly wished to check Germany's rise to power, and Germany appeared unable to prevent this from occurring at the negotiation table. War was the only solution. In the end, Germany turned to its military planners for an answer as to how to break the encirclement, and they delivered. The answer was predicable. Enemy nations must be crushed one at a time before they could form a unified front. The east offered few prospects of a successful German offensive. To strike a blow against Russia meant a land battle of undetermined scale and peril. Russian forces at the least could withdraw and gain strength while German armies weakened in the chase. On this front, the Russians could determine when to fight and in this way dictate the German timetable. This would not do. In the west, the prospects were much better. France did not enjoy the great expanse of land as did Russia. A massive German blow here would lead to a war on French soil. This outcome had the advantage of forcing France to fight an early decisive battle. When Germany won this battle, and it would thanks to its great military strength, the war in the west would be over and German attention could return to the east. All told, Germany could face a two-front war with confidence. It remained only to identify the most opportune moment to launch a preemptive strike.

In 1914, German political and military leaders concluded that the moment was right for launching such a preemptive strike. Germany would violate Belgian neutrality as a matter of military necessity. This reason excused the offense of aggression: it was necessary to wage the war forced upon Germany. German war planners agreed that if the war in the west was unjust at the onset, its overall purpose was just. Germany faced war anyway; that was certain. It was a war of national survival, and the only task now was to make sure Germany won the war. Military exigencies excused all other cautions. For this reason, Schlieffen's plan was a godsend as both a means to win a battle of envelopment and as a way to keep the rationale of preemption intact. Massive German armies would attack France via Belgium as soon as hostilities erupted and would defeat France in six weeks. Germany would then turn its attention to the east. German military planners, Moltke in the lead, embraced the Schlieffen plan since it offered a quick war in the west that then allowed Germany to confront Russia. Any wrong Germany committed in initiating the conflict by violating Belgian neutrality paled in comparison to the good Germany would accomplish by winning the war and ensuring its own survival and that of Europe with the repulse of the Russian hordes.

All the pieces were in place by August 1914. German influence netted a tough response from Austria-Hungary to the Serbian government. The Austrians did not believe Serbia was doing enough to right the wrong of the assassination of Archduke Ferdinand, and threatened that state with invasion. Conrad von Hotzendorf, the chief of the Austrian general staff, and therefore the most important military leader in Austria, asked for German support in the event that an Austrian attack provoked Russian intervention on the side of Serbia. Germany, at this point ready to risk war with Russia and France, offered the "blank check," a guarantee of German support. The dream of preemption was so prominent as to push Germany to look for war. In a final comment several years into the war, the Kaiser turned to a confidant and put things bluntly: "Whoever in the case of a European war was not with me was against me." He then pushed the military argument further, enshrining it in history by reminding his advisers that Napoleon and Frederick the Great had had to fight wars "forestalling their enemies."* Germany would do so versus France via Belgium. The encirclement would be broken by military force and done quickly so that Germany avoided any negative consequences of a two-front war. Violating the territory of a neutral country in the name of preemption had carried the day.

The Attack

As tensions rose in the summer of 1914, the question of mobilization became paramount because it helped dictate the timing of the outbreak of hostilities. All nations assumed Germany would complete its mobilization first, so they planned to counter German actions. When the Kaiser heard the Russians had mobilized part of their army in response to Austria-Hungary's partial mobilization designed to confront Serbia, he ordered full mobilization. He had little choice. So tied were the Germans to the Schlieffen plan and its timetable of six weeks, that they could not afford to lose an hour of the assumed advantage to be reaped from this first act of war. Russia's mobilization was an obvious flash point since the Germans counted on a slow Russian preparation for war, enabling Germany to fight in the west before having to face east. France mobilized as well and so in rapid succession, in a matter of days, Europe was poised for war.

As expected, the Germans completed their mobilization swiftly and soon two million German soldiers assembled on the frontier between France

---

* Barbara W. Tuchman, *The Guns of August* (New York: Macmillan, 1962), 24.

and Germany. Formed in seven armies, the plan was simple enough. Once launched into action, the bulk of the German forces would sweep into Belgium and past the French frontier defenses. With this maneuver, the German high command hoped to turn the French left flank and advance toward the Channel coast. The jaws of the trap would then clamp down by swinging back toward Germany, the French armies caught in between the Germans in their rear and the fortifications protecting the German border. It was the classic battle of envelopment in the tradition of Hannibal, Schlieffen hoping to duplicate on a grand scale Hannibal's victory at the battle of Cannae in 216 BC, where the Carthaginian leader destroyed Roman forces totaling 80,000 men. That this battle did not bring Carthage victory in the war against Rome apparently was an outcome the Germans considered unimportant. Germany could not afford such introspection, given that once France was defeated another war against Russia still had to be fought. Avoiding a two-front war was the reason for the Schlieffen plan in the first place. That Germany might not win the battle it sought in the west and that it might be left with the reality of a two-front war was the great gamble. To lose this wager meant they probably would lose the war.

The strategic risk of having to fight a two-front war was but one problem inhibiting the successful implementation of the Schlieffen plan. Timing was another. The plan did not allow for any disruptions. If these arose, the Germans would not meet the six-week timetable of defeating France and then sending their armies east. Two considerations made the inability to meet the timetable likely. The first involved counting soldiers. Schlieffen believed Germany needed an additional 200,000 men on its right flank to make the envelopment successful. Germany did not have this number of men. And even if it did, there was no place to put them. The roads already were occupied by the existing German armies heading through Belgium and beyond into France. In short, the advance could not be executed to Schlieffen's satisfaction. Yet he clung to the plan much as Bethmann Hollweg clung to the fiction that Britain would not enter the war if Germany attacked France. Britain's role raised the second consideration. Should Britain fight and send an army to France, might that army oppose the German advance toward Paris and upset the German timetable? The fact was that no matter the preemptive nature of the attack, the attack would probably fail to knock France out of the war in the period of time desired by Germany. What was more probable was an extended fight with France, albeit on French soil. This lone gain of acting preemptively was not enough to justify the German faith in the Schlieffen plan, and a two-front war loomed.

This pessimism contaminated German thinking, Schlieffen himself succumbing to this negative thinking in the "Great Memorandum" he wrote in December 1905 that voiced concern over the troop numbers mentioned above and simply ignored the possibility of a British contribution to the French battle line. In short, the plan was not a guaranteed prescription for success. The fact that Moltke treated it as such is normally a sign of the limited imagination of this successor to Schlieffen. And Moltke was to prove a poor commander, lacking nerve and therefore unfit to direct the great advance that symbolized the risk inherent in the German attack in the west, a failing Moltke admitted to others before the war broke out. His limitations meant that here again was another German leader captivated by wishful thinking. The plan would succeed because it was Schlieffen's plan. But blaming Moltke excused the shared German problem of being incapable of rational thought as its leaders planned to break free of encirclement in 1914. The time to do so had either been missed or was yet to come. German leadership believed otherwise, no matter the evidence to the contrary, ignoring the almost certain failure of the execution of the Schlieffen plan.

As feared, in the beginning of August, after the German army mobilized successfully, things quickly went awry. First, the staunch Belgian defense of Liège delayed the Germans by four days, a devastating blow to their plans. Second, Britain landed an army of five divisions in France much faster than anticipated. With the addition of the British Expeditionary Force (BEF), the Allied resistance grew stronger and threw the German timetable off schedule once again. These problems were partially offset by a serious French mistake. The French commander, General Joseph Joffre, ordered an advance from France into Germany across the shared border, one heavily fortified on both sides. The French suffered terrible losses. Worse, they indeed had done the "favor" Schlieffen believed they would not do for Germany, massing their forces along the frontier. In so doing, the French put themselves further at risk of envelopment, giving the Schlieffen plan a greater chance to work. Fortunately for France, Moltke's limitations as a leader again surfaced and harmed the likelihood of German success. The German commander along the frontier wished to advance after successfully blunting the French advance, and Moltke allowed him to do so, even reinforcing him with units needed to keep the right wing strong. The great single-envelopment had now become a double-envelopment, to what degree with the understanding and blessing of Moltke remaining unclear. But the Germans could make no more progress there against French resistance than had the French when attacking the German lines, and the German advance stalled, but not before dealing a great blow to the Schlieffen plan.

Insufficient German strength on the right flank now surfaced as a major problem at a pivotal time. As the Germans approached Paris, Moltke redirected the German advance south of the French capital, the natural inertia of the German attack unable to carry it north of Paris due to a simple loss of momentum from lack of troops. In making this fatal decision, Moltke tampered with the Schlieffen plan in remarkable fashion given that he had refused to modify it just before the outbreak of hostilities, so sacred did he deem his duty to protect the plan. The change now offered the French a chance to launch a counterstroke, and the climax of the campaign approached. Joffre jumped at the opportunity to turn the German right flank, and this is what occurred at the Battle of the Marne in early September 1914. It was a closely contested fight, the French use of Paris taxis to transfer soldiers to the front representative of French desperation. But the French stopped the German advance. The defeat of the Schlieffen plan undid German resolve and exposed the desperation on the German side as well, certainly at the highest levels of command. Moltke suffered a breakdown and was relieved. Moltke's successor, General Erich von Falkenhayn, managed to stabilize the battlefront, but the German bid for a great victory against France in the opening weeks of the war had faltered. The German high command now had no choice but to contemplate a long war on two fronts with uncertain results.

Success

The German offensive against France in August 1914 was the last time the Western Front, as it now became famously known, would feature a battle-field of maneuver until the war entered its final year in 1918. With the German defeat at the River Marne, the opposing sides quickly extended their defensive lines from the Swiss frontier to the English Channel. The fortifications, or trench system, erected by both sides then endured a series of tests as military commanders looked to break the deadlock with a battle that breached enemy lines and restored a war of maneuver. These "tests" led to battles where thousands and thousands of men perished. Only after the great battles of 1916, Verdun and the Somme, did the respective sides understand the formidable nature of the trench system. There would be no great breakthroughs until 1918, and when this occurred it did so for three main reasons. First, American forces arrived and gave the Allied powers a decided manpower advantage. Second, the Allies would use a new weapon, the tank, to aid them in breaking through German defenses. And third, German exhaustion would finally sap its ability to fight effectively along the Western Front.

German defeat in the west came only after a series of dramatic battles on the Eastern Front that almost allowed Germany to wrest victory from the shambles of the Schlieffen plan. This opportunity occurred immediately since Russia refused to cooperate with German expectations once hostilities commenced and confine its military activities to the Austrian front. In a matter of weeks two large Russian armies advanced on East Prussia, bringing the war home to Germany. However, a pair of German generals, Paul von Hindenburg and the newly arrived Eric Ludendorff, crushed one Russian army at Tannenberg and expelled the other, ending the threat to Prussia by the first week of September. This success came just in time to bolster the failing war effort of Austria. The Austrians faced a war on two fronts as well, one against Serbia and the other in Galicia against the Russians. Both went badly and the Austrians found themselves heading to defeat early in the war. Only German assistance prevented their collapse. Of course, in providing this assistance, the Germans had to weaken their effort in the west, and this meant a lesser force sweeping into the French rear. In sum, the fighting in the east invalidated a series of German assumptions when starting this war: one, that Austria-Hungary could hold Russia at bay while Germany overwhelmed France; and two, that Germany could not achieve a decision on the battlefield in the east against the Russians—clearly it could have done so. These two revelations did more to deflate the triumphal optimism surrounding the Schlieffen plan than did its actual failure. German determination to launch a preemptive strike in the west meant a missed opportunity in the east.

The idea that Germany could have gained a decisive victory in the east did not reveal the full extent of the failure of preemption. Other consequences did, however. The German attack on Belgium meant that from the opening stages of the war, the Germans faced too many enemies. The only plan to offset this great disadvantage was the Schlieffen attack. When this strategy failed, the Germans faced the two-front war they feared and that they had hoped to avoid by implementing the plan. This strategic failure meant that even battle successes on the Eastern Front could not be turned to strategic benefit. The picture darkened as the war continued. Britain's naval blockade increased the hardships facing Germany. In a desperate bid to end the British advantage at sea, the Germans turned to submarine warfare. This escalation of the conflict eventually produced another great negative, the entry into the war of the United States on the side of the Allies. The weight of Germany's enemies had dramatically increased, and German defeat was only a matter of time.

Before the arrival of American forces in Europe, Germany tried one more bid for victory and it did so by striving to end the war in the east so it would only have to fight in the west, the complete inversion of the Schlieffen plan. With this goal in mind, Germany ensured that V.I. Lenin reentered Russia in the hopes of his being able to overthrow the Russian monarchy and so disrupt the Russian state that it would have to end its involvement in the war. This scheme came to fruition by early 1918. Consequently, Germany had the chance to launch one last great offensive on the Western Front in that year under the direction of Hindenburg and Ludendorff, the famed team from the Eastern Front. When it did so, these two demonstrated the obsolete nature of the Schlieffen plan. A sweeping advance as in 1914 was not possible. Now, infantry advanced in clusters, the "storm troopers" probing for weaknesses in enemy lines. The German plan for victory was to win one more battle as a means to break the will of the opposing side. It was a vain hope and that one more victory never came despite the fact that the Germans did win a number of battles. But the will of the Allies held firm, in no small part thanks to the arrival of American units. The new armies fielded by the United States ensured that Germany's will broke first, not that of the Allies.

This result came in November 1918 as the Central Powers sued for peace. In over four years of fighting, much had occurred to reshape Europe. The war weakened all of the great powers in Europe to such an extent that global changes became possible. Colonial possessions changed hands. The United States and Japan emerged as great powers. Conversely, Europe's stature declined. The Great War also meant a retrenchment in European spirit as well and to such an extent that Adolph Hitler became possible a generation later. The Treaty of Versailles that formally ended the war did not recognize these profound changes. It brokered an unrealistic peace in so far as Europe remained a volatile entity, and one that could well start another global conflict, but it hardly would be able to determine the outcome of such a war. The decision would be left to other nations.

That European statesmen paid no attention to this new reality in 1919 meant a larger war in the future with greater negative consequences for both Europe and the world. To argue that Germany's failed preemptive attack produced the great changes emerging from World War I is an obvious overstatement. But to stress the failure of preemption and the consequences as a result of the ensuing war is not an exaggeration. The Germans risked much with their preemptive attack in August 1914. Their failure to win a quick, decisive war against France meant a carnage that left Europe with a declining influence in world affairs starting on November 11, 1918, the day the guns fell silent.

Conclusion

To a great extent, Germany after 1870 played the role of a great European power and, by so doing, threw Europe into war a generation later. But from the point of view of the Germans, the war was a preemptive one.

Why should Germany not rise to great power status during an age where this eventuality was a norm, at least for western powers? The path had been clearly defined by Britain and to a lesser extent by other nations such as France and Russia. Colonies generated the wealth necessary for industrial development that meant the modernization that produced enormous military strength. The competition this shared goal created could benefit Germany as much as any other power. In so doing, Germany could assume its rightful place in Europe as a great nation.

This step Germany was determined to take, given a reading of history that looked favorably upon German ascendancy in Europe. Russia and France clearly were in decline. Britain remained strong but Germany, as a newly rising power, could challenge its standing. The only check to Germany came from a conscious effort on the part of the European powers to hold the German state at bay. Britain believed in a balance of power on the Continent, and so stood against Germany. Russia posed a great threat as it recovered from internal unrest and disastrous wars and again looked to dominate Western Europe. France was a nation that had long opposed Germany and it was ready to join with Russia to limit, perhaps destroy, German power. The magnitude of German strength registered on these powers in the alliance they created to deny Germany its rightful European stature. The Triple Entente of Russia, France, and Britain meant hostile powers had encircled Germany.

The Reich had no choice but to act and to do so in military fashion. Not to stand firmly with Austria-Hungary could mean the loss of this state as a German ally. The loss of its closest ally would ensure the defection of other Balkan states from the German circle, such as Turkey. If this happened, German encirclement would be complete. On the other hand, a stand to preserve the union with Austria-Hungary staved off encirclement. But given the weakness of this state, and the inroads of France, Russia, and Britain in gaining influence in the Balkans, its value as an ally was limited. States in this part of Europe could turn on Germany as soon as support it, and then German isolation would be complete. As a succession of Balkan crises passed prior to 1914, this conclusion appeared more likely. Germany looked for a favorable opportunity to ensure the support of Austria-Hungary, and German leaders believed they had found it in July 1914.

The prospect of having to act militarily meant a German war on multiple fronts, a clearly undesirable situation. Here preemption gained added importance since it could conceivably solve this military problem. France should be attacked first since its destruction was more feasible than was an attack into the endless spaces of Russia. Once Germany achieved victory in the west, it could turn east and win a similar victory. The Schlieffen plan gave Germany the strategy it needed to win its preemptive war. The main problem with the plan was that it required the violation of Belgium's neutrality. Only by advancing on a broad front in the west could German forces turn the French flank and win a great battle of envelopment. Transgressing on Belgian territory mattered little but for the larger impact of prompting Britain to join the war on the side of France and Russia should the Germans ignore Belgian neutrality. Germany in the west, as in the east, was held hostage by a minor state. German leadership decided this would not be tolerated. Violating the sovereignty of a state mattered little in comparison to the gain of vanquishing an enemy of the Reich and winning the war in the west against France. Any wrongdoing at the onset of the conflict was outweighed by the good of a German victory.

Germany reasoned it had few other choices. The home front was volatile, and a war defending greater Germany would bring unity to an otherwise fractured state. To delay meant increasing Russian strength with unknown consequences for Germany. The Russian threat imperiled the very existence of Germany, threatening a great people with extinction. To delay an attack invited this catastrophe and only lessened German chances of success. France might further prepare for war and prove too formidable to defeat in a quick campaign. Given enough time, its encirclement would be complete and Germany would stand alone. Clearly Germany had to fight, and do so in the summer of 1914. The war plan was in place and Europe appeared destined to face German greatness.

A more sober reckoning found problems with German reasoning. The encirclement was largely a German creation and believing otherwise blinded Germany to its role in fostering war in Europe in 1914. Its policies pushed Britain into an alliance with France. German naval construction threatened Britain with an arms race it wished to avoid. By allying with France, and therefore adding French naval forces to Britain's, Britain staved off an arms race while still keeping in the lead overall at sea. For this reason, British policy earmarked France as a key ally, one that ensured a balance of power on the Continent, a long sought-after British goal. A German defeat of France meant the end of a counterweight to Germany and a dominant power on the Continent. British policy was anti-German in this respect, although it had no other cause for personal malice directed against that state. Any power looking for Continental domination would face British suspicion, and therefore find itself the target of a tested British staple in diplomacy, coalition warfare. France no longer aspired for this end, and so peace, even alliance, was now possible with this nation. This goal of British policy also refuted German claims in another respect. Should Russia have wished to overrun Germany, as the Germans feared, Britain would not allow this to occur in order to preserve a balance of power on the Continent. To protect itself from any Russian threat, Germany could have allied with Britain against Russia, ending its "encirclement" through this diplomatic stroke.

German leaders refused to see this simple calibration in British policy. Instead, right up to the outbreak of war, Germany believed Britain would stand aside even as Germany launched a war to establish its control of Europe. The wishful thinking here centered on Bethmann Hollweg. He had successfully defused another Balkan crisis in 1912 by working with Britain. Bethmann Hollweg cautioned Austria not to resort to force if it could be avoided, allowing Britain to hold a conference that forged a territorial agreement in the region. He also tried to ease British fears of a German naval build-up. Believing he had made great progress, a month before the July crisis, Bethmann Hollweg wrote to his ambassador in London in very confident terms: "Sometimes you see things too pessimistically if you believe that in the case of war England will undoubtedly be found on France's side against us."* Neutrality was more likely, he believed. Yet, this was the same man who backed the "blank check" to Austria, and he did so for several reasons. Losing Austria as an ally was one concern, so too was his fear of growing Russian power. Accepting the two chief tenets of the encirclement reasoning meant risking war, something he had tried to avoid. Why now? It was less an acceptance of Germany's encirclement than it was a pessimism that gripped the man and made him unable to staunch the flow to war. Austria-Hungary would be dissatisfied with Germany no matter the policy: German support would be viewed as pushing that state into a war while German caution would be viewed as abandoning an ally. This "no win" situation contrasted sharply with his positive hopes of winning Britain over to neutrality. Bethmann Hollweg's mercurial personality impeded his ability to clearly face the consequences of Germany's actions.

He was not alone. The decision for war rested on the whims of some key individuals who were not always up to the task. Moltke's rigid adherence to the Schlieffen plan at the outbreak of war also stressed this point. This factor was famously captured when the Kaiser summoned Moltke and ordered him to cease the mobilization for war in the west because Britain had agreed to stay neutral. Now Germany could focus on war in the east and not worry about a two-front war by having to engage France. Moltke refused to change the plans. The mobilization would continue and France would be the target. It would be unsound to leave that enemy on Germany's

---

* Craig, *Germany, 1866–1945*, 333.

flank, he argued. The Kaiser was stunned by a desire to face an enemy where none existed at present. He dismissed Moltke from the meeting and continued the political discussion that shaped the looming war, without the cooperation of his army chief of staff. When the British guarantee of neutrality proved illusionary the next day, Moltke again received the Kaiser's acceptance of the mobilization for war with France as the primary target. The Schlieffen plan remained intact, but this clash made it clear that the military was leading the push for war, its preemptive doctrine supreme. Moltke's slavishness to the Schlieffen plan exposed a man of limited talents.

The problem of this pronounced military influence on German policy made its impact in another manner. Germany, by attacking Belgium, was an aggressor since it violated the territory of a neutral state. For the Schlieffen plan to work, all German planners deemed this a necessity. The threat of encirclement gave these military leaders a reprieve: legality did not matter. The diplomats did not enjoy such a luxury, and Bethmann Hollweg worked hard to convince himself that Britain would overlook Germany's violation of Belgium's neutrality and not join with France and stand against Germany. Lafore, in *The Long Fuse*, described this state of denial in pursuit of German grandeur in as kind terms as possible: "There was undoubtedly a kind of dreaminess about Germans' views of world affairs."* The dreams also fostered acute paranoia, and in this way very serious consequences arose out of Germany's daydream. Foremost in this regard, German military planners and statesmen alike exaggerated the threat posed by Russia, overstating its recovery from war and internal chaos. Casting the looming apocalypse at Russian hands in racial terms surely fed Germany's fear of the Slavic menace from the east. But feeding such fears also quelled a volatile home front, promising a united Germany in the face of a mortal threat. The use of war to foster a more cohesive Germany meant that if necessary, Germany's decision makers could employ some cold reasoning when planning for war. By 1914, this combination of planning for war but pretending it would not come or that it would be fought strictly on German terms meant that when war did erupt, it arrived largely because of Germany's doing.

Thanks to the desire to strike preemptively, Germany assumed the burden of starting World War I. Still, Germany maintained that its preemptive attack in the west in the opening days of August was a justified attack because France had attacked Belgium. Germany merely acted to protect that country. Few believed this then, no one now. But German aggression had a close tie to preemptive warfare. Preemption had taken on

---

* Lafore, *The Long Fuse*, 194.

a life of its own to the point where it was no longer a tool to fight the war successfully. Instead, Germany relied on preemption as the larger purpose of its war, protecting itself from encirclement. This call to arms came from perhaps the most unbalanced of Germany's leaders, Emperor Wilhelm. The simplicity of the Kaiser's belief that nations either stood with Germany or against it meant Germany would gravitate to preemptive war to meet a greater threat, willingly engaging in an act of aggression to do so. The Kaiser would commit his nation to an ever-expanding war that sapped its strength and helped to usher in a revamping of the world order, although in what respect remained unclear. In early August 1914, the lights had indeed gone out.

CHAPTER 5

A Question of Survival: National Socialism Takes Germany to War, 1939

Introduction

A few soldiers neared the checkpoint. They ignored the warnings from the sentries to halt. Instead, they approached and opened fire. The defenders had no recourse but to defend themselves by returning fire, killing a few of the attackers. When the shooting ceased and the assailants withdrew, German infantrymen advanced to look over the Polish soldiers they had killed. A few hours later, German motorized columns were advancing into Poland to defend the Reich from the clearly pending Polish attack. Had the heroes defending Germany looked closely at the soldiers they had killed, they would have noticed an important curiosity. These men were Germans in Polish uniforms. The "attack" they had just withstood was no more than a Nazi ploy to saddle Poland with the responsibility of starting a war by using German prisoners to stage a border incident. On this shaky ground, Adolph Hitler would initiate World War II, telling the world that Germany had a right to defend itself from aggression. It would be a preemptive strike directed at Poland. Only after the war ended would the extent of Nazi duplicity be clear. Not only was the Polish attack on Germany a Nazi fabrication, but the right of Germany to wage this war in the name of self-defense would rest on a different understanding of preemption altogether.

With the attack on Poland, Nazi Germany started World War II in September 1939. When it ended six years later, 57 million people had died. The conflict had reached every continent save Antarctica and laid waste to numerous nations. This reach came gradually. In the first few years of the war, German armed forces appeared unbeatable. Poland collapsed in four weeks. France fell in six. While Britain held firm in late 1940, Russia bore the brunt of the German juggernaut in 1941. By the end of that year, Japan made the conflict global with its attack on the US fleet at Pearl Harbor, Hawaii. Siding with Germany, these two Axis powers, in conjunction with Italy, challenged the world order at a minimum. At a maximum, they appeared on their way to global conquest. The Allied powers of Russia, Britain, and the United States dealt the first serious setbacks to Axis ambitions in 1942. Soviet forces destroyed an entire German army in southern Russia at Stalingrad, while the British defeated a combined German and Italian army in Egypt at El Alamein. In the Pacific in the same year, the Americans turned back Japan, first at the naval battle for Midway Island, then at the vicious, sixth-month land and sea battle for Guadalcanal in the Solomon Islands in the South Pacific. 1943 was a year of Allied resolve. Blunting Axis advances would not be satisfactory; only the complete defeat of the Axis powers, or vanquishment at their hands, would end this conflict. After 1943, it was clear that an Allied triumph would mark the end of this war. American and British armies forced Italy out of the war in 1943. Russian forces withstood another German attack that year at Kursk, before going on the offensive themselves. In 1944, Russian advances in the east accelerated, supported by an Allied invasion of France at Normandy. A final push by Allied armies from both east and west ended all German resistance in April 1945. Four months later, Japan surrendered as well under constant American attacks, the last featuring the use of the atomic bomb. The carnage, loss, and suffering reminded all combatants that the war had been total not just in its scope, but in its purpose. Opposing sides engaged one another with the only goal being the complete defeat of the enemy. When it ended, one side had met this goal, the Allied powers. The world order indeed had been defended, even if irrevocably lost in the process.

Most observers usually blame Nazi Germany for the destruction arising from this catastrophe and this is where it belongs. World War II may have started at different times in different parts of the world, but the catalyst for this violence was Germany, the pivotal year, 1939. The account of the origins of the war offered here is no different in this respect. Certainly Hitler's depraved sense of mission propelled Germany into a war that soon engulfed the world. Yet this view of Hitler at the head of an aggressor state in pursuit of some greater Germany takes on a decidedly different view when examined through the lens of preemption. Hitler convinced the German people that they faced an imminent threat to their security and, given this threat, Germany needed to defend itself. This defense would be a defense of civilization. In short, preemption reverses Germany's role as aggressor to that of assuming a defensive posture, carrying with it the moral weight of that stand. However, the war Germany unleashed was immoral, of course, in the purpose of that war, no matter the label of preemption.

The Case for Preemption

There is no question that Germany's post-World War I situation helped Hitler galvanize Germany into military action in the years after his elevation to power in 1933. The Treaty of Versailles that ended World War I attacked German identity in every way possible. Politically, the new German government, the Weimar Republic, offended German sensibilities of order and authority. Economically, capitalism contributed to this political disorder by failing to provide sustenance for the nation. This loss of German self-sufficiency teamed with restrictions on the size of the military meant a weakened Germany. As Germans reckoned with the diminished status of the fatherland, their society faced psychological trauma in that their leaders had accepted the sole blame for starting World War I. Hitler certainly found a society in crisis when he came to dominate affairs in Germany. He then elevated this crisis to hitherto unimagined levels.

This escalation was not hard to achieve given the hostile intentions of Germany's enemies. Britain resisted any increase in German strength. France wanted German military might eliminated. The peace in the aftermath of World War I gave these nations this chance to keep Germany weak. Acting in tandem, the Allies restricted German war-making capacity, allowing it only a very small army and insisting on the demilitarization of the Rhineland, Germany's industrial heart. This loss of power meant Germany could do little about the territorial restrictions it suffered as well, ones that strengthened its neighbors. France gained Alsace-Lorraine. The new small states of Czechoslovakia and Poland contained large portions of former German territory and, obviously, a large number of German inhabitants. The corresponding reduction in size of the German state was more than a ploy to emasculate Germany. France hoped to use Poland and the Czech state to contain German expansion. These new small states would draw the ire of their German neighbor so these countries would be forced to look west for aid in the form of a military alliance. Additionally, the USSR with its multiplying "lesser peoples" could overrun Germany at some point in time. Even across the Atlantic danger loomed since the United States appeared to be willing to enforce the post-war order as well. Hemmed in on all sides, stripped of the ability to defend itself, Hitler had little trouble convincing Germany that it faced a grave situation in the wake of World War I.

The lone bright spot was that the treaty recognized German unity and therefore legitimacy at the center of Europe. This concession on the part of the victors was remarkable, given their great fear of German power. But Allied statesmen mocked this great power status with the limitations and changes they heaped on Germany. At best, Germany was to remain a latent power. At worst, Germany was to exist at the behest of its overseers, France and Britain. By acknowledging German power but seeking to control it, the Allied powers offered the German people a powerful incentive to redefine themselves one way or another in the aftermath of World War I.

The peace forged in 1919 became a lasting testament to a potentially dominant Germany on the Continent. Clearly an expansion, or more accurately a reestablishment, of German influence in Europe was inevitable given its location and size. That this redefinition of Germany would embrace war came from Hitler. Undoubtedly he found a German population dissatisfied with its role in European affairs. The Treaty of Versailles was universally hated in Germany. Most Germans agreed that expunging this disgrace required an adjustment of German territorial boundaries. However, this motive fell far short of Hitler's more ambitious aim of European domination by Germany. Hitler conflated these two ends. He asserted that Germany endured more than humiliation at the hands of its European enemies; it also faced cultural extinction. The failure to act against its enemies would mean the end of German civilization. Hitler left unclear to the public the extent of the actions he believed necessary to forestall this bleak future. But to his inner circle Hitler made clear the violent nature of how he perceived this reemerging German "influence."

Hitler's assumptions of Germany's ideological and racial superiority drove his plans for Germany and drove the need for war. The Aryan race identified German culture as the best culture. So virtuous was this culture that it must triumph and survive the struggle of race relations that beset the world. Germany's failure in this regard meant the end of all of civilization. For this reason, the fate of "world civilization" was at stake and Germany had a moral duty to assert its rightful place in the world. This claim meant increasing the size of Germany and imitating the great powers that benefited from a large land mass as a means of self-defense. To remain small, a boundary dictated by enemies of Germany, invited the destruction of the state. A coalition of hostile powers could simply overrun Germany at a time of their choosing.

The need to expand grew out of more than a need to acquire territory as a matter of self-defense. The enlargement of Germany also was mandated by Hitler's vision of German greatness. Its people must multiply and to do this they must enjoy additional land and raw materials to support this population increase. Once in possession of *Lebensraum*, or living-space, Germany could flourish as a nation. According to Hitler, Germany had a moral right to a universal expansion in territory, an entitlement of a great civilization. And Hitler warned of the great peril facing Germany if it failed to take its place at the center of the world. He also recognized the need for war. Germany's enemies on the Continent would resist this expansion, so war was inevitable.

Having decided on the expansion of German territory and to do so by force of arms that would result in war, the question was where to strike. The main goal lay in the east. Here, in the USSR, the German people could gain what they needed to thrive as a nation in terms of raw materials and the land needed to sustain an increase in population. As always, the benefits of expansion went hand-in-hand with the practical motive of self-defense. To hesitate waging war in the east invited disaster because the "eastern hordes" would eventually overwhelm Germany. German sacrifices and technological superiority had prevented this catastrophe from overtaking Europe to this point, but time was running out. While advancing east was the goal, into Russia specifically, Germany's vulnerable strategic position complicated this plan. To move east invited attack from the west and vice versa. Should the western powers object to Germany attacking east, then Hitler would make peace with Russia and Germany would attack west to defeat these powers before returning east. Should German efforts in the east meet no western resistance, then these allies would be added to the German order of battle and the war in the east pursued with utmost vigor.

The key was to fight only one war at a time, either in the east or in the west but not in both places simultaneously. In this way, Germany would avoid a two-front war and certain defeat. If possible, Hitler would not strike west at all. By turning east, he engaged the main enemy, the USSR. At other times, Hitler rearranged his priorities. France, a steadfast enemy of Germany, had to be defeated first. Britain could be brought in line as an ally. With Western Europe firmly under German control, Germany could fight the war in the east. The allowance extended to Britain was subject to change, however. Since the Reich's ultimate goal was world domination, allies would have to bow to German suzerainty just as did enemies of the Reich. The fanciful goal of Nazi world supremacy rested on some hard rationality. One, Hitler did not delude himself into thinking he could conquer the world in his lifetime. That end fell to future generations that would finish what he started. Two, he was Bismarckian in that he would parley with nations even ideologically opposed to Germany, the USSR being the most important example. His diplomatic flexibility underscored a shrewd political skill. Third, he strove to limit the number of enemies Germany faced at any one time. In this way, a two-front war would not cripple Germany's chances of victory as it had done in World War I. With these considerations in mind, the goal of universal German power might still appear absurd, but the means to German expansion suddenly appear very feasible. The questions were how far would Hitler get in his lifetime and how much bloodshed and carnage would he inflict on Europe, Germany and its enemies alike?

The weighing of options of where to attack first put Poland in Germany's sights. Victor Rothwell, in his *Origins of the Second World War*, wrote that as early as November 1937, Hitler "appeared to be thinking out loud about some 'pre-emptive' attack on Poland."[*] By 1939, the attack and defeat of Poland were within German capabilities and its defeat had a measure of certainty. This point had been reached because of a series of steps Hitler had taken that strengthened Germany militarily. German repudiation of the arms limitations imposed upon it by the Treaty of Versailles had produced a significant rearmament by 1936. On Hitler's orders, a revitalized German military then reoccupied the Rhineland in 1936, the key industrial center of Germany. At this point there could be no mistaking a German intention to rearm, and no missing the lack of will of France and Britain to stop this development. Germany was further strengthened, and the lack of will of German opponents in the west further validated, when Germany annexed Austria in March 1938. Piece by piece Hitler strengthened Germany and sounded out the will of his enemies. Their unwillingness to go to war to stop Germany meant a further gain for Germany: its enemies were not as formidable as was believed.

Much the same story unfolded when Hitler occupied Czechoslovakia in 1938, with an important qualifier. Germany was again strengthened by seizing Czech armaments and eliminating a hostile nation from the list of Germany's enemies. The will of Britain and France to stop Hitler also appeared impotent, as the famous Munich Conference underscored. To many, at the time and in retrospect, the appeasement of Hitler at the expense of the Czech Republic paved the way to the greater war to come a year later over Poland. However, Gerhard Weinberg points out in controversial fashion in *Hitler's Foreign Policy*, this view of Munich misses the main point. Hitler walked away from Munich believing he had failed to achieve his objective of starting a war because Britain surprisingly had agreed to what Hitler thought were his excessive demands.[**] Hitler understood that Britain's negotiation was not appeasement but amounted

---

[*] Victor Rothwell, *Origins of the Second World War* (Manchester: Manchester University Press, 2001), 92.

[**] Gerhard L. Weinberg, *Hitler's Foreign Policy: The Road to World War II, 1933-1939* (New York: Enigma Books, 2005), 775.

to shrewd policy. The more time the Allies had to prepare for war, the more time they had to rearm. Hitler believed that Germany had to strike now while it had a military advantage in armaments. Should others reequip over time, then all was lost. Total readiness varied, Hitler at times stating that Germany would be ready for war in 1945, at other times arguing that a nation was never totally ready for war, so one may as well go to war immediately. Since Allied will in stopping German expansion was lacking, Hitler planned for war sooner rather than later. As scholar Norman Rich put it in his book, *Hitler's War Aims*, Hitler believed that "Germany was faced with the harsh alternatives of striking now, while the chances of success were still favorable, or allowing events to take their course and facing certain annihilation in the future. 'Time for a solution now ripe. Therefore strike!'"* The Allied capitulation at Munich denied him this first strike opportunity.

The result was that by 1939 a general war over Poland was virtually certain because Hitler wanted it to be so. Poland could not be trusted to back Germany in any scenario envisioned by Hitler. Should Hitler attack west, Poland could stab Germany in the back and seize Silesia, Pomerania, or East Prussia or all three. Should he turn east, Poland would prove a feckless ally. In fact, Hitler's plans for war in the east merely assumed the defeat of Poland and its incorporation into the Reich as a conquered province. While Hitler prepared himself and Germany for all possibilities leading to war, Poland was now the key to the pending outbreak of hostilities in Europe. The German attack on Poland would do more than merely reclaim the portions of Poland that belonged to Germany. It would be more than a repeat of the German occupation of Czechoslovakia. The goal was the complete destruction of the Polish state and a general state of war denied to him at Munich. If the Western powers objected to a German attack on Poland, then Hitler would make peace with the USSR, then attack west and end this threat before returning to make war in the east. Should the western powers stand aside, then the larger war in the east would begin. Either way, the time for the war of German expansion had come.

Some last-minute diplomacy clarified the order of the upcoming war. The Soviet Union agreed to a non-aggression pact with Germany on August 24, 1939. When learning of this development, Hitler slammed his fist on the dinner table and exclaimed, "I have them!"** The victims he identified in this shriek were the western powers. Hitler now assumed that Germany

---

* Norman Rich, *Hitler's War Aims: Ideology, the Nazi State, and the Course of Expansion* (New York: WW Norton, 1973), 129.

** Richard Overy with Andrew Wheatcroft, *The Road to War*, rev. edn. (London: Penguin Books, 1999), 69.

had a free hand to fight in Poland. Should Britain and France decide to go to war against Germany over a German attack on Poland, they would do so without the aid of the Soviet Union. Hitler did not think they would take this risk. German absorption of Austria and its occupation of Czechoslovakia without a French or British declaration of war had convinced Hitler that no conflict would erupt over Poland in the west. He understood the statesmen opposing him and believed they would shrink from war. Even should they fight, with no threat in the east, Germany would not face a two-front war as it did in World War I. A German victory in the west was very probable for this reason. Since France and Britain understood this, Hitler believed they would not fight over Poland. It was indeed a good time to go to war.

When both of these governments reaffirmed their intentions to fight over Poland, Hitler still believed they would back down. When they did not, World War II erupted in the first few days of September 1939. Although bent on war, Hitler was still surprised how things played out over Poland—that France and Britain had gone to war. The strongest evidence in this regard has been proven false: when informed of Britain's ultimatum for war after Germany attacked Poland, Hitler scornfully asked his foreign minister, "What now?"* This had served as evidence of his dismay that his gamble to eliminate Poland without western intervention had failed; clearly, he had desired another localized war. If this exchange never occurred, additional evidence suggests the opposite. Eyewitnesses describe Hitler as worn out and troubled in the week leading up to war with Poland. Yet he slept soundly the night before the invasion of Poland. These observations speak to his comfort with events moving beyond another localized war. He would not be cheated out of war, his main worry up to the outbreak of fighting with Poland.

When it came to Poland in 1939, Hitler may have been surprised by Allied intervention and embarrassed that those around him had seen his intuition fail him, but he also realized that the most important factor was not timing, but how to fight his war of expansion. Enemies were to be faced one at a time and this strategy was still intact even after the German invasion of Poland. Hitler realized that war in Poland meant war in the west, and he was determined to have this war. Germany would attack east, the main target, after German victory in the west. Therefore, the intervention of France and Britain in the war in Poland did very little to disrupt German plans of expansion, as Hitler saw things. It merely accelerated the timetable. This may have been unforeseen by Hitler, but it was hardly undesirable.

---

* Overy, *The Road to War*, 70. Weinberg calls attention to the doubtful veracity of this outburst by Hitler. See his, "Preface to the Combined Edition," in *Hitler's Foreign Policy*, 9.

In fact, a war in 1939 offered three benefits. First, Germany would maintain its rearmament advantage. Other nations would not be able to use additional time to catch up with Germany. Second, after hostilities ended in Poland, the war for German expansion would no longer have to hide in the shadow of an unjust peace. Without this rationale of righting the wrong of the Treaty of Versailles, the ostensible motive for war up to Poland, Hitler's preemptive purpose of expansion for living-space would have been more transparent and might not have survived close scrutiny from within Germany, let alone from a passive Europe. Now the war over Poland meant he could go ahead; it was too late to stop him from pursuing his quest for living-space once general war erupted. Third, a wider war in the west over Poland underscored the importance Hitler attached to himself in waging this war. He believed that Germany must act now before he was too old to be vital and capable. Only he possessed the will to set Germany on this historic course. It was a great moment demanding a great man who did not shrink from the costs of war. Hitler did not underestimate the sacrifices and woes Germany's path to greatness would entail. In fact, he welcomed these eventualities. This war would benefit Germany as it had other great civilizations birthed from similar trauma. So a general war in 1939 was a good thing even if it came sooner than Hitler had expected.

Poland was the final step to putting Hitler's goal of a war for *Lebensraum* into action. The irony surrounding the German attack on Poland was that a war against Poland made sense to the German public. It would settle the "Polish question" once and for all. Germans could tell themselves that they were merely correcting the injustices of 1918. But the case for preemption made sense only to Hitler. He relished Polish resistance as the opportunity he wanted to launch his war for the control of Europe. Germans hoped he could get more land but avoid a general war. Hitler sought the opposite, a state of hostilities in Europe to get more land. The track record of Hitler's successful expansion of German power without war up to the attack on Poland obfuscated the contradictory notions each party held surrounding the purpose of Germany's attack on Poland. The German people could tell themselves that with the defeat of Poland, German expansion was complete. Hitler understood that the German conquest of Poland would launch a preemptive war in the name of *Lebensraum,* and that German expansion was only beginning, just as he desired.

The Attack

The cause of the war in Poland was the free city of Danzig. Poland refused to return to Germany this city and the German population caught in the "Polish Corridor," the land Poles used to access Danzig and that cut off

Germany from East Prussia. The city was in some kind of limbo status after World War I, but the Germans had a clear reason for resentment; Danzig was lost to Germany. Therefore, Hitler made the pretense of war with Poland the same as that of Austria and Czechoslovakia. Germans severed from the fatherland demanded their return and Hitler was determined to make this happen. However, this time around, Hitler took no chances of repeating his mistake at Munich. There would be no negotiation over Poland's borders. Poland would fight and Germany would invade. Britain would not be allowed to convince Poland to meet the German demands and avert war. The famous episode where the British ambassador to Germany could not even get the list of demands from his German counterpart on the eve of the German invasion of Poland made this intention perfectly clear. For Hitler, the war in Poland was much bigger than Danzig. A general war in the west over Poland meant the clock had started on Hitler's push for living-space.

Postponed a week while Hitler sounded out British intentions, German forces entered Polish territory on September 1, 1939. Germany offered no declaration of war. This breach of protocol delayed the response of France and Britain. Both nations issued an ultimatum to Germany to withdraw its forces or face war. The ultimatum was ignored and they declared war on Germany on September 3. Poland, of course, had been at war for several days and immediately faced a dire situation. The German attack came from three different directions at once: Germany, East Prussia, and Czechoslovakia. The three-pronged offensive was made feasible by the German occupation of Czechoslovakia, validating Hitler's fixation on eliminating the threat posed by countries positioned in Germany's rear or flanks. The Poles now faced an almost impossible task of defending themselves on three fronts.

While the launching point of the German attacks gave Germany a key strategic advantage, tactically the Germans stumbled badly and almost forfeited this benefit. The German armored units, so crucial to a rapid advance that promised a quick end to the war, were dispersed on the three fronts. The German superiority in mobile forces was frittered away, weakening the intended *Blitzkrieg* offensive. Air power compensated for this mistake. German forces did break through the Polish river lines of defense thanks to complete German mastery of the air. Soon German forces threatened Warsaw. Even at this point, despite heavy losses in manpower, enough Polish forces remained intact to defend the city. Polish reinforcements from the east could stymie the Germans yet. A prolonged Polish resistance might be rewarded with relief from an attack by France and Britain on Germany itself. The situation was dire but not hopeless.

It soon became hopeless. On September 17, 1939, the USSR invaded eastern Poland. Russian forces met little opposition and quickly linked up with German units. Poland was overrun and any further resistance futile. The end of Poland came in the first week of October 1939, the result of a remarkable bit of diplomacy by Hitler, the two ideological enemies of Germany and the USSR agreeing to end the existence of a neighboring state. Hitler also showed flexibility by postponing his ultimate goal of eastern expansion. The Soviet Union now gained territory at the expense of Poland obviously, but also that of Germany. Even though the soldiers of the Reich did the majority of the fighting, Germany settled for less Polish land than Russia. Worse, the USSR had increased its territorial holdings in the east, the very region Hitler identified as so important to Germany's defense. This concession appeared to blaspheme the entire purpose of Hitler's preemptive war against Poland, a war to acquire living-space in the east. However, Russian gains were the product of a temporary arrangement from Hitler's point of view. Germany would turn east soon enough once it settled the war in the west and did so without Soviet intervention.

The sudden German victory allayed any unease Germans may have felt from the overkill of the attack. Hitler indeed had addressed the Polish question but the German onslaught conquered a substantial portion of the country, not a small part of it. If this outcome could be accepted as a longstanding German goal that predated Hitler, the settlement with the USSR to carve up Poland with Germany could not be so explained. A key enemy of the Reich was now a partner in settling a German issue. And of course Hitler's decision for war in Poland meant a general war in the west. Germans had good reason to ask just what their Führer intended by starting this war. Had his luck run out, and with it that of Germany's? Had he not intended to start a general war? Or was there a larger purpose in attacking Poland?

Now committed to war, now on the path to restoring the greater Germany, Hitler told them his purpose. Preemption was not needed to defend Germany from an imminent Polish attack. Polish defensive positions testified to this fact, and when Germany attacked, Poland withdrew its forces to the interior of the country. Moreover, the Polish government had delayed mobilization in order not to provoke Germany. The German attack was preemptive only in the context of a war for *Lebensraum*. Poland was but the first step. Hitler now had the opportunity to launch a general war in Europe to fight the war of German expansion. Of course, the German people had believed there was a crisis over Poland, and this helps explain their gravitation to Hitler. That he had redefined the crisis facing Germany into a reason for preemptive war only slowly became apparent. Up to Poland, Hitler made sure to keep his larger mission muted. After Poland, he was much more overt since it was too late to debate the merits or meaning of Hitler's preemptive attack on Poland. Hitler did not put German thought into action when he implemented his extreme racist policies or sent Germany down a path to dominate Europe, as historian A.J.P. Taylor argued in his book, *Origins of the Second World War.** The converse was true. Germans put Hitler's thought into action. Once war broke out over Poland, Germany and its leader were now firmly tied together, and if this was unclear to the German people, it was clear to Hitler. He soon would make the Germans and the world understand the full meaning of his preemptive war.

Success

Given Hitler's reason for preemptive war in the name of securing *Lebensraum*, Poland's defeat was not enough. It was only a beginning. More wars would follow to ensure that Germany achieved its goal of acquiring living space in the east. After the attack on Poland, the German war of expansion continued but with more alacrity. Hitler got his war for expansion and largely on terms of his choosing. The west was to be engaged first, and then the east. Over time this last criterion, fighting enemies on one front at a time, which would prove the most important criterion, failed him and doomed his strategy for fighting his preemptive war. But this outcome arose from circumstance, not by design.

War in Poland now meant a general conflict in the west, given the obdurate stand of France and Britain. Yet, when Germany did strike Poland, Britain and France did little to support the Polish state. They did declare war but they stood idle as Germany overran Poland. They stood idle into 1940, hoping that Germany had satiated its demands, that the legacy of Versailles had been expunged to Hitler's satisfaction. German attacks against Demark and Norway in April 1940 dispelled this hope. Hitler ordered the conquest of these Scandinavian nations for a number of reasons, including the prevention of an Allied amphibious landing in the German rear. German forces overran the two countries in just a few weeks and Hitler turned his attention to France.

Hitler attacked France in May 1940, ending nine months of tense standoff along the western front. With the USSR immobilized given its pact with Germany, Hitler went to war in the west confident of victory. Still, a fortunate military development aided this assault. The original German plan called for a repeat of the Schlieffen plan of World War I.

---

* A.J.P. Taylor, *The Origins of the Second World War* (New York: Atheneum, 1962), 71.

German forces would race through the Low Countries, turn the French flank and win a battle of envelopment. This attempt could possibly have succeeded but it would be a close contest since the Allies anticipated this German maneuver. In 1940, the Germans did win a battle of envelopment but from an unexpected direction. Hitler changed the locus of the attack when an air mishap allowed the German war plans to fall into Allied hands. He now embraced a strategy of striking though the Ardennes forest and heading to the coast of France. This drive would split the Allied forces in two and lead to the decisive victory Germany sought in the west.

Mobile forces were not supposed to be able to negotiate such rough terrain as that found in the Ardennes. The Germans were able to do so given expert planning, impeccable air cover, and complete surprise. Allied commanders simply disregarded the reports of German forces attacking in this area. They could not believe it was the main attack. When the German breakthrough occurred, surprise was total. In a matter of days, German tanks reached the French coastline. Now, Allied forces advancing into the Low Countries to meet the assumed major German attack there were cut off. While Britain extricated most of their forces in an emergency evacuation at the port of Dunkirk, French resistance collapsed rapidly, leaving only Britain against Germany in the west.

So far, things had gone largely by design for Germany. The goal was to face the enemies of the Reich one at a time. It was "conquest by installments," as scholar H.P. Willmott labeled it in his book on World War II, *The Great Crusade.** True, the German attack on Poland had led to Britain and France declaring war on Germany in September 1939. So from the outset of a general state of hostilities, Germany faced multiple enemies. Still, the idea of fighting in the west and not in the east remained intact. In this way, Germany avoided the two-front war that had so badly crippled its war effort and chances for victory in World War I. After 1940, Hitler's ability to choose his opponents and fight them on only one front failed. Britain refused to make peace with Germany no matter that it stood alone after the Allied disaster suffered in France. Hitler ordered an invasion of the island but to do this Germany needed control of the air to neutralize British sea power. When Britain defeated the German air force in the fall and winter of 1940, Germany's bid to invade Britain soon passed.

Although not completely victorious in the west, Hitler now focused his attention east. He believed the time had come at last to gain the eastern territory so necessary for German survival. He now risked war in the east

---

* See the chapter by that name in H.P. Willmott, *The Great Crusade: A New Complete History of the Second World War* (New York: The Free Press, 1989).

and the west. Hitler dismissed the fears of his generals of a two-front war—exactly what he had avoided to this point—for two reasons. First, Britain was too weak to trouble Germany anytime soon. Additionally, Britain would come to realize that its interests lay in fighting with Germany, not against it. Should it not realize this, it would be defeated in the near future anyway. Second, the USSR was too weak to withstand the German *Blitzkrieg*. It would be subdued in just a few weeks. Germany could then utilize the benefits of living space in the east to equip its armed forces for a final showdown with Britain. World domination would be possible as well after this series of successes. The fruition of Hitler's preemptive war was seemingly at hand.

Very quickly, however, circumstance overtook design. Germany attacked Russia in June 1941, but that nation did not collapse in six weeks. It continued to fight and war in the east soon became Germany's main battle front. This commitment facilitated the recovery of Britain. Granted a reprieve, Britain first contested German supremacy in North Africa, then in Italy, and finally in France. When teamed with the growing power of the United States, the west again became a front that Germany had to reckon with. By late 1942, Germany found itself in a two-front war—one in the east and another in the west—and much as was the case in World War I, the battle lines stretched German resources to the breaking point. In just a few years, a two-front war would prove fatal to Germany. Allied air armies destroyed German cities. Allied offensives first contained and then pushed back German armies. Soon, Germany fought on two fronts to hold onto the land it had conquered. By late 1944, Germany fought desperately merely to defend its borders. It would lose this fight by April 1945.

Hitler's failure to localize each war he fought meant German defeat in its preemptive war for living-space. But this point was reached, not with war in Poland, as Weinberg argued in *A World at Arms*, but with Britain's stand in late 1940.* Until this point, Hitler successfully clung to his strategy of fighting on one front at a time. The general war in the west in 1939 had come without fear of Russian intervention. It had been very successful. Poland had been destroyed and occupied. Western Europe was soon under German control. Only Britain remained an enemy of the Reich in the west. At this point, Hitler risked everything, broadening the war by attacking east. It had always been the main target, so with Britain seemingly in check, the temptation was too great not to begin the war for *Lebensraum*. From this decision came German defeat. Hitler's vision of preemptive war in the name of expansion came to an end once the Nazis had to fight on two fronts.

---

* Gerhard L. Weinberg, *A World at Arms: A Global History of World War II* (Cambridge: Cambridge University Press, 1994), 44.

Instead, Germany faced the war of survival that he had feared, although it came about largely of his own doing.

One more point needs to be stressed in regards to measuring the success of Hitler's attack on Poland. While circumstance derailed Germany's expansion, rendering its preemptive war unsuccessful, this lack of success must be measured more carefully than this. Germany did overrun a great amount of territory. It did seek to implement a new order throughout its conquered lands. In the east, this meant the Third Reich started its program to secure *Lebensraum*. To pursue this effort the Germans killed millions of people by using extermination methods targeting Jews and Slavic peoples, and anyone else deemed subhuman by Nazi doctrine, and by dislocating those deemed undesirable from their lands which were then stripped of all resources to fuel the German war effort. By this measure, Hitler's preemptive war enjoyed a measure of "success." Over the period of several years, he put Germany on the path to using outlying territories in the east to serve a greater Germany, the purpose of the war in the first place. The horrific cost in lives merely amounted to preparing now empty lands for colonization by the anticipated new stock of Germans destined to rise out of the great experiment. But the loss of life did much more than this. It ensured that German preemptive warfare fell from the category of success to that of a crime. The crimes the Germans committed in the time allowed to them in the lands they had taken vitiated any claims of success. The absolutely disastrous German rule in foreign lands makes one grateful that circumstance undid Hitler's expansionist designs as soon as it did.

Conclusion

The war Hitler launched against Poland in September 1939 was in many ways one he viewed as an act of preemption. Germany was surrounded by enemies that looked to keep her weak and at their mercy. France and Britain enforced a punitive peace that absorbed German financial resources while depriving Germany of the opportunity to create an economy that could pay its debts and rid it of foreign oversight. German efforts to point out this contradiction merely earned it threats of a harsher peace still. The superiority of France and Britain rested on the military might of these two nations and a number of smaller states they had created to contain German power. Poland and Czechoslovakia were two examples. When added to the western powers, Germany faced a formidable coalition. Nor could Germany be certain that the USSR would remain indifferent to European events. A resurgence of the power of this nation threatened Germany. And across the Atlantic the United States clearly backed a world order that helped Germany's enemies. From Hitler's point of view, Germany had to strike or face obliteration.

This glum picture helps explain the rise of Hitler to power. His nationalism was supported by the majority of the German people. The efforts to free the nation from the humiliation of 1918, to rejuvenate Germany, and to protect it at the same time, all received the broad support of the German people. By making these ends his own, Hitler assured himself an opportunity to reshape Germany and make it strong again. A reshaping of Germany was certainly one way to look at Germany's revival after 1918. Rearmament spoke to German greatness. Reconstituting a Third Reich spoke to German greatness. That Hitler managed to do this without war over the Rhineland, Austria, or Czechoslovakia meant that, in the eyes of many Germans, Hitler was a great man too. The war that erupted over Poland stemmed from Allied intransigence as much as from German aggression. In the post-World War I era, Hitler had returned Germany to the status of a great nation despite the efforts of its enemies. This fact was resented by most if not all of the European nations since they always had feared German power. Hitler's call to arms merely exposed this resentment, the desire to hold Germany in check.

The insult of Germany's enemies trying to deny the German nation its rightful place in the world was all the greater given the changed political landscape of Europe. Russian power had receded and it no longer played an important role in European affairs. France and Britain endured internal chaos from the paralysis of democracy. That these two nations had saddled Germany with this same problem in the form of the Weimar Republic only reaffirmed their hostile intentions. The peace appeared arbitrary indeed to most Germans. A new world order based on liberal democracy had been created in the aftermath of war. Germans could well ask themselves why they should not create a new world order, one that benefited Germany and did not exclude it or seek to deny it a key role in shaping the future. Why not the German vision of centralized authority enforcing law and order that allowed for orderly societal development? Why not export this idea throughout Europe? In this context, German expansion amounted to an act of self-defense and Hitler's preemptive policy certainly made sense to most Germans.

"Most Germans" is a vague definition of Hitler's supporters both in terms of numbers and composition. It is not easy to qualify it further but it is important to try because it is possible that Hitler exaggerated the threat Germany faced from outside attack merely to shore up his rule at home, not because of some fanatical belief in his preemptive war. Acting preemptively rallied Germans to his side to meet the ominous threat. At the very least, this political device quieted opposition to the Nazi regime since Germany would feel compelled to remain united in the face of danger. Hitler's complete control of the state was still a dream far from realization. Hitler needed to sedulously guard his popularity in the years leading up to 1933 when he took power, and in the years before 1939 when Germany went to war. In fact, this concern remained a Nazi priority during the war years as well. Keeping Germany in a permanent state of crisis over the threat of war, even if there was no threat or the threat was greatly exaggerated, was one way to ensure Germans remained loyal to the *Führer*. Keeping the nation always at war was another. Given this perspective, preemption was not a necessary act of self-defense to fend off outside foes, but a manipulative tool to gain and hold political power.

Hitler desired all the public support he could get because many questioned his rule for several reasons. He was an outsider, after all, an Austrian looking to rule Germany. He was also a commoner. While Hitler turned this commoner status into a badge of honor and enjoyed much political acclaim by representing himself as a man of the people, Germany remained a class-conscious society. He was not accepted by the elite of German society, particularly the industrial sector. His generals had the same reaction. They believed in their elite status based on Prussian nobility. This outsider and commoner had nothing to offer Germany but could hurt the nation badly with his reckless plans for reestablishing the great German nation. Hitler sensed this animosity and quickly acted to politically outmaneuver the opposition. He won over most of the elite with basic successes: establishing law and order, reviving the economy. Winning the allegiance of the military was more difficult. They opposed his reoccupation of the Rhineland as too dangerous because this rash act would provoke an invasion of Germany by France and possibly Britain, one that the German military could not stop. Hitler pushed for this decision anyway and in so doing stood alone. This act meant he reaped significant benefits when Germany first reoccupied the Rhineland in 1936, and then in 1938 annexed Austria and crushed Czechoslovakia, all without war. One of the chief benefits Hitler earned from this string of successes was the deference now shown to him on the part of the officer elite. Many of them reconsidered their view of Hitler. Perhaps the upstart did know something after all. If given more opportunities, he might win more concessions from France and Britain and further strengthen Germany. This latitude the military extended to Hitler was a key turning point. He now had the blessing of those in control of the tool he needed most to start a war.

Hitler's political perspicacity should have been apparent to all rivals and doubters long before 1936 because, after his election as chancellor in 1933, he very quickly consolidated his power. There would be no controlling this man, as the elites had expected they could do. If they had underestimated him initially, they took him very seriously soon enough. Though he was hated, they still allowed him to remain in place. True, there were a few attempts to assassinate him or remove him by other methods, but these came to nothing. What they point to is that German elites, and most Germans at the very least, tolerated this man in control of the nation. The question is, why? The answer is that Hitler skillfully remedied outstanding German grievances. Unsettling political change was real enough, economic dislocation was real enough, and the burden of carrying the guilt for having started World War I was real enough. Social chaos indeed surged in this environment, oftentimes sparking open violence in German cities. In the tumultuous post-1918 world, this vulnerability was a dangerous course to run. Internal collapse was possible even before an attack launched by an external enemy allowed it to conquer Germany. Hitler ended both of these fears. He made stability of government a priority. He made addressing economic woes a priority. He made German rearmament and war with Poland a priority. All of these goals met with German approval because they predated Hitler's rise to power. Hitler had largely cured Germany's identity crisis and in so doing he consolidated his political power. Only then did he feel confident that he could embark on his preemptive war. But the priority was clear. For Hitler, preemption was about political control first, his vision of a greater Germany second.

If Hitler demonstrated significant political savvy in a short period of time, his motives were more difficult to pinpoint. He clearly felt illegitimate as Germany's leader and found the outside threats facing Germany useful to keeping him in power. So he exaggerated the crisis facing Germany. In this way, the German people would be willing to accept something new. That may have included an Austrian leader promising an end to the humiliating Treaty of Versailles. But world conquest requiring a great cost in human life was another matter entirely. Here was a point of profound separation between him and the German people. For this reason, Hitler emphasized the threat of imminent attack facing Germany, the humiliation of not being able to meet this threat, but not the preemptive war he wished to wage, a testament to the shaky hold Nazis had on power. Close confidants were enlightened, pliable generals were informed, but the public remained shrouded in hazy calls for sacrifices in the name of a return to German splendor. The implication of Nazi rule was certainly ascertainable, but few Germans took this step. They contented themselves with the belief that Germany, under Hitler's guidance, was merely assuming its rightful place as a great power in Europe. The blurring of these two ends worked to Hitler's distinct advantage: he got to stay in power and launch his preemptive war. He may well have been a true believer that Germany faced a threat to its existence that could only be dealt with through expansion.

He may well have believed in his preemptive war, but the politician over-shadowed the visionary. He wanted to retain power and preemption came second to this goal.

Hitler's preemptive rationale of expansion in the name of preserving a German culture threatened with extinction failed to qualify as an act of self-defense on two additional accounts. First, Hitler exaggerated the external threats facing Germany. France and Britain together posed the greatest challenge to a German resurgence. But they hoped to preserve and contain Germany, not destroy it. The smaller states created to contain German power posed no threat either. They were too small individually to challenge even a weakened Germany. They also showed no inclination to ally with one another. Only when allied with France or Britain could they pose a threat to Germany. But these two states would hardly unleash this coalition in an attack to destroy Germany. If anything, France and Britain would act to restrain any adventurism on the part of these lesser states. Russian weakness meant Germany did not have to fear being overrun from the east. For all its financial muscle, the United States clearly favored an isolationist stand and was unlikely to intervene militarily on the Continent under any circumstances, let alone to crush Germany. There was no imminent threat facing Germany and no need to strike preemptively.

Hitler found a need. The extinguishing of the German nation was the price of inaction because a defeated German culture could not flourish and defend itself. Germany must strike preemptively to ensure its survival. If preemption appeared to give Hitler a cause for action—self-defense—war was still unnecessary. Germany was a great power. It could exert its influence and secure a dominant German culture on the Continent without war, given its size and location. That it continued to do just this even in its weakened state following World War I underscored this reality. But a peaceful assimilation of Germany back into Europe, one even leading to a German ascendancy, did not suit Hitler. Nazism pursued war as an end in and of itself. The crisis was perpetual and demanded ever more acts of war. There was never to be an end to the Nazi war for *Lebensraum*. But, here again, the reasoning for a preemptive war failed since Germany could return to great power status without war at all.

A preemptive strike that rebuffed Germany's looming enemies made sense to most Germans. But there were limits to the extent of the emergency from the point of view of the German people. Once German honor was restored, Germany could cease its preemptive attacks and take its rightful place in European affairs. Not so from the perspective of Hitler. Ending these external threats and reestablishing a Germany that played a key role in European affairs was only part of Hitler's preemptive policy. His goals were much more ambitious. He took Germany to war to try and assert an ideological and racial supremacy that he believed was morally valid. This end was more than correcting injustices arising out of past wars. This vision meant a necessity for German expansion far beyond its borders and a murderous war of extermination of inferior peoples. To his everlasting damnation the goals Hitler set for German expansion were obscene and immoral. It is surprising to what extent his cultural arguments in favor of the necessity of German expansion relied on the destruction of other cultures. Given the racial imperative, nothing would stand in the way of Germany. This expansion was preemptive only in the context of a war for *Lebensraum*, a war that appealed to the morality of German expansion in the name of defending the majesty of a German culture destined to spread throughout the world. Germany would pay a great price for this assumption of cultural superiority.

German war plans went astray and that is a good thing. Germany was defeated and its monstrous and murderous vision of the world defeated as well. But Hitler's claims of a moral purpose in expansion are not so easily dismissed. Hitler did not start these wars with an act of preemption. He fought these wars in the name of preemption. The difference was crucial. Germany did not enter World War II under the mandate of Hitler's preemptive war. However, Germans did fight this war for that purpose. From Hitler's point of view, the moral purpose of expansion exonerated any transgression in starting a war, and apparently any crime when fighting the war as well. Hitler was protecting German civilization. Hitler remained convinced that this mission constituted a moral end in and of itself. War may well be an evil, but it now bowed to a noble purpose. Hitler believed he sought the greater good for Germany and for the world once it was endowed with the gift of German culture, a belief he clung to in spite of the crime inherent in his preemptive war.

CHAPTER 6

Choosing Enemies:
Japan Accepts the US Challenge
for War, 1941

Introduction

Japanese pilots faced a disconcerting sight when they returned to their ships after participating in the second wave that attacked Pearl Harbor. No other planes were preparing to take off and strike the naval base a third time. Why was there no third wave? The question cut to the core of Japan's preemptive attack on Pearl Harbor. The aim of the attack was to destroy the American capacity to make war, but a third strike was needed to do this. The task force commander, Vice Admiral Nagumo, held a different view. The United States already had enjoyed a reprieve that day: its carriers were not present and escaped destruction. He now had to worry about a retaliatory strike from the air, not from Pearl Harbor, but from the missing carriers that might be in the vicinity. He decided to stop the attack and withdraw, believing that Japan's preemptive strike had accomplished enough. Here lay the seeds of the Pearl Harbor attack as a Japanese setback, if an American disaster as well. But for Japan, these signs were present before the first bomb fell at Pearl Harbor. Nagumo always had opposed the attack, believing it risked too much. By pulling back prematurely before inflicting maximum damage on US war installations, he reflected the larger Japanese trepidation about fighting a war against the United States. A preemptive strike was supposed to allay these misgivings. That these doubts surfaced anyway, even before the completion of the attack, underscored the limits of the utility of the Japanese preemptive strike at Pearl Harbor and that country's bleak future in a war against the United States, no matter the results on December 7, 1941.

Japan's decision to target Pearl Harbor grew out of its campaign on the Asian mainland for control of Manchuria that it formally initiated in 1931. Six years later, Japanese military forces advanced into China proper and started a war with that nation, even if hostilities were officially known in Japan by the euphemism of the China "incident." The Japanese offensive quickly led to an early atrocity in an era of violence that would be known for many atrocities when Japanese soldiers committed acts of barbarity against Chinese citizenry collectively known as the Rape of Nanking. Despite sharing this disgraceful characteristic with its soon-to-be Axis counterpart Germany, and despite a formal alliance with the Nazi state, the Sino-Japanese conflict became a part of World War II only after Japan attacked Pearl Harbor. The Japanese offensive that then unfurled throughout the Pacific rapidly left Imperial Japan in control of an expansive area. But the reversal of the fortunes of war in this theater of operations would be stunning indeed. Japan's new Greater East Asia Co-Prosperity Sphere came under rapid American counter-attack first at Midway Island in June 1942, and then in the Solomon Islands at Guadalcanal in August 1942. By early 1943, the Americans had secured the initiative and Japan faced a two-pronged US offensive, one in the south Pacific under the command of Army General Douglas MacArthur, the other in the center of the Pacific under Admiral Chester Nimitz. The ensuing American successes at the expense of the Japanese army and its accompanying air and naval forces propelled the US military across the Pacific and into position to threaten the Japanese home islands by mid-1945. But the American advance faced a growing Japanese resistance that resulted in one of the last key developments of the Pacific war, the United States using the atomic bomb against two Japanese cities in August 1945. If World War II had begun with all eyes fixed firmly on Europe, it ended with that attention riveted on the war against Japan in the Pacific.

Much as is the case with Germany, Japan's role in World War II is that of a villain, its "sneak" attack at Pearl Harbor an emblem of its aggression. To call this attack by Japan an act of preemption, and by extension to call its war in the Pacific a preemptive struggle, is to offer a moral reprieve to a much vilified state, again as is the case with Nazi Germany. Since there is much validity in the charge that both of these nations committed heinous crimes while waging war, the view of preemption as giving Japan a valid reason to start World War II in the Pacific requires careful consideration. It is not a task that has been addressed satisfactorily in the literature. H.P. Willmott, in his analysis of World War II, *The Great Crusade*, labels the

Japanese air strike at Pearl Harbor a preemptive attack, but says little else to define or explain what he means.* This chapter looks to offer an explanation for Japan's "preemptive" war in the Pacific. This account also tries to echo the early call in the historiography to bring balance to the examination of US–Japanese relations in the decade prior to war in 1941, best exemplified in the published proceedings of the Lake Kawaguchi conference in 1969, *Pearl Harbor as History*. These scholars believed that "American–Japanese relations were a two-way street that had constantly to be looked at from both ends."** The end emphasized here is the Japanese point of view.

The Case for Preemption

In several important ways, the Japanese preemptive attack in the Pacific resembled Hitler's rationale for preemption in Europe. For the sake of national survival, the Japanese nation had to expand its territory into neighboring Asian countries to allow Japan to accumulate the raw materials it needed to sustain its industrial development. Coal and iron could be attained from Manchuria, oil and rubber from Southeast Asia. These goals in different locations reflected a desire to secure an inner perimeter consisting of Korea, Manchuria, and Taiwan. The outer perimeter would include the French colony of Indochina, the British colony in Malaya, and the Netherlands colony in the Dutch East Indies. Without the resources culled from all its military objectives, Japan would not be able to sustain itself as a great power. Japan would cease to develop as a nation, and its people would suffer. For this reason, Japanese expansion was a necessity.

Japanese leaders teamed this economic imperative with a cultural one, just as did Germany. Japan's objective was the expulsion of colonialism in Asia and the end of white oppression resulting in the establishment of a "New Order." This Greater East Asia Co-Prosperity Sphere required the military defeat of the colonial powers present in Asia since France, Britain, and the Netherlands would never capitulate to Japanese demands. With the expansion of Japanese power and establishment of a sphere of influence, the best people of Asia would finally drive out the white presence and all of Asia would benefit.

There were, of course, extraordinary differences between Japan's aims and those of Germany. The liberation that Japan offered other Asian nations

---

* H.P. Willmott, *The Great Crusade* (New York: The Free Press, 1989), 165.

** Dorothy Borg and Shumpei Okamoto, eds., *Pearl Harbor as History: Japanese–American Relations, 1931–1941* (New York: Columbia University Press, 1973), xiv.

stood in contrast to Hitler's vision of spreading German culture at the expense of the peoples he conquered. Japan offered a more inclusive expansion, a good development for the peoples of Asia suffering at the hands of western imperialism. The members of the new order in Asia would graciously support Japan with the resources it needed because of that nation's gift of freedom. Japan's vision included the complete rejuvenation of Asia so that the entire region could aspire to enjoy an equal footing in the international system, its subservient position due to colonialism having come to an end. Thanks to Japan, Asia would leave behind its backwardness and poverty and assume a western disposition without incurring the abuses previously inherent in the relationship between east and west.

Perhaps most importantly as far as differences were concerned, few of the members of the Japanese elite plotted a course of world domination, as did many of their Nazis counterparts. From Japan's point of view, the Greater East Asia Co-Prosperity Sphere was an effort to establish a defensive perimeter. Japan already had control of Korea, Manchuria, Taiwan, and part of the Sakhalin Islands. No nation had stopped her yet. Why not continue to expand and secure a larger sphere of influence, much as other great powers had done, including the United States so dominant in the Western Hemisphere? Surely the Americans would understand the need for this perimeter. As Japan considered possible enemies opposed to its expansionist aims, it hoped the United States would not have to be added to the list since Japan's "good-neighborly union" mirrored a similar push by the United States in Latin America with President Franklin D. Roosevelt's "Good Neighbor policy."* The United States could not but be supportive of such a Japanese plan.

No matter its close emulation of the West and the limited aims Japanese expansion entailed, Japanese leaders anticipated that the western powers would fight to prevent Japan's ambitions from being fully realized. They would not respect Japan's right to a sphere of influence in the Far East. The inconsistency in American thinking in particular on this point—enjoying a sphere of influence while denying this to Japan—resonated in Japanese reasoning. Japanese officials again offered comparisons between the two nations. Much as was the case of American expansion in the preceding century, Japanese objectives in Asia were an outgrowth of a natural expansion of Japanese power in Asia. Certainly there had been costs to this growth, but such had been the case for the nations the United States impacted in its development. Foreign Minister Matsuoka put it this way: "Ask the American Indian or the Mexican how excruciatingly trying the

---

* Robert J.C. Butow, *Tojo and the Coming of War* (Princeton, NJ: Princeton University Press, 1961), 120.

young United States used to be once upon a time."* In a similar vein, Japan was only "trying" its neighbors at present. The comparisons accomplished little. Few Japanese believed that flattering the United States won them any favor with that nation. In American eyes, the Japanese were inferior. Close adoption of western culture by Japan meant little to them. Far from earning their respect, Japan would incur the wrath of the country it most hoped to emulate. To make its defensive perimeter a reality, Japan had to face war with the United States.

A fear of the potential military might of the United States did not stop the push for war. The reason was simple. Japan faced destruction either way. To act might invite a war that Japan could not win. But not to act meant the demise of Japanese fortunes as an empire anyway since it would not be able to acquire the resources needed to sustain itself. Given this belief, war was an attractive option simply because of the honor that lay in making this fight, or at least from not shirking from it. In this thinking lay the seed for a preemptive, military strike that would mean a great Japanese triumph at the commencement of war.

Additionally, the Japanese did not delude themselves into believing that they would win a war against the United States. America was too formidable a foe for Japan to realistically believe it could defeat its rival in the Pacific. This pessimism extended far beyond that of the chief of the navy, Admiral Yamamoto, who voiced strong reservations over going to war against the United States even while planning the attack at Pearl Harbor. Others concurred. Facing this dissent, the government forced from office Naval Minister Oikawa, in April 1941, or just as the country geared up to go to war against the United States, because he had doubts about the possibility of a successful war with America. The naval command was reconstituted by 1941 to include those most supportive of an advance in the Pacific. No matter this purge, the question persisted. How could Japan triumph against such military might? Granted this power was latent and embedded in a powerful isolationism. But the potential for great military power was within the grasp of the United States should it seek to move in this direction.

There were signs that American leaders, no matter the opposition of the majority of their population, intended to do just this. At the Washington conference in 1922 and the London conference in 1930, Japan and the western powers brokered a series of naval arms agreements. These treaties reflected the interests of all parties in avoiding an expensive arms race. But the last treaty now suffered eclipse at the hands of American rearmament plans initiated in 1934. If allowed to come to completion, America's Vinson

---

* Butow, *Tojo and the Coming of War*, 107.

Bill appropriated enough funds for a two-ocean navy. In 1940 alone, the number and type of ships on order were impressive: nine battleships, eleven aircraft carriers, forty-two cruisers, and 181 destroyers. Japan could not match this build-up in the long term, scheduled to be completed by 1948. It could match the number of American ships, however, in the short term. Parity in numbers would be achieved by late 1941 thanks to the Third and Fourth Replenishment Programs initiated by Japan after it abrogated the London naval agreements. Taking advantage of such preparedness was one benefit to striking sooner than later. Additionally, Japanese ships could claim a qualitative advantage as well. The super-battleship, the *Yamato* class, could out-range any American ship. In this weapon lay a distinct Japanese advantage in a naval war with the United States. Yet, if given enough time, due to the rapidly changing nature of war at sea, such qualitative superiority might be lost in the near future. Japan's naval leaders convinced themselves that they could look forward to victory if they went to war against the United States now and if, as Admiral Kondo, vice chief of the Navy general staff, said, "we fight an early, decisive battle."* In the balance of armed forces came the rationale for preemption.

In sum, Japan could not count on a peaceful United States content to do nothing should Japan act to protect its interests in Asia. Harmful American intentions already could be seen, the American support of China the most egregious from Japan's point of view. True, the American efforts on behalf of China had been largely rhetorical to this point. When Japan acted to bring Manchuria under its control starting in September 1931, American opposition amounted to a strenuous denunciation of this "aggression." Japan failed to understand this opposition given the internal political chaos afflicting China. The war between the Nationalist leader Chiang Kai-shek and the Communist leader Mao Zedong so destabilized China that it threatened Japanese interests in Manchuria. The volatile situation there meant the possible end of Japan's coveted trading position, leaving Japan no choice but to act to restore stability. It was a step America had taken in Latin America on many occasions, most flagrantly with the Roosevelt Corollary, President Theodore Roosevelt's addition to the Monroe Doctrine in 1904 that ensured the United States the right to intervene in the affairs of Latin American countries to ensure stability.

Japan took careful note of American protests and moved forward with its plans in China. When forced to make further inroads on the mainland to try and end what was turning into a debilitating conflict, an open war erupted between China and Japan in July 1937 just outside of Beijing. Japan

---

* Stephen E. Pelz, *Race to Pearl Harbor: The Failure of the Second London Naval Conference and the Onset of World War II* (Cambridge, MA: Harvard University Press, 1974), 218.

again faced vocal American opposition, President Roosevelt, in a speech he gave that October, calling on the international community to "quarantine" aggressors to prevent war from spreading. Tensions threatened to escalate into more than an exchange of words when the Japanese sunk the American gunboat *Panay* in December 1937. This US vessel was escorting tankers up the Yangtze River when Japanese planes struck and killed three American sailors. No matter the belligerence of the Japanese attack, the Americans simply accepted a hurried Japanese apology and indemnity. The tame American response to the Japanese admission of guilt made it clear that neither country had an interest in fighting a war against one another, at least at this time. It would be other factors that pushed Japan to seek this war, all the while claiming the hostilities met the requirements of preemption.

US rhetoric may have been just that but what mattered more was the very real financial aid America offered Chiang in 1938. In December of that year, the Roosevelt administration extended a US$25 million credit to Chiang. Japan reasoned more would follow. Clearly American policy hoped to sustain Chiang to tie down Japanese forces on the Asian mainland and in this way curb Japanese aspirations in Southeast Asia and the Pacific. If this was the American strategy, it was working. Japan's war in China already had lasted far too long and the United States bore much of the blame. The Americans, by stubbornly defending their "open door" policy of not allowing one power to dictate trade relations with China, propped up Chiang and seriously impeded Japanese plans to enjoy the fruits of its Asian empire. Originally, the Japanese offensive to compel Chiang to negotiate or to force him from power was to be undertaken by three Japanese divisions, take three months, and cost 100 million yen. A year after attacking Shanghai in 1937, Chiang was still fighting and the Japanese army requested twenty divisions costing 2.5 billion yen with no end to the fighting in sight. The economic strain that the China "incident" placed on Japan was great. Moving south would solve this problem. This advance meant cutting off China from the external support coming from Britain over the Burma Road and from the railway in northern Indochina. In this way, Japan could end the war in China by forcing the collapse of Chiang's government, or by forcing it to make a settlement favorable to Japan once it was isolated from outside assistance.

To move south raised international concerns, however. Japanese leaders believed that the United States was tied to Britain and that any threat to Britain would cause the Americans to enter the war on the side of Britain. To make war on Britain was to make war on America. Japanese war leaders calculated all options based on this assumption. This conclusion amplified the problem of the American territory of the Philippines. A Japanese

offensive south could not bypass these islands for fear of American intervention in a war involving Japan and the western European nations. It
provided a base for American naval power that, once present in the area,
could disrupt if not prevent Japan from achieving its objectives. President
Roosevelt's shift of the American Pacific fleet from San Diego, California,
to Pearl Harbor in Hawaii in April 1940, appeared to confirm this American
intention. Once Japan headed south, the American fleet would sail from
Hawaiian waters to the Philippines and interdict the Japanese attack. One
way or the other, should Japan move south, this step meant war with the
United States.

The collective strength of these western nations led to additional
considerations. The ABCD powers, the Americans, British, Chinese, and
the Dutch, obviously were working in collusion with one another to deny
Japan the resources it hoped to attain in the south in a peaceful manner.
The British and Americans objected to Japanese efforts to settle a border
dispute between Thailand and Indochina, suspecting that Japan would ask
for permanent bases in the region as compensation for brokering a peace.
Such opposition in Southeast Asia helped Chiang continue the fight since
supplies from both powers could reach him from this location. Britain's
temporary closure of the Burma Road for three months starting in July 1940
was not enough in Japanese eyes. US actions were more alarming. That
same month, July 1940, in response to Japan pressuring French authorities
to make concessions in northern Indochina, the Americans initiated a trade
embargo against Japan of iron and steel and it limited exports of scrap-
metal and petroleum products as well. On top of this, the Dutch refused
to listen to reason regarding Japanese efforts to negotiate rights for more
oil in the Dutch East Indies, the colony obviously responding to pressure
applied by Britain and the United States. The obstreperous actions of the
ABCD powers underscored that diplomacy would not be able to secure the
economic materials Japan needed. The Japanese concluded that they faced
a threat on this front from multiple powers. The rationale of engagement
appeared clear. Japan had a right to a sphere of influence to secure the
resources it needed to flourish as an empire. To safeguard itself from
isolation leading to collapse meant a preemptive war against all those
standing in its way.

The course of World War II in Europe gave Japan an opportunity to
strike south. With each Nazi victory, the ability of the western powers to
sustain themselves in Asia came rapidly in question. France felt the first
blow. In September 1940, in the wake of French collapse in Europe, Japan
occupied the northern portion of Indochina, closing the railway to China
that Japan estimated delivered just over 40 percent of all supplies still
reaching Chiang. The French acquiesced to Japanese pressure; given their

weakened state, they had little choice. But the other European colonies remained defiant. The Netherlands managed to remain in possession of the oil-rich Dutch East Indies. While Britain fought off a potential German invasion, it kept its Asian empire intact. Yet, given German occupation of the Netherlands and the mortal threat from Germany now facing Britain, these nations appeared so exposed to complete defeat that the time for Japan to act was ripe. Britain in particular had no fleet to stop Japan. German intelligence had confirmed this view by passing onto the Japanese naval command captured minutes of a British war cabinet meeting of early August 1940, calling attention to British naval weakness in the Pacific since the Royal Navy was needed to protect the home islands from a German invasion. This was the proceeds from the newly created Axis alliance between the two powers. The usefulness of this relationship exceeded a bit of timely intelligence. Thanks to German successes, Japan could use its military power to expand south and it could look forward with confidence to defeating the now weakened European powers there.

The hopeful picture in the south was dampened by one other factor. In the north lay a great enemy of Japan, Russia. The formidable nature of this long-time foe had been clearly demonstrated in a series of military clashes between Japanese and Soviet forces, first along the Korean and Soviet border in 1938, and then along the Mongolian border with the Japanese-sponsored state of Manchukuo in 1939. In each case the Japanese faced sharp defeat. This experience meant that Japanese army planners hungered for revenge but also feared the consequences of a renewed war with the USSR. The latter consideration won out and by 1940, the army and navy were in agreement that an advance south was the best course of action to take. The army looked forward to ending the fighting in China by completely isolating Chiang's regime and forcing its collapse; the navy hoped to secure the oil it needed to fuel its ships. Given army and navy concord on the issue, Matsuoka completed a non-aggression pact with the USSR in April 1941. This diplomatic stroke enabled Japan to attack south since it no longer needed to concern itself with a Russian attack along its northern border.

Matsuoka's success freed Japan from its strategic problem of encirclement: to head north invited attack from Britain, France, and the United States; to head south invited attack from the Soviet Union. This arrangement lasted but a few months, however. When Germany attacked the USSR in June 1941, Japan had to revisit the question. To join with its Axis partner in an attack on Russia appeared attractive. Once this northern threat was eliminated, Japan could then enjoy not just security in the north, but resources that would facilitate a push south. The army naturally relished this chance to avenge its humiliating defeats along the Korean and

Mongolian borders, but it had to acknowledge a number of practical obstacles. Japanese forces on the mainland simply were not strong enough to challenge the USSR militarily. Given its setbacks in 1938 and 1939, the army desired a tremendous increase in strength prior to confronting the Russians in battle, and this could not be accomplished prior to the time when changing weather conditions made such an attack impractical. As usual, the navy pushed in the opposite direction, coveting the oil that came with a drive south. With the USSR in a mortal struggle with the Nazi regime, it could hardly threaten Japan. Now was the time to strike south, gain the resources in this region, and then return to fight in the north.

Japan decided to let the fighting in Russia determine its policy. Should the Russians clearly be facing collapse at the hands of Germany, then Japan would attack north and complete the destruction of this state. Should the USSR manage to survive the German onslaught, then Japan would pursue the southern course of action. For another three months, the Japanese observed the fighting in Russia closely, until deciding that Russia would survive and that Japan's best course of action was to head south.

As arguments over how best to proceed continued on the Japanese side, America soon struck a blow that Japan could not tolerate and one that settled the issue of where to advance once and for all. The absolute line had been reached and crossed in the summer of 1941 when, in response to the Japanese occupation of southern Indochina, the Americans froze Japanese assets in the United States in July, and then embargoed oil in August 1941. Previously the US government had restricted the sale of steel products and scrap iron to Japan in response to the Japanese advance into northern Indochina. The increasing American embargo that now included oil under-scored Japan's vulnerability to this type of economic threat and emphasized Japan's need to move south to secure the resources that the empire depended upon. The American action merely confirmed Japanese think-ing: the empire was too vulnerable to economic disruption. A war was needed to remove this threat hanging over its head. Once the threat was realized and the embargo in place, the choice to act was settled. A senior naval officer, Admiral Nagano Osami, put it this way—the American embargo meant that Japan faced a chain of encirclement so that "there is no choice left but to fight."* The Greater East Asian Co-Prosperity Sphere would be extended far into the Pacific in an effort to deter American interference in Japan's war plans.

The navy now contemplated how best to fight the United States. The aim evolved into first deterring the United States from fighting at all. But

---

* Pelz, *Race to Pearl Harbor*, 223.

how to achieve this purpose particularly since Japan did not expect to defeat the United States, only to discourage it from seeking to re-conquer the territory Japan did take? Somehow the Americans must be dealt such a blow that two things would occur. First, its fleet could not impede Japan's liberation of the Asian countries that would compose its Greater East Asia Co-Prosperity Sphere. Second, from behind this defensive perimeter, Japan could make any American counterattack so expensive in lives that the United States would give up the effort. Not only would the newly secured raw materials fuel Japan's economy and put it nearly on par with American industrial strength, but Japanese leaders believed that the American will to fight could be sorely tested with a first, great defeat. At the outset of war, Japanese forces must inflict such losses as to discourage any American challenge, and do so at minimal cost to Japan. After such a success, Americans might not even offer a challenge to Japanese actions in the Pacific. A preemptive strike that made such a statement might stop the war even before it began.

Negotiations with the United States gave Japan no reason to reconsider these conclusions. Discussions in May 1941 went nowhere because the United States remained inflexible. Japan would have to offer guarantees that it would not attack the United States should America become involved in a war in the Atlantic against Germany. Yet American assistance to Britain was not banned, an obvious problem should Britain become an enemy of Japan, which was likely. Trade issues became as lopsided. The Americans offered no promises of resuming their economic agreements with Japan, all the while demanding concessions in China in the form of a renewed Japanese declaration in favor of nondiscriminatory trade practices. This was bad enough for Japan but the key issue of the war in China was left to future discussions. When these came in September, the issue was still not resolved despite substantial Japanese concessions. Japan offered to withdraw most of its troops from China in two years, staying in only three key regions for twenty-five years. Japan also agreed to the non-discriminatory trade demand in regards to resources in China. Last came the question of Manchuria. Japan's hope that negotiation could be premised on its independent status contrasted sharply with the American insistence that Chiang settle this issue with Japan, implying that Manchuria was a part of China and would have to be so again. Clearly negotiations merely confirmed the American desire to force Japan out of China and to keep Japan from achieving its co-prosperity sphere. The American resistance to any Japanese sphere of influence was paramount in determining the Japanese decision for war. Without its empire, Japan faced the imminent threat of economic collapse. It had to act in preemptive fashion to forestall this calamity.

After much debate, Japan made three monumental decisions. First, that war was inevitable. Second, that war should come first in the south against the western powers including the United States; after this success, war could be waged in the north. Third, to have any hope in being successful versus the United States, Japan must deal the Americans a crippling blow at the onset of war. This thinking led Japan's military planners to target the US fleet at Pearl Harbor, Hawaii.

The Attack

Vice Admiral Nagumo felt deeply the responsibility of command. He had at his disposal all six fleet aircraft carriers equipped with over 350 planes. It was the cream of the Japanese air arm. Its loss would be a catastrophic blow to Japanese naval power and to the Japanese war hopes. Preemption ran the risk of losing the war as much as winning it at the very outset of hostilities.

Japanese planners minimized the risk as best they could when striking Pearl Harbor. Ships sailed from different ports at different times. Radio silence was in effect. The strike force followed a route to the target notorious for bad weather. Thanks to a gale, Nagumo managed to bring his command to within 275 miles of Hawaii undetected by American aircraft or ships. Most importantly, the Japanese high command gave the timing of a declaration of war special consideration. An announcement of the cessation of diplomatic ties was to precede the Japanese air strike by half an hour. This was not much notice but it would help ensure the safety of the task force. By the early morning of December 7, 1941, all appeared in order, the Japanese preemptive strike at Pearl Harbor needing only daylight to proceed.

Nagumo ordered two strikes against the island. The first of 214 planes arrived over Pearl Harbor at 7:55 am on Sunday. Total surprise meant an unopposed attack and in a short period of time Japanese aircraft hit a number of American vessels, leaving them burning and either sunk or sinking. Japanese pilots also attacked the airfield on Ford Island and very quickly neutralized American airpower. The second wave of attack aircraft totaling 170 planes arrived at 9:15 am. It faced a more robust defense from anti-aircraft fire but continued to wreak havoc in the port, completing the destruction of the American fleet. In total, the attack lasted two hours. At the end of this time, the Japanese had sunk or damaged eighteen American ships, including all of the battleships, had destroyed hundreds of aircraft, and had killed over 2,400 Americans while wounding almost 1,200. The destruction was as complete as was the element of surprise.

The success of the military component of the attack quickly unraveled, however. Japanese pilots reported the absence of the American aircraft carriers. Nagumo now had good reason to worry, fearing discovery and an American strike from the air that could greatly harm his task force. He headed home at 1:35 pm, breaking off the attack prematurely. The termination of air strikes left the installations at the base intact, including the oil storage facilities and the dry docks, so Pearl Harbor still remained operational, even if the ships at the base had been obliterated. The importance of this reprieve would tell quickly in the months that followed, since many American ships sunk or damaged on December 7 would be repaired and rejoin the fight, and since Pearl Harbor would be a key base sustaining US military operations in the very near future.

Any military success garnished from preemption quickly encountered diplomatic effacement even before the attack was completed. Japanese diplomats in Washington DC fumbled the transcription of the memorandum terminating negotiations, and failed to deliver it on time to the US State Department. Consequently, the attack preceded the initiation of hostilities by twenty-five minutes. The American Secretary of State Cordell Hull responded tersely to the Japanese note, saying, "In all my fifty years of public service I have never seen a document that was more crowded with infamous falsehoods and distortions—infamous falsehoods and distortions on a scale so huge that I never imagined until today that any Government on this planet was capable of uttering them."* He captured the American mood that would now dictate this struggle. The Japanese "sneak attack" at Pearl Harbor galvanized American resistance as no other act could have done. Horrified by the extent of the damage, offended by the diplomatic treachery facilitating the strike, Americans looked to war eagerly as a matter of revenge. Japan may have won a great opening battle, but the chances of intimidating the United States to the point that it would then sit out the ensuing conflict evaporated in the process. Clearly, the Japanese preemptive strike at Pearl Harbor so enraged Americans that US forces would test the Japanese defensive zone willingly and as soon as possible.

Success

No matter the outrage on the American side after the Pearl Harbor attack, the initiative still lay with Japan. The Japanese strike at Pearl Harbor indeed had so staggered the United States that it could not stop Japan's

---

* Akira Iriye, *Pearl Harbor and the Coming of the Pacific War: A Brief History with Documents and Essays* (Boston, MA: Beford/St. Martin's, 1999), 105.

assaults elsewhere in the Pacific. These were numerous and effective. The American island possessions of Wake and Guam fell to Japanese assault forces in the days after Pearl Harbor. The Philippine Islands came under Japanese air attack and then invasion. When Japan compelled the last American defenders there to surrender in May 1942, the American position in Asia faced retrenchment on a grand scale. The American defeats, however, paled in comparison to British disasters. The British garrison at Hong Kong, 12,000 Commonwealth troops, surrendered to Japanese forces on Christmas Day. The British defense of Singapore collapsed several weeks later on February 15, 1942, and the loss in prisoners was great: over 130,000. Once Japan had chased British forces from Burma, and overwhelmed Dutch resistance on Java, the colonial apparatus of the western powers in Asia came to a sudden end. In this way, Japan dealt a shock to the region that heralded the arrival of the new order of the Greater East Asia Co-Prosperity Sphere.

The spectacular Japanese course of expansion rivaled that of Germany and perhaps exceeded it given that Germany had needed a considerably longer period of time to occupy the regions of Europe it coveted. Nor were German successes complete, as continued British and Russian resistance made clear. The Japanese could claim the opposite. The defensive perimeter was a reality, and the Japanese could now await the expected American counterattack.

The only thing that compared to Japan's military success in the opening stages of the Pacific War was the rapidity with which the United States did counterattack. From a battered US military came the American challenge to Japanese supremacy in Asia. First, Japan's carrier arm suffered disaster at the battle of Midway Island in June 1942. A combination of shrewd American planning and luck meant American planes sunk four Japanese aircraft carriers in two days and turned away the Japanese invasion force headed to that atoll. At the end of the summer, American marines landed on Guadalcanal to blunt Japanese expansion in the Solomon Islands in the South Pacific. After a six-month battle, the Japanese gave up the contest there but not before its naval forces had been bloodied and its carrier arm further weakened.

The American counteroffensive had not been long in coming and when it did come, it undermined Japanese expectations of creating a defensive zone that would be too formidable to assault. The Japanese could blame themselves for this development. The attacks in the Solomon Islands leading to the disastrous Guadalcanal campaign grew out of ambitious aims to threaten Australia. Expansion for this dubious end meant that Japan's military leaders compromised the defensive perimeter before it was even tested. Completely vanquishing American power from the Pacific region as was the larger implication of an advance toward Australia had never been the Japanese purpose; defending the perimeter had been the goal. The battle at Midway at least attempted to meet this parameter since that island was needed to complete the defensive perimeter in that part of the Pacific. Instead, the Japanese thrust in the South Pacific represented offensive-minded objectives that exceeded Japanese capabilities and transgressed on the purpose of war in the south. It mattered little that Japanese planners recognized this error and labeled this overconfidence "victory disease." By late 1942, it was too late. What mattered most was that the Japanese successes in the aftermath of Pearl Harbor had led them to over-extend themselves, thereby compromising their limited forces that made it very difficult to look forward to successfully defending their newfound gains. Success in the aftermath of Pearl Harbor was short-lived indeed.

The rapid American curtailment of Japanese ambitions in the Pacific that shattered Japanese expectations of how the war would proceed did not mean the conflict would be short, however. Japan always had looked askance at victory in favor of stalemate. Its goal was to prolong the conflict and so bloody American forces that that nation would give up the fight. At a minimum in this struggle, Japan hoped to hold onto its inner perimeter of Korea, Manchuria, Taiwan, and its dominant position in China. At a maximum, it hoped to defend an outer perimeter stretching from Southeast Asia to the Aleutian Islands. As stated, its dissipation of strength in the summer and fall of 1942 greatly dimmed the chances of a successful defense in either respect. Nevertheless, the Americans anticipated a bloody struggle along the long road back to the Japanese home islands. That both sides found their expectations realized did mean a long war. The Japanese mounted a stubborn defense no matter where the Americans struck, and the Americans adopted a flexible strategy that accelerated their advance. The "island-hopping" campaign American forces waged against selected targets allowed the United States to bypass more heavily defended islands. Even so, by early 1945, as the Americans drew closer to the Japanese home islands and attacked Iwo Jima and Okinawa, the fighting had assumed such ferocious proportions that after this campaign the Americans could consider the use of the atomic bomb a life-saving proposition. When this weapon helped bring the war in the Pacific officially to a close in September 1945, the reckoning of preemption achieved clarity. What the Japanese accomplished in the first six months of war in the Pacific thanks to its preemptive strike at Pearl Harbor was one of the few times in military history that the attacking power set objectives that it believed would make it successful, actually attained these objectives, but still suffered catastrophic defeat.

Conclusion

Japan dreamed of establishing a new morality by expelling a hated occupying power and ending the colonial legacy of Western Europe in Asia. That Japan could do this was of monumental significance. From its point of view, an Asian power, a great people, would now stand up to European rule. Japan would benefit from this change but so too would all of Asia. The problems arose from the expected resistance. Obviously, the western nations would never allow their colonies to fall without a fight. But Japan insisted on "liberating" them as a necessity for Japanese national survival since the trade relationships sought in the south meant sustaining Japanese industrial production and growth at home. Without the raw materials of iron ore, steel, oil, and rubber, the Japanese nation faced great peril. Japan had no choice but to challenge western domination of the Asian region. Japanese leaders preferred diplomacy and negotiation. When these efforts failed, the clear demise of Japanese fortunes lay at hand. Therefore, war was inevitable. Not to fight invited disaster, and while fighting might invite disaster as well, Japan had to meet this struggle as a matter of honor. It had to wage preemptive war to secure Japan's future.

The purpose of the war was preemptive and so too was the act of preemption that would initiate hostilities. To advance south meant a confrontation with a great adversary, the United States. Aware of the tremendous power this nation could wield, Japan only reluctantly moved in the direction of war with the United States and did so only after enduring numerous provocations. The anti-war sentiment in America, so prominent in its isolationist stance, was undermined by US governmental leadership when it put that nation on a war footing with the rebuilding program of its naval assets. This rearmament meant the end of the Washington Treaty and the London Conference negotiations, both designed to deter an arms race. Japan had to match the US build-up and since the long-term prospects of doing so obviously pointed to futility—Japan could not match US military production—a short-term effort promised Japan military parity with the United States, and therefore pushed the Japanese government toward a consensus of striking sooner than later while the numbers were in Japan's reach.

Nor did Japan have to look very far to find other examples of American hostility. The war Japan waged against China mattered most in this respect since American moral support and financial aid bolstered Chinese resistance. Chiang's ability to continue fighting presented great problems for Japan. The ongoing war sapped Japanese military strength and financial resources. The entire purpose of fighting in China, which was to fuel Japanese industry, was compromised by this debilitating war. Ending outside aid to the Chinese regime clearly became a matter of great importance to Japanese leaders for this reason. Isolating Chiang meant the end of his regime and the end of the war in China. Japan made this aim a great priority after 1937, and it understood that such a goal meant more confrontations with the western powers. The British and French refused to stop allowing aid to reach Chiang from their colonies of Burma and Indochina. Japanese threats managed only to force the British to agree to the temporary closure of the Burma Road and little else. When Japan went further than this and occupied Indochina, the United States responded with increasing hostility, implementing an economic embargo that threatened Japan's entire empire. It was again another lesson in American interference resulting in the validation of Japanese logic: their economic lifeline was at stake, and only military force could secure it. A showdown with the United States in particular was inevitable, and Japanese military leadership gave serious consideration how best to engage the United States in a war. Naval officers now contemplated a preemptive strike designed to neutralize American military power at sea.

Identifying the United States as the primary target grew out of compelling circumstances. The resources coveted by Japan lay in the European colonies of French Indochina, British Malaya, and the Netherlands' Dutch East Indies. Japan assumed an attack on these colonies would provoke a military clash with the United States as well because the Americans would come to the aid of these countries. Altogether these nations curbed Japanese needs at every point in the south. The logic of striking south to break the hold of the western powers assumed even more urgency in the wake of the eruption of the fighting in Europe in 1939. Once Nazi Germany overran the Netherlands, France, and threatened Britain with invasion, the precarious state of the Asian colonies of these nations invited a Japanese attack. But to take this step meant Japan had to consider the response of the United States. Given the support of China by this nation, and its sympathies that lay with Britain and France in containing Japanese power, a Japanese advance south meant hostilities with this nation as well. Since an advance must be undertaken in order for Japan to survive, the war plans had to include a clash with the United States. Preemptive war to protect the future of Japan now meant a preemptive strike against the United States to make the success of such a war possible.

The move south left one other consideration open-ended. What was Japan to do with the USSR? This northern front already had caused much disarray in Japanese planning. Soviet military success at the expense of Japan in 1938 and 1939 clearly established the USSR as a dangerous foe to reckon with. To move south with this front unsettled invited military disaster. The Russian problem received careful review and consideration from Japanese war planners, and the preferred solution shifted depending on circumstance largely of Germany's creation. This ally of Japan acted unpredictably, so much so that it sided with Russia in 1939, but attacked that country in 1941. This latter action settled Japanese thinking to a great extent. With the USSR in a death struggle with Germany, the northern front was no longer an issue. Once Japan secured a neutrality pact with the USSR, the path to the south was open.

Still, it took one more act of belligerence on the part of the United States to make the war in the south a reality. When the United States cut off its delivery of oil to Japan after the Japanese occupied southern Indochina, the threat the Americans presented to Japan was clear. The American embargo underscored not only Japan's economic vulnerability, but also the threat it faced from the ABCD powers. On their own, the US economic restrictions were debilitating enough, particularly in the area of oil. But American and British efforts went further than this. They pressured foreign tankers to stop doing business with Japan and then banned the export of steel drums used to carry the oil. These actions pulled other nations along in the slowly increasing embargo of oil to Japan, including the Netherlands. The Japanese, of course, in the face of this economic collusion, openly talked about the need to secure their interests in the near future by ending this economic dependence.

Curing this economic weakness was the main rationale behind the Greater East Asian Co-prosperity Sphere. American actions merely confirmed Japanese reasoning. If this was a service, the gratitude was short-lived given the prospect of war with the United States was something the military leadership of Japan understood to be a daunting, almost foolish endeavor. But to shrink from this challenge was not an option, given the need for preemptive war to safeguard the future of Japan. The Imperial Navy had to cripple American military strength—even if only temporarily —and this task now assumed paramount importance. Not to act meant Japan faced encirclement and its empire extinction. The necessity to act took the Japanese navy to the Hawaiian waters near Pearl Harbor. Preemption would be both the blow that initiated war in the Pacific and the purpose of that war.

In too many ways, Japanese self-assurance of acting defensively and therefore acting morally given the preemptive nature of its war in the south suffered from severe inconsistencies. A co-prosperity sphere designed for the betterment of all of Asia had baser motives that served primarily Japanese interests. Foremost in this regard was the value Japan placed on the economic resources it needed to sustain its national development. Having watched the eclipse of German power after World War I for this very reason, a lack of economic resources, the Japanese hoped to ensure this problem would not happen to them. That the Japanese implemented policies that subjugated the inhabitants of the regions they occupied as well as harnessed the resources they demanded, underscored the exploitative purpose Japanese ascendancy brought to those caught in the expansion of Japanese power. The belief that Japan was a more inclusive liberator than was Germany was hollow rhetoric. Japanese expansion in the name of economic gain was a hegemonic end as much as a benevolent one of liberating beleaguered peoples from white oppression for the betterment of all of Asia. The rationale may have been preemptive but the morality was in question, given the singular purpose of ensuring Japanese domination of the Pacific.

Japanese rearmament revealed the martial overtones to their drive to hegemony. They abrogated the naval treaties already in place that were designed to forestall an arms race. Any subsequent American rearmament program could be seen as merely a necessary step to meet a Japanese build-up. That Japan had made the decision to abrogate such treaties by 1934 underscored this point since the Americans found themselves too burdened by economic woes stemming from the Depression to make rearmament a priority. Some long-range thinking on the part of the Roosevelt administration certainly moved that country in this direction, but it did so only after meeting much congressional opposition that promised rearmament in starts and stops. Japan could look forward to enjoying an advantage in naval assets to make war feasible with the United States in the years after 1934. That this superiority would eventually dissipate meant little since the preemptive rationale lacked substance given that Japan did much to foster the imminent threat to its interests by provoking an American arms build-up.

Japanese resentment against American interference reached absurd levels when it came to the issue of China. The moral support and very limited financial assistance the United States extended to China needed to be set alongside American support of Japan. The United States continued to send war materials to Japan while calling for the Japanese to end their aggression against China. In a way, US economic aid to Japan made Japanese aggression in China possible. For this reason, the American China policy was even-handed and too limited in influence to make much of a difference on either side. The reality the Japanese had to face in China, one they did not face, was that they had undertaken too much there. Vanquishing Chiang's government was beyond their reach. They did not have the military power to do this and this failure underscored that Japan was not a great power. More modest goals should have been in order and these could have been attained at least in part from trade agreements secured through diplomacy. Well might scholars call attention to the economic fallout of the worldwide depression legitimizing Japanese militarism at home, and therefore allowing a more war-like policy abroad, but a social reality was at work here. War was a cover for the limits of Japanese power, a weakness vanquished by notions of cultural superiority as much as the opportunism inherent in economic dislocation. Autarky may have been the call in the 1930s, but Japan labeled it a co-prosperity sphere to cushion the folly of waging war to overcome weakness that would only be accentuated by conflict.

The circumstances growing out of World War II provided Japan with further opportunity. Britain, France, and the Netherlands all faced defeat in Europe, which weakened their ability to defend their colonies in Asia. Japanese willingness to expand its war south grew out of these favorable circumstances, favorable indeed except for the stand taken by the United States. When that nation teamed with the other western powers, Japan's risk in moving south was great. The rationale of an attack south may have been ending the war in China, but a clash with the United States meant another war, one that Japan could not win. Yet Japan came to other conclusions regarding war with the United States. That country's efforts at "self-defense," such as reinforcing the air defenses of the Philippines, or repositioning the Pacific Fleet at Pearl Harbor, represented a determination to stop Japanese expansion in the Pacific. So too did the American retaliation of an oil embargo directed at Japan after Japan occupied southern Indochina. The American refusal to meet Japanese demands during negotiations meant an effort by the United States to work with other powers to stop Japanese expansion. The Japanese could wonder why they should not rule in Asia rather than the colonial powers. But US resistance did not represent an effort to destroy Japan. These American measures did not pose an imminent threat to that state. The dire consequences that Japan believed came out of its failure to expand were largely of its own creation.

The opponents Japan identified in its preemptive war also spoke to this folly. The supposed coalition of American, British, Chinese, and Dutch military forces never amounted to much of a threat. First, Japan received plenty of oil from the United States and from the Netherlands colony of the Dutch East Indies, no matter Japanese claims that these two nations were working together to implement an oil embargo against Japan. This flow was greatly restricted by 1941, of course, but not before Japan had the opportunity to stockpile oil and hold it in reserve. Second, the United States and Great Britain disagreed over naval deployments to contain Japanese expansion, the Americans favoring a stand-back approach based on Hawaii and one willing to abandon the Philippines, which amounted to very little containment at all. The British insisted on a defense centered on Singapore, a stand clearly favoring British colonial interests and therefore frowned upon by the American high command. In short, there was not much cooperation. Third, the larger perspective is just as telling. Russia never became a partner in the efforts of the western powers to stop Japanese expansion until the last days of the Pacific War. That Japan believed this nation an enemy contributing to its "encirclement" resulted from Japanese actions and decisions toward the USSR long before December 1941, and did not stem from a coalition seeking to encircle Japan. The best the Japanese could argue was that they needed resources and anyone who opposed this end was an enemy. But to admit this meant the preemptive purpose of the war evaporated in the face of base opportunism.

For Japan to argue that the attack on Pearl Harbor initiated a war that could not be avoided made little sense. When its commanders weighed the decision of attacking north or south before finally settling on moving south with the attack on Pearl Harbor, the preemptive purpose of war now opened a third front against the ABD powers since the war in China continued and the threat of the USSR remained in the north. Japanese alarm at the encirclement it certainly faced after December 7 again was largely of its own creation because Japan's war did not start with a preemptive strike at Pearl Harbor; the war was ongoing and a new front was merely added. Once shorn of preemption in the name of self-defense as a cause of its war against the United States, the morality in the purpose of preemptive war could only rest on cultural assumptions that Japanese ascendancy benefited all peoples it contacted. The resistance it faced from those it identified as enemies in its preemptive war, and the resistance it encountered from those it "liberated," called into question the benevolence of its cultural assumptions, and therefore the preemptive nature of its war in the Pacific. By finding morality in a preemptive war to defend civilization, Japan clung to its preemptive purpose only by insisting that its cultural norms represented civilizational goals universally desired, even as the fighting belied this hoped-for truth.

CHAPTER 7

The Soviet Monroe Doctrine: The Russo–Finnish Winter War of 1939

Introduction

A massive artillery barrage began at 6:50 am. Just over an hour later, hundreds of Russian tanks supported by infantry crossed the Soviet border with Finland and advanced toward the Finnish lines. The few Finns in forward positions fled before the assault could reach them, panicked by the great show of force. It was indeed an impressive display of military strength. The Russian offensive extended along the entire Finnish–Soviet border. Russian planes also attacked Helsinki, the Finnish capital, meeting virtually no resistance. The air strike underscored Russian superiority. In fact, the odds appeared overwhelming, the disparity in numbers so great, that it seemed pointless for the Finns to resist the onslaught. Yet, in a matter of days, the Russian attack faltered and then stopped. Whole columns were halted by lone snipers. Fast-moving Finnish ski troops then harassed and assaulted the stalled vehicles or attacked Russian soldiers at night as they huddled around huge fires. Russian tanks milled about allowing Finnish soldiers to creep up and destroy them with mines or "Molotov Cocktails." These setbacks occurred at every point of contact and so often that it soon became clear that the Russian soldiers were not executing a preemptive attack, but fighting for their lives. Preemption had taken an unexpected turn indeed.

The Soviet Union confronted Finland in a separate war fought in the midst of World War II. This isolated clash arose from the non-aggression pact between Germany and Russia. Signed in August 1939, the two powers dismembered Poland the next month. Joseph Stalin, the Soviet leader, now believed he had a free hand to settle security issues on the northeast border of the USSR. After subjugating the Baltic states of Estonia, Latvia, and Lithuania, he turned his attention to Finland in October 1939. Finland was to come into the Soviet orbit and bolster Russia's national defense. The Finns refused to yield to Russian requests for territorial concessions and security guarantees, and the two sides prepared for war. The fighting erupted at the end of November, as the Soviets unleashed their massive ground attack designed to quickly subdue the upstart Finns. Initial success was fleeting, and the Soviet ground troops soon found themselves in a desperate struggle against a determined and capable enemy. A severe winter set in, adding to Russian miseries and increasing the chances of a spectacular Finnish victory. However, massive Russian reinforcements five weeks later pushed the Finns to exhaustion and they agreed to a settlement in mid-March 1940. The Russians won this winter war of 1939, a victory that created more problems for them in the next stage of World War II. When Germany attacked the USSR in June 1941, Finland was a willing ally of the Third Reich.

The portrayal of this war in the literature overwhelmingly depicts a valiant Finland resisting the Soviet Bear. Democracy, for a fleeting moment, stood up to aggression. The Finnish resistance failed, but the message was that if properly supported, a democratic state could triumph over tyranny. How else to explain the Finnish success in so bloodying the Russians that certain victory became doubtful? This view buoyed up the spirits of the western democracies, reaching across the Atlantic Ocean to America. These countries would need such hope in the days ahead, as Nazi Germany swept to victory after victory. Still, the picture was never as clear as desired. Once attacked by Germany, the USSR became a friend of the democracies, and Britain and the United States had to overlook the inconsistency of this aggressor state turned ally. But long before making this leap, the Soviet invasion of Finland could arguably be cast in the sympathetic light of preemption. William R. Trotter's account of this war, *A Frozen Hell*, noted that the Russian diplomatic overtures to Finland sought to ensure a forward defense, "a veiled reference to the strategy of preemptive attack."* In Anthony F. Upton's version entitled, *Finland: 1939–1940*, he commented that if Finland had proved receptive to German designs prior to 1939,

* William R. Trotter, *A Frozen Hell: The Russo-Finnish Winter War of 1939-1940* (Chapel Hill, NC: Algonquin Books of Chapel Hill, 1991), 12.

"Russia might be compelled to launch a pre-emptive move into their territory."* In this light, the USSR acted to gain a buffer zone since it feared an imminent attack by a nation trespassing on Finnish territory and Stalin looked to deflect such a blow before it occurred. This chapter examines the war in the north to try and find the morality that defined the massive Soviet attack on tiny Finland as preemption.

The Case for Preemption

Distrust permeated Soviet thinking in the arena of foreign affairs. Ensuring the survival of the Communist state in the face of certain aggression from the west preoccupied much of Stalin's time. The question was: what country posed the greatest threat? Germany at the head of an anti-Comintern alliance that included Poland certainly menaced Russia's borders, particularly along the Baltic front, maybe reaching to Finland. On the other hand, the superior naval strength of Britain and France troubled the Soviet leader as well since this advantage at sea allowed those nations to move north, intimidate Finland, and use this nation as a base to attack the USSR at Leningrad. Either way, Finland represented an unacceptable risk to Russian security. This reality would be particularly true when the war expected in the west between Germany and the allies France and Britain ended. The victorious side would then be free to direct its attention to the USSR. Should the Germans win, a land battle in the Baltic region loomed large, and should the western nations win, a naval force was sure to enter the waters near Finland.

While there were a great many threats the USSR had to face near its borders, Finland by itself was not one of them. Its population of only three and half million spoke to its limited threat potential, as did its small armed forces. What concerned the Soviets most was not a Finnish offensive directed at the Soviet Union, but that another country would seize Finland and attack Russia from this vantage point. The military weakness of Finland compounded this fear. It would not be able to prevent this scenario from unfolding. During negotiations with the Russians leading up to the crisis of November 1939, Finnish delegates remained adamant that their nation would resist such an invasion, but this guarantee did little to convince the Soviets that their northern flank was secure, given the USSR's low regard for Finnish military capability. Of course the Finns would resist, but this defense would do little good and the USSR would have to contend with a difficult security problem unless steps were taken to avoid this development

---

* Anthony F. Upton, *Finland, 1939–1940* (Newark, NJ: University of Delaware Press, 1974), 17.

all together. Preemption became that necessary step if the Finns refused to listen to reason.

To prevent the use of Finland as a springboard for the invasion of Soviet territory, Stalin requested naval and air bases on Finnish territory to safeguard the waterways to Leningrad, a city whose population of three and half million people matched that of all of Finland, and one that represented cherished Russian and Soviet traditions and ideals. The Russian port of Murmansk farther to the north served as a key outlet of trade for the USSR and Finnish territory again presented an obvious axis of advance to threaten this strategic point. From Finland a hostile nation indeed could inflict serious blows against the USSR. To remedy this problem, the USSR looked for very limited territory. It asked the Finns to cede 70 kilometers of the Karelian Isthmus, pushing the Finnish border back from Leningrad. To interdict sea travel nearby, the Soviets insisted on occupying Hanko on Finnish soil, a rocky promontory jutting into the Baltic Sea with a harbor at its tip. In this way, the USSR's navy could block passage to Leningrad. A second port, Porkkala, was coveted for the same reason. Far to the north, Finland was to cede its portion of the Rybachiy peninsula, this to safeguard Murmansk and Russian access to the Arctic Sea. In exchange for these concessions, the Russians would surrender a large portion of land on Finland's eastern border, territory where many Finns lived. Given the modest terms and the offer of an exchange in territory, the Russians believed this to be a very reasonable offer.

In making these demands, Soviet strategists incorporated Finland into a larger picture of Russia's security. Overall, the Russians hoped to carry any fight with Germany into the territory of another country, and in this way spare the USSR the devastation of war. The Soviets desired control of the Baltic states for this reason alone. But Soviet thinking went past merely adding a buffer zone. Should the Germans attack the USSR, they reasoned that the most likely objective would be the Ukraine. To stop this southern thrust, the USSR would strike the exposed flank of this German offensive by attacking through the three Baltic states. This "forward defense," as the Soviets called it, meant a preemptive strike against Estonia, Latvia, and Lithuania before any such German attack.* Finland sat on the extreme edge of this Soviet offensive, and therefore could not be left alone. It was a Baltic state, and all such states had to be secured to allow Russia to face a war with Germany.

Finland preferred to think of itself as a Scandinavian nation and outwith the fray engulfing Russia and the Baltic states. In early 1939, Finland turned

---

* Carl Van Dyke, *The Soviet Invasion of Finland, 1939–1940* (London: Frank Cass, 1997), 2.

to Sweden to foster this gravitation but it accomplished very little. The Swedes hesitated to accept the Finnish offer to fortify the Aland Islands, a demilitarized group of islands strategically located between the two nations, because it would offend too many nations. The Germans worried that such defenses potentially would block its access to iron ore deposits in Sweden. The USSR believed the defenses would do little good to stop Germany or Britain and once an invading country like Germany was in control of these defenses, it would occupy a key position from which to continue to advance toward Leningrad. Even Britain took an interest and objected to the alliance because should its navy wish to interdict the iron ore shipments to Germany, fortifications in German hands on the islands would make this almost impossible. The Swedes balked, not wishing to entangle themselves in a war. And while they did not refuse the Finnish offer, they did nothing to make it a reality. The Finnish hope of an alliance of neutral Scandinavian powers went nowhere. What they did accomplish was to create further alarm in the USSR. Stalin now believed that the Finns were looking to fortify the islands at the expense of the USSR. Perhaps it would be a first step toward inviting German protection. Soviet offers of working in tandem with the construction teams and keeping observers in the area were rejected by the Finns. In this case, Finnish efforts at forging their own security had weakened their position in that it encouraged the USSR to strike first in preemptive fashion.

Finland maintained a hard line in negotiations and refused Russia's territorial objectives. Finland countered the Soviet proposal with only minor concessions: it would share the island of Suursaari in the Gulf of Finland, yield no territory on the Finnish mainland, and allow a 12-mile adjustment of the border along the Karelian Isthmus. It offered nothing regarding the Rybachiy peninsula in the north. The Finnish government did this despite the advice of Field Marshal Mannerheim, a soldier and statesman of long and distinguished service. He urged compliance with Soviet demands, stressing the unprepared condition of the Finnish army. He also believed the concerns the Russians expressed regarding how their security related to Finland to be real and valid. Mannerheim concluded that not to act in conciliatory fashion might well invite a Soviet attack that Finland could not defeat.

It did not require a particularly astute analysis of the international scene to support Mannerheim's view of making concessions. Soviet efforts in entering into an agreement with one of the western camps, Germany or Britain and France, had come to pass. The USSR's August 23, 1939 signing of a non-aggression pact with Germany prompted Russian action. It joined in the German destruction of Poland. It then targeted the Baltic states starting on September 25, 1939. The three states offered no resistance and

Soviet military forces occupied these countries in a matter of days. Finland's turn was clearly next. On October 5, 1939, Stalin's trusted confidant, Vyacheslav Molotov, presented the Finnish ambassador with a note that asked for a meeting to discuss "concrete political questions."* The Russians then reiterated their demands. Finland's overture to Germany, presented as the Russians forced the collapse of the independent Baltic states, had been rejected on October 7 when the Germans confirmed their alliance with the USSR in a diplomatic note to Finland. Finland now stood alone.

The fact was that the situation in the later portion of 1939 greatly favored the USSR. With Russia no longer worried about German intentions after signing the non-aggression pact, it could direct all its resources toward Finland. Additionally, Russia had recently ended its border war with Japan in Manchuria. This meant the Russian defeat of Finland appeared certain. Still, the Russians trod lightly, promising not to change Finland's government, civil institutions, or interfere in the internal affairs of Finland should that nation allow Soviet armed forces on its territory for the purpose of defending Finland from an attack by outside invaders. This was a kind gesture, one not extended to the Baltic states.

Soviet leniency toward Finland was all the more remarkable given the Russian belief that the historically volatile nature of the Finnish home front left it vulnerable to attack. A bitter civil war over the founding of the nation that included a struggle between communists and anti-communists had coincided with, in fact grew out of, the climate of World War I. This timing meant that Finnish independence from Russia came when that country could do little to prevent this eventuality. Lenin, in fact, immediately recognized the new state so as to win its allegiance to Russia. He also hoped to galvanize the resistance of the proletariat in that country that promised to make Finland communist. Only the timely intervention of the German armed forces allowed the "Whites" to defeat Finland's communist movement. Many of the survivors then fled to the USSR. They now, twenty years later, hungered for a chance to return to their country and establish a communist government. These émigrés assured Stalin that once the USSR attacked Finland, much of the population would join with the Russian soldiers in a show of solidarity and welcome them with "flowers and banners."** Finnish resistance was doomed given that this internal threat compounded its already immeasurable difficulty in defending itself from a Russian attack. For the Russians, the risk of leaving the Finnish question

---

* Leonard C. Lundin, *Finland in the Second World War* (Bloomington, IN: Indiana University Press, 1957), 51.

** Max Jakobson, *Finland Survived: An Account of the Finnish–Soviet Winter War, 1939–1940* (Helsinki: The Otava Publishing Company, 1961), 143.

unresolved was great while the solution to the problem appeared easy. Should they play their cards right, a Soviet attack would secure the state at little cost. The greatest hazard facing a Soviet attack would be driving down some snowy roads.

The Finns did not help their case by allowing the visit of German dignitaries and assuming an obvious pro-German stand. In August 1937, a German naval squadron composed of submarines entered Helsinki. The following year, in April and May, a large German delegation traveled to the Finnish capital to commemorate the Finnish civil war victory in which the Whites had crushed their communist opponents with German help. In June 1939, the German chief of staff, General Halder, visited Finland and observed Finnish army maneuvers opposite the Karelian Isthmus and received a decoration from the Finns as well. Such overt courting of German dignitaries had the obvious connotation of soliciting German aid against a Soviet attack. As such, Soviet officials could not dismiss these entreaties as merely highly offensive banter.

Further developments deterred Russia from taking a light view of Finnish–German relations in the mid to late 1930s. The Finnish overtures to Germany stretched over two governments. The Svinhufvud administration clearly was tolerant of the Nazi regime and hostile to the USSR, which Svinhufvud characterized as the eternal enemy of Finland. However, the Soviets expected the succeeding Kallio administration to be more suspicious of the resurgence of German power and therefore open to establishing better relations with the USSR. Assuming power in 1937, President Kallio promptly reassured the Russians of his government's good intentions. But the Halder visit clearly undid this call to good will. So too did the demonstrations of the Finnish people in support of Germany, including a youth group singing songs predicting fascism's pending victory over communism, this while they built fortifications along the Karelian Isthmus. The Russians could see that Finnish neutrality had a clear pro-German bent to it. The Soviets asked themselves, why they should wait until a German army appeared in the north? Preemption gained credibility and urgency.

Even so, Stalin pursued a settlement, not war. On October 23, he presented an offer to the still unyielding Finnish delegation that reduced the proposed Russian garrison on Hanko to 4,000 men and promised to withdraw this force once the war in the west was over. He also asked for less territory on the Karelian Isthmus. A new round of talks began on November 3, but the Finns offered no concessions. Stalin did. He repeated the security needs of the USSR, and offered to buy Hanko from Finland. Rebuffed again, he asked if another island nearby would be acceptable to Finland. Still the Finns did not relent. In a final meeting on November 9,

Stalin pointed to an island and asked in exasperation, "Is this island vital to you?"* The Finnish delegates merely replied that they had no authority to accept a compromise. The telling flexibility of Stalin is more apparent when these later requests are compared to the earlier Soviet demands. These goals included a mutual defense agreement, Soviet control of Hanko with 5,000 soldiers stationed for thirty years and the right to deploy Soviet warships in nearby ports on the Finnish mainland, all of the islands in the Gulf of Finland, the 70-mile concession along the border of the Karelian Isthmus, and Soviet control of the Finnish part of the Rybachiy peninsula, this to safeguard Murmansk. To ask for merely one island was indeed an enormous concession. True, the Finns would have had to cede more than this to complete an agreement, but Stalin's willingness to negotiate was clear. The Finns refused to budge and the Finnish delegation left Moscow on November 13.

The Russians believed that the western powers, France and Britain, had stiffened Finnish resistance by promising to support Finland in the event of war. How else to explain the uncompromising Finnish stand? Stalin now had no choice but to resort to the military option. Up to June 1939, the only contingency plans available were those designed to occupy Finland as part of the "forward defense" strategy should war commence with Germany. At this time, Stalin ordered a new plan, one designed to ensure the defeat of Finland in advance of Russo–German hostilities. General Shaposhnikov, chief of the general staff, recommended a massive force of fifty divisions involving a carefully planned operation along the entire Soviet–Finnish frontier. This approach would stretch Finnish defenses to the maximum and ensure victory by a steady strangulation of the country. Stalin considered this plan overkill. He believed the Finns were weak and would collapse in a matter of days, their army crushed by superior Soviet forces. Internal factionalism meant most Finns would welcome the Soviets as liberators and these Finns would turn their guns on landlords and the bourgeoisie class. Because of these advantages, a successful Russian offensive could be accomplished by the Leningrad Military District alone, and Stalin issued orders for it to do so. The commander of that district, General Meretskov, soon had a plan ready, a clumsy assault relying primarily on an advance through the Karelian Isthmus. To do this he deployed but 60 percent of the forces that Shaposhnikov had determined would be needed for a successful Soviet invasion of Finland. This plan received Stalin's endorsement in July 1939, anticipating that if forced to go to war, it would take only a couple of weeks to gain a favorable result.

---

* Upton, *Finland, 1939–1940*, 41.

The folly of believing in an easy victory over Finland would soon be demonstrated. But rather than pointing to a certain degree of arrogance in his aggressive designs, Stalin's military plans pointed to the opposite, a reluctance to attack and undertake a preemptive offensive in the first place. Stalin's contempt for Finnish military preparedness again speaks to his sincerity in wishing to negotiate a settlement. The Finns were so weak as to invite attack, but Stalin ordered an attack only after repeatedly trying to negotiate. His frustration mounted given his personal involvement in the negotiations, and given Finnish inflexibility. His suspicion peaked as well, since he became convinced that Finnish intransigence could only stem from promises of military aid from Germany or Britain and France. Clearly he believed that Finland posed a security threat to the USSR, and he only reluctantly accepted the need to use military force to eliminate this threat. With Germany allied to Russia, the time to strike had arrived. The Soviet attack would be preemptive, designed to forestall another power from using Finland as a base to attack the USSR. It was indeed a dangerous world by the end of 1939, but one that promised some tangible gains for the USSR, territorial concessions in Finland foremost among them.

The Attack

Evidence of the imminent threat facing Russia along its long border with Finland came on November 26, 1939. A number of artillery shells landed on a border town along the Karelian Isthmus, killing several Russian soldiers. Molotov told the Finnish delegates in Moscow that the border must be pushed back immediately. Finland demurred and requested a joint investigation. They thought it more likely that the Russians had fabricated this incident as a pretense for renewed discussions to then pressure Finland to make concessions. For Russia, this latest instance of Finnish hostility could only be dealt with through military force. This came on November 30, as large Russian forces attacked Finland along the entire length of the 1,000-kilometre border.

The Leningrad Front mounted four different attacks. The main thrust came opposite Leningrad on the Karelian Isthmus. Another arm of this attack advanced north of Lake Ladoga in support of the attack on the Isthmus and was designed to turn the flank of the Finnish defensive line that rested on the southern shore of that lake. Two more Russian thrusts came further north and strove to achieve strategic ends. A Russian army attacked the center of Finland and hoped to cut the country in two and isolate it from Sweden so as to deny Finland any aid from that country. A final Soviet army advanced on the Finnish port of Petsamo in the far north as a way to protect Murmansk. In all, the Russians deployed 450,000 men,

2,000 tanks, and 1,000 planes. The Finns mustered 180,000 troops, a few antiquated armored vehicles, little modern artillery, and just a small number of planes. The material disparity measured something on the order of 3 to 1 in troops, 80 to 1 in tanks, 5 to 1 in artillery, and 5 to 1 in planes in favor of the Russians. To achieve this preponderance of strength, the USSR committed only 25 percent of all of its forces. Success appeared certain and it required little exertion by the Soviet Union.

The Soviets expected to encounter weak Finnish resistance for a number of reasons, among them the anticipation that the two additional thrusts far north of Lake Ladoga would divert Finnish resources away from a defense of the Karelian Isthmus. But such dispersion of effort tends to forfeit offensive momentum more than it stretches a defense. This problem rebounded here due to the terrain. The attacks in the north and center of Finland proceeded along single roads and into the inhospitable terrain of endless forest. The result was that a handful of Finnish soldiers first delayed these attacks, and then a small number of soldiers disrupted them. Anything more on the part of Finnish resistance in that area proved unnecessary since the war north of Lake Ladoga became irrelevant early on. The Russians did take Petsamo in the north but this was a minor success. In the center, Finnish troops stopped the Russian forces well before they could interdict Finland's north and south communications, let alone its communications with Sweden.

In a matter of weeks it was clear that the Russians had dissipated precious military strength in areas of dubious value, while the Finns had conserved their own resources and concentrated them in the area that mattered most, the battle around Leningrad. Nor did the émigré threat serve any purpose. The Russians created a new Finnish government, but few Finns rallied to its banner. Otto Kuusinen, an exiled Finnish communist and the leader of the Russian-sponsored government, remained little more than a spectacle, a man whose authority existed only in those areas where there were Russian forces. In this opening phase of the war, this amounted to very little land indeed. In the post-1939 war settlement, Stalin ignored him altogether.

The inescapable reality was that the war would be decided in the vicinity of Leningrad. Here the Russians enjoyed the advantage of numbers and nothing else. The disadvantages quickly became apparent and overwhelming, dooming the attack. Given the narrow isthmus, only 70 kilometers wide, the avenues of attack were obvious and well defended. Consequently, the Russians encountered strong Finnish resistance from the very beginning of the attack. No amount of armor, artillery or infantry could assail the Mannerhein Line, as the Finnish defenses became known. On this front alone, the Russians deployed 200,000 soldiers and 1,500 tanks as well as an abundance of artillery, some 43 percent of the total strength of the

Leningrad Military District. They even used aircraft in large numbers when the weather permitted.

This collective strength had little effect on the Finnish defenses. Sheer weight of numbers merely added to staggering Russian losses. After two weeks the offensive lost momentum. Worse, a heavy snowfall soon made the roads impassable. Now the exhausted and strung-out Russian forces, bloodied from the incessant fighting, faced increasingly effective Finnish counterattacks. Entire Russian divisions were cut off and destroyed at the leisure of the Finnish commanders. It rapidly became apparent to even the most diehard communist that no amount of men and material would penetrate the Finnish defensive lines. The question became, could the Soviets ward off further disasters?

This was the state of affairs given that the expected breakthrough never came. Russian gains measured only a few miles, and this came at great cost. The losses were so large as to be damning in their own right, but they pointed to greater problems within the Soviet military. Clearly, training, leadership, tactics, and equipment all lacked capability in one way or another. Fixing these problems was a worrisome and presumably time-consuming venture. The trouble was that Stalin feared the USSR did not have enough time. The Russian debacle in Finland was being watched by the world; the war that raged in the frozen north during the winter of 1939 took center stage since there was no fighting in the west as the French and British engaged in what became known as a "phony" war with Germany. Stalin worried greatly that the obvious Russian weakness would encourage an attack from the west by either Germany or France and Britain. His response was to try to win in Finland as quickly as possible. It was clear that to do this Stalin would have to disregard Russian losses. Even by Russian standards of tolerating a large number of casualties, preemption threatened to become cost prohibitive.

A new Russian commander, General Timoshenko, stressed this point because he accepted the post only after being assured he would not be held responsible for losses. This condition spoke to the grim fate that awaited the Russian soldiers involved in a new offensive. No matter the Soviet examination of their initial failure in Finland that generated a move toward doctrinal reform, the reality was that such changes could not be implemented satisfactorily in the short period of time—twenty days—that elapsed from the end of the first Russian offensive to the beginning of the second, launched on February 11. Now 600,000 men and 2,000 tanks tested the Finnish defenses along the Karelian front alone. The attacks to the north ended and the focus of attention rested on the fighting around Leningrad. Massive artillery support and air assets completed the Soviet arsenal. The numbers at the disposal of Timoshenko made it clear what strategy the

Russians were following: the Soviets resolved to overwhelm the defenders. A further bloodying of the Soviet military could be expected, but Stalin reasoned this was a price worth paying to end the conflict before foreign intervention of some form or another greatly complicated his preemptive war in the north. It already was complicated enough, a preemptive strike designed to ease Russian security concerns that had made those concerns more acute and plunged the Soviet military into crisis. The winter war had become costly indeed.

Once the Soviets renewed their attack, Mannerheim believed Finland had a limited time to continue fighting. The field marshal did not think the Allied powers would come to his aid despite the rumblings in France and Britain to that effect. So no matter the success of the defensive war to date, Soviet numbers would spell the difference. The Russians appeared willing to pay any cost to win. And this they did, the opposing sides coming to terms in mid-March 1940. A month into the new attack, the Russians still had not gained much ground. But they did stretch Finnish defenses to the breaking point due to the sheer exhaustion of men and ammunition. It was not so much a victory as it was a successful test of endurance. The Soviet Union lasted longer, and given their larger population and material advantage, this outcome was foreordained. The cost had been high, over 48,000 Russian soldiers dead, another 158,000 wounded. Finland suffered more than 22,000 fatalities and over 43,000 wounded. These were stunning totals for a conflict that lasted just 105 days. From the Russian point of view, the mass casualties left them asking whether Stalin's preemptive strike was worth it.

Success

One answer had to be yes, because from the Russian standpoint the sacrifices had not been in vain. Having won the war, Stalin dictated a harsh settlement. The islands in the Gulf of Finland, so much in dispute before the war, came under Soviet control. The Soviets also gained Hanko and made this port a Russian stronghold on Finnish territory. The USSR won a large land concession near Leningrad both north and south of Lake Ladoga. Further north, the Soviets acquired some high ground that in their hands would allow them to defend more easily the rail line between Murmansk and Leningrad. And finally the Soviets gained control of the Finnish part of the Rybachiy peninsula. Altogether, these terms met the Russian security concerns voiced before the conflict and therefore amounted to success. Leningrad now appeared more secure and so too did Murmansk.

These Russian "successes," however, raised the issue of the value of pre-emption. Finland was to serve as a buffer zone, a defensive area of particular importance to Stalin given the proximity of Finland to both of these cities. But the Soviet effort at securing a buffer zone largely accomplished the opposite. A German front was established in Finland, and this came after the Russian attack of 1939. It is likely no German presence would have existed had the 1939 attack not taken place; before 1940, there were no German plans for such a deployment. After 1939, both Germany and Finland did plan for this eventuality, the Germans seeing an opportunity to deploy minor forces in Finland and so stretch the Russian defenses. Additionally, they hoped to protect their access to the iron ore coming to Germany from Sweden. The Russians understood this failure of their policy. They left a sizeable army of fifteen divisions along the border to safeguard their new gains. Obviously, the threat of a power occupying Finland and striking the USSR remained and it was not just a worry but a likelihood.

Worse, that power would probably be Germany. The Finns craved revenge for the 1939 war, and an agreement with Germany was not hard to forge, or to accept, given this motive. True, they were careful to minimize the German presence in their country; Germany as a foreign power was no more welcomed than was the USSR. Additionally, Finnish leaders worried that too overt a shift to Germany would provoke another Soviet "preemptive" attack. But Finland became a front the Russians had to contend with during the anticipated showdown with Germany because of Soviet actions in 1939. Russia's preemptive war forced Finland to turn to Germany in the aftermath of its conflict with the USSR, creating the threat the Russians had wished to avoid. This reality emphasized a great failing of the Russian strategy of preemption: creating an enemy front where none existed before. Such an outcome contravened the very purpose of preemption, to eliminate a threat. Instead, it pointed to the dangerous consequences of an ill-advised preemptive attack.

With the Germans established in Finland, the two key Soviet cities in the north did come under attack when Germany launched their offensive against Russia in June 1941. The ultimate German objective was Murmansk, Germany recognizing it as a crucial port of supply for the USSR. Murmansk did prove to be part of a vital shipping lane during the war since the majority of Allied lend-lease equipment came through this port. The many planes, trucks, tanks, and supplies made a valuable contribution to Soviet success during the war. As the Soviets staggered from the savage German blows in the first two years of the war on the eastern front, this material aid did indeed give the Soviet Union a much needed lift. At the very least, it allowed Soviet industry to focus on the production of tanks and other vital instruments of war given this additional source of supply. German forces came close to taking the city, but failed to do so. A heroic Russian resistance stopped them, as did the same daunting terrain that had handicapped Russian attacks in this area in 1939. The Soviets also benefited from the land it had taken from Finland to such an extent that it helped them successfully maintain the rail link between Murmansk and the rest of the country. The success of defending this city, however, could not undo the near disaster that again questioned the wisdom of the Soviet preemptive strike against Finland. Had the 1939 attack not taken place, the Germans might not have been in position to threaten Murmansk or the rail line to Leningrad at all.

Leningrad also came under German attack. German forces approached the city in the first days of September 1941. Unable to take the city by storm, the Germans decided to bomb and starve Leningrad into submission. Given this purpose, it faced a particularly severe ordeal during the war, some 900 days of isolation. The Finns did their part by advancing on Leningrad from the north and northeast. But a Finnish-German army advancing on the city through the Karelian Isthmus did not become a reality. The Finns never launched an offensive toward Leningrad at all, and with no German forces in the vicinity, the city was not hard-pressed from the northern side. This situation called attention to the fact that Finland never did threaten the city, nor would it allow a foreign army to use the Karelian Isthmus to attack Leningrad without its permission. Once again the need for preemption proved questionable. Worse, a pliable Finland might well have been able to ease the plight of the city once the Germans isolated it from the south. Instead, Finland's army bolstered the German siege, making Stalin's fear of the loss of Leningrad a near reality.

The city held on and it continued to anchor Russian defenses in the north. But the successful defense of the city had little to do with the islands taken from Finland after the 1939 war. These sites did little to no good. They obviously could not prevent German advances on land through the Baltic states. In fact, the Russian position on Hanko, the point of so much contention leading up to the Russo–Finnish war of 1939, proved useless. The Soviets abandoned it after the loss of Tallinn in Estonia; Hanko had been outflanked from the opposite shore. Such was the case with most of the islands in the Gulf of Finland. This German ground maneuver had been anticipated by Russian admirals who were not impressed with the proposed plan to acquire Finnish soil that brought about the 1939 war with Finland. In fact, many of these commanders had dismissed the rationale of needing any such bases as amateur in the extreme. Here was a damning return on preemption, the acquisition at great loss of blood and treasure of land that did nothing to prevent the end that was feared: a threat to

Leningrad that furthered its isolation. In the end, German land bases in Estonia were enough to make the Baltic Sea a dangerous place for the Russian fleet to operate and to help the Germans isolate the great city.

Given the limited returns on the occupation of Finnish territory gained after the 1939 war, the buffer zone approach had failed in the north. The war had pushed Finland into the German camp and created a front that had not existed before. This problem was compounded due to the fact that other powers also considered entering the war in Finland. During the fighting in late 1939 between Russia and Finland, the western allies, France and Britain, considered sending five or six divisions to Finland and help this fellow democracy survive the winter. The Allies decided against this step given the difficulty in transporting troops there, and worries of violating Swedish neutrality thereby spreading the war to that country. Such caution by France and Britain again meant a different tack. They furnished material aid that arrived in significant quantities to better equip Finnish defenses, particularly in the air. Nevertheless, a force of 30,000 to 50,000 allied troops would have disrupted Stalin's plans. But more than this, the threat of this deployment was enough to expose the shallowness of his motive for preemption. The Allies had not planned such intervention before the attack, only after it. By this measure, preemption appeared a total failure. It provoked the very thing it hoped to discourage, possible foreign intervention in Finland by France and Britain, to say nothing of the German threat of intervention.

In the string of failures that characterized the Russian attack in 1939, there was one bright spot. The performance of its military forces was so poor as to induce widespread reform. The coordination between the services was greatly improved, and armor, infantry and air power worked together much better thereafter. The tactic of mass attacks persisted as Soviet doctrine, but some sophistication was introduced to at least mitigate casualties; camouflage was adopted and frontal attacks discouraged. Since leadership was so poor during the war with Finland in 1939, many officers disgraced in the recent purges were re-inducted into the army after this date. Equipment of poor quality was jettisoned. These lessons and improvements helped the Red Army survive the German attack in 1941. Yet to cite such an indirect benefit from preemption does little to minimize its failure as a strategy.

Conclusion

By the winter of 1939, the Soviet Union believed it faced a threat that it could no longer ignore. Should an enemy of Russia successfully overrun the Finnish state, hostile military forces would come too close to some key geography in the USSR. Leningrad could be directly threatened, and this important population center and economic hub, not to mention its value historically and symbolically, would be difficult to defend should an invasion come from Finland. Murmansk in the far north represented a key economic asset, an outlet to the sea that the USSR could not afford to lose. An offensive from Finland could go far to hurting the USSR and contribute mightily to its collapse. To resolve this threat it acted preemptively and attacked that nation before another state could launch such an attack.

Before committing this act of violence, the USSR requested a series of meetings with Finland to reach an agreement that satisfied both parties. While they participated in the talks, the Finns refused to negotiate. They would not allow the USSR to occupy a few key islands and harbors that would put naval assets of the USSR in place to block the approach to Leningrad from the sea. Stalin showed great flexibility in deciding which islands the Russians would utilize, but the Finns refused all of his requests. Nor did the Finns cede any significant territory opposite Leningrad or near Murmansk. The Finns also refused Soviet offers of land along the shared eastern frontier as an exchange for the loss of Finnish territory. This land mass far exceeded the territory demanded by the USSR. Given the status of the respective countries, one a great power, the other a small one, Stalin's flexibility toward the Finns meant that he was being generous in the extreme during negotiations.

Finland's refusal to negotiate emphasized two additional points. First, Stalin did not fear Finland in its own right. He understood that its armed forces were very small and under-equipped and that it posed little threat to either Leningrad or Murmansk. However, this military weakness was the point that drove Soviet policy in regards to Finland. Another nation, a greater power, would take advantage of the Finns' weakness and attack and occupy Finland. From there, they would direct their military advances at the USSR. The international scene was volatile to say the least, and a threat from Finnish soil appeared a real possibility no matter which side won the war that erupted in September 1939. Russia, and therefore Finland, had to anticipate the worst and this caution required a Soviet presence in Finland.

Second, Finnish unreasonableness confounded Stalin. Try as he might to explain his concerns to the Finns, they would not yield. Stalin understood this stubbornness as evidence that Finland was plotting to work in tandem with another nation. Should the Germans move east, perhaps Finland intended to welcome them onto its territory. Or, just as likely, Great Britain might try to use Finland to wage war against the USSR in the north. Finnish actions had given some credence to both of these possibilities. Its government, no matter its political orientation, had demonstrated strong pro-German tendencies. At one time or another in the years after the Nazi rise to power in 1933, Finland had invited German military personnel to visit Finland to celebrate past feats of military prowess or witness military maneuvers. In each case, these events appeared directed at the USSR. Such demonstrations fell off in the wake of the Nazi–Soviet pact in 1939, but this only increased Stalin's suspicion that Britain was working with Finland. Why else would the Finns not come to terms when otherwise completely isolated and facing certain defeat should the USSR be forced to attack it?

Stalin considered one other scenario and that was one where Germany, France, and Britain acted in unison against the USSR. They had done so in 1938, dissecting Czechoslovakia, the sole Russian ally in central Europe, without even inviting the USSR to the accords. In 1939, they might reach some agreement that brought one or more of these powers to Finnish soil. The Munich Agreement meant that troubled times had accelerated the pace toward war and that such a conflict might soon engulf the USSR. It was possible that a united front in the west could attack the Soviet Union and use Finland as one launching pad for such an assault. It was best to plan for all eventualities and if possible to circumvent them before they occurred. The Russian need to preemptively attack Finland grew stronger in order to neutralize this looming threat in the north.

When the imperialist powers went to war against one another in the west, this generally was considered good news from the Russian point of view. Tied up in a war, these countries could not now threaten the USSR. But Stalin understood the joy from this development to be temporary. When that war ended, the winning side would be in a stronger position to directly threaten Russia. Stalin believed the USSR had to prepare for this moment. When he made his non-aggression pact with Hitler, the time to safeguard the USSR had arrived. As part of its "forward defense" strategy, the USSR had to convince, or bully, as the case may be, its neighboring states to agree to defense terms acceptable to the Soviets. Estonia, Latvia, and Lithuania agreed to Stalin's demands. Finland did not. This lone holdout now became of primary importance, a vulnerable Achilles' heel to an otherwise well-defended frontier. With the west tied up in a war, and the Finns recalcitrant, the time to act preemptively had arrived.

To describe the Finns as uncooperative and therefore deserving of the attack the Russians unleashed on them on November 30, 1939, dismisses Finnish fears that the USSR could not be trusted to merely establish a few bases on its soil. For many reasons, their suspicions were justified. They needed only to look across the Baltic Sea to understand what Soviet "protection" meant. Estonia, Latvia, and Lithuania all had allowed a USSR military presence on their soil. They soon found their independent status put on hold in the name of Russian self-defense, then revoked altogether when annexed to the USSR. Finland could expect the same treatment. Moreover, the Soviet requests were such as to rob the Finns of excellent defensive terrain. This weakness would be most pronounced opposite the Karelian Isthmus, the famed Mannerheim Line being rendered useless in any surrender of territory on Soviet terms. And once able to land forces on Finland's soil through the occupation of Finnish ports, the Soviets could then reinforce their garrisons and eventually absorb Finland in the same way they had crushed the Baltic states. The Russian land concession on the border in the north meant nothing given the erosion of Finland's defenses elsewhere. Surely a capitulation to the USSR's demands doomed Finnish security and therefore Finnish independence. Stalin's insistence that he was being flexible—almost generous—conveniently overlooked this reality.

Defensive terrain was at a premium given the impact both sides knew it would have in a war. The USSR would have to attack under very difficult circumstances. The heavy winter snows would block roads. To move off the tracks meant an advance over land studded with heavy forest and lakes. These terrain features benefited the defenders in two ways. One, they made the use of tanks almost impossible. Two, they acted to channel advancing forces down obvious routes and therefore into readily identifiable kill zones. The Finnish army may have been outnumbered and under-equipped, but nature would prove a valuable ally, neutralizing the mechanized forces of the USSR, reducing the effectiveness of its artillery. The days would be short, the weather overcast, grounding the Red air force. In short, the Finns could force an infantry to fight on their terms, and they could expect to fare well in such a confrontation since Finland's limited numbers and resources could be deployed to maximum effect. Under these favorable circumstances, it was possible to organize a credible defense. Moreover, Finland's leaders concluded that the Russians would not attack during winter for the very reason that it would too much favor the defense. Soviet demands did not need to be taken seriously until the spring of 1940. Stalin's willingness to compromise grew out of this reality, his patience a mere bluff.

While most of these calculations proved correct, the last one did not. Finland underestimated Stalin's determination to solve the Finnish "problem." To seize upon Finland's supposed intransigence revealed a willingness to go to war on the part of the USSR, and the sooner the better to take advantage of Finland's isolation. Stalin's non-aggression pact with Germany had paved the way to undertake this offensive without the likelihood of German intervention. For the Soviets to then suggest that the attack was necessary to forestall a German invasion of Finland was the height of insincerity. Stalin, when speaking with the Finnish delegates, merely deflected this point by remarking that while the USSR and Germany were at peace now, "anything in this world can change."* Clearly the non-aggression pact was an agreement between two dominant powers that had divided much of Europe between them. Stalin intended to secure his spoils before the international climate shifted again and he found himself at odds with Germany.

French and British efforts to work with the USSR and to guarantee the defense of Finland went nowhere. These discussions dragged on for some time. What they indicated was that neither France nor Britain wanted to intervene unilaterally in matters related to Finland. In fact, Britain candidly made this point during negotiations with Stalin prior to the outbreak of war in the west in September 1939. To curry Soviet favor, both France and Britain agreed to a Russian sphere of influence that included Finland, in effect agreeing to a Soviet Monroe Doctrine in the north. As it turned out, prior to the outbreak of the Winter War, the Finns spurned Russia, France and Britain's offer of guarantees of Finland's security because they did not put any stock in those guarantees. More likely, they believed Finland would be sacrificed at another "Munich." No accord was reached. Still, what is telling is the willingness of the western powers to make concessions to the USSR in the months leading up to the Russian attack on Finland. Plainly Stalin's fear of British military action in the region was another fabrication designed to mask his overt aggression against what he assumed was an easily outmatched neighbor.

The Finns tried to assure the USSR that it had no reason to suspect a Finnish opening to the west, either to Germany or to France and Britain. By robbing the Soviets of the need to act preemptively, they hoped to deter a Soviet attack. The Soviets dismissed Finnish neutrality as feigned, or as a useless gesture given the inability of the Finns to prevent the arrival of another power on their soil. Either way Russia had to attack to protect itself by preventing a foreign power from occupying Finland. What this meant was that to preserve its independence, Finland believed it would have to fight. They expected to be able to defend themselves well if necessary. Should an invasion come, it actually offered a bit of good news for Finland and this again helps explain why the Finns opted to fight in 1939. A Soviet attack would produce a political advantage in that the home front would rally behind the defense of Finland to fend off what would be perceived as Soviet aggression. Any pro-Soviet element in the country would drop this stand in favor of defending Finland's independence.

The Russians expected to be greeted as liberators since a number of Finnish émigrés assured them of Finnish discontent at home. Not believing

---

* Olli Vehviläinen, *Finland in the Second World War: Between Germany and Russia*, trans. Gerard McAlester (New York: Palgrave, 2002), 37.

this propaganda, some Russian generals asked for a large force to make the attack. Stalin and his closest advisers deemed this preparation unnecessary to defeat puny Finland. Soviet military forces were greatly superior to Finland's, and the expected turmoil on the Finnish home front doomed any chance of a successful defense. Consequently, the Soviet leader sent an army into Finland that was ill-prepared to face staunch resistance. When Finland did not yield in the opening days of the offensive, he soon had a longer and more costly war on his hands than he had anticipated. Stalin recovered from his shock to order a renewed offensive with all the resources the USSR could spare, and Finland submitted. He remained focused on his strategic goal of denying Finland to other nations wielding greater military resources. However, that few Finns welcomed the spectacle of Russian "liberation," that national unity served as a key to an effective Finnish defense, again revealed the Soviet attack as nothing more than an act of aggression.

Certainly, from Finland's point of view, the Soviets did not launch a preemptive attack in November 1939, but an offensive serving a policy of aggression. Two other points make this clear. First, one of the main purposes of the war from Stalin's point of view was to forestall foreign intervention in Finland, a Soviet attack being necessary because of Finnish weakness; it could not prevent its takeover by an outside power, one undoubtedly hostile to the USSR. The Finns did not threaten Russia by themselves. But in November 1939, the Soviet pretense for war became an act of Finnish aggression—the shelling of a border town—more than likely instigated by the Russians. To suddenly blame hostilities on Finland, as the Russians did when launching their invasion, belied the need for preemption at all and called attention to Soviet aggression. Second, Stalin held ambitions no different from past Russian monarchs and leaders. The Czar had been forced to relinquish control of Finland in the turmoil of World War I. The same turmoil left Lenin no choice but to allow Finland and a number of other states to break away from the Russian empire. To turn and avenge this setback to communism only revealed one layer of Russian interest in Finland. This northern state represented an age-old part of the Russian empire, formally divorced from Sweden and attached to Russia during the Napoleonic Wars of the early 1800s. Before this point, Peter the Great, the Russian monarch who did so much to build a modern, Russian state, had dueled Sweden for the right to control Finland. In 1939, Stalin may well have told himself and the world that Finland posed an unacceptable security risk, but his path was that of Imperial Russia. In short, his offensive was an act of recreating Russian hegemony in the north, and therefore an act of aggression.

In the Winter War of 1939, the USSR exaggerated the threat Finland posed to its national security and this alarm fueled a Russian preemptive strike that masked a drive to achieve Soviet hegemony along the Baltic seafront. The rationale of self-defense eroded in a number of specific ways. Most importantly, Soviet arguments that Russia faced an imminent threat due to the possibility of another nation occupying Finland to then strike at the USSR did not hold up. Neither Germany nor Britain and France had moved in this direction prior to the Winter War. Nor could Finland pose an imminent threat to Russia, the military odds between the two nations so overwhelmingly in the USSR's favor that numbers alone denied the logic of Soviet preemption. The supposed limited Russian territorial demands appeared reasonable only to Stalin, since Finland worried that once it allowed these first gains, renewed pressure from the USSR would soon mean the loss of its independence. What all of these points add up to was that Finland was not being irrational as they considered their position versus the USSR in the winter of 1939 and remained intransigent during negotiations. Finland understood that it represented a national security concern to the USSR only if Russia was prepared to act as an aggressor. So they understood the fiction of preemption. Clearly Stalin had hegemonic goals in mind when it came to safeguarding Russian territory by reducing the "threat" coming from Finland. This aim undid any bid for morality coming from the self-defense inherent in preemption and saddled Russia with the odious label of aggressors.

CHAPTER 8

Fighting on Ground of Its Own Choosing: The PRC Opts for War in Korea, 1950

Introduction

The first contacts represented a probing effort. Should Chinese soldiers face United Nations (UN) personnel in the field, especially American troops, they would need every advantage to offset the superior firepower of the enemy. Surprise was essential, as was the cover offered by rough terrain. The central mountains of North Korea allowed for both conditions. Chinese forces could mass in the area and still avoid detection, then strike the unsuspecting and overconfident enemy. Even better, perhaps a show of Chinese resolve amounting to no more than a skirmish would be enough to stall the UN advance and to avoid war with the United States and its allies. Should this not be the case, and a war erupted instead, Chinese generals could confirm the belief in their soldiers' ability to confront and stop these western invaders. The first attacks in October 1950 did just that: Chinese soldiers fought well and could clearly stand up to the enemy. There was still a chance that war could be avoided. UN forces appeared timid, road-bound, and lacking the stomach for combat and they quickly came to a standstill. Perhaps they would go no further. But the UN advance resumed in late November and as UN forces moved closer to the Sino-Korean border, the Chinese high command gave the order for a full-scale offensive. This preemptive strike brought Communist China into the Korean War in dramatic fashion, and face-to-face with its main rival, the United States.

The Korean War erupted in mid-1950 and it dominated the early stages of the Cold War. It was an unlikely place for a pivotal battleground, far away from Europe, which was the focus of this ideological struggle between the United States and the USSR. But the Korean situation demanded attention in its own right, a hold-over from World War II that left Korea divided in half at the 38th parallel. Since 1945, a Communist North Korea had faced an anti-Communist South Korea in an uneasy standoff along this political demarcation line. Both sides wished for reunification, and North Korea attacked its neighbor in June 1950 to achieve this end. The offensive was spectacularly successful. But the United States quickly intervened, believing this to be an offensive directed by the Soviet Union. American military forces first prevented a North Korean victory by holding onto the key port of Pusan in the south. The United States then led a counter-attack that expelled the North Koreans from the southern half of the peninsula and threatened the Communist regime in the north with attack. When US troops, under the banner of the United Nations, crossed the 38th parallel and attacked North Korea in October 1950, the armies of Communist China, the People's Republic of China (PRC), crossed the Yalu River, the border between China and Korea, and soon engaged the American army and its UN allies. The Korean War now assumed a different form, a local battleground serving as a main front of the Cold War. For almost three more years the PRC and the United States waged war on the peninsula, killing several million people before agreeing to an uneasy ceasefire in 1953. The Cold War carried on, with Korea smoldering in the background.

The early literature addressing PRC intervention in Korea stresses that Mao's decision revolved around issues of national security. Allen S. Whiting, for example, in *China Crosses the Yalu*, argues that Mao entered Korea to fight a defensive war. This view gained credence due to the numerous studies like William Stueck's *The Road to Confrontation*, or James Matrary's article, "Truman's Plan for Victory: National Self-Determination and the Thirty-Eighth Parallel Decision in Korea," which emphasize the reckless American motives for crossing the 38th parallel, the act that provoked the Chinese to intervene.* In the 1990s, scholars such as Chen Jian, in *China's Road to the Korean War*, and Shu Guang Zhang, in *Deterrence and Strategic Culture*, gained access to Chinese records that allowed them

---

* Allen S. Whiting, *China Crosses the Yalu: The Decision to Enter the Korean War* (New York: Macmillan, 1960); William Stueck, *The Road to Confrontation: American Policy Toward China and Korea, 1947–1950* (Chapel Hill, NC: University of North Carolina, 1981); James I. Matray, "Truman's Plan for Victory: National Self-Determination and the Thirty-Eighth Parallel Decision in Korea," *Journal of American History* 66, no. 2 (September 1979): 314–333.

to offer a more complicated view of the Communist Chinese decision to enter the Korean War. Thanks to this scholarship, the picture is very different. Far from looking to fight a defensive war in Korea, Mao hoped to reconstitute a Chinese nation destined for wars of expansion. The hostilities in Korea served as an early testing ground to achieve this end.* This chapter views Mao's decision to intervene in the Korean War from the perspective of preemptive war. In the process, it casts considerable doubt upon Mao's rationale for war in Korea as one of self-defense in the name of national security, that is, in the name of preemption.

The Case for Preemption

Korea represented an old battlefield for China. At one time a Chinese vassal, in June 1950 Korea stood at the center of the Cold War, a divided peninsula whose two countries, North and South Korea, fought each other to rule one nation. This internal struggle already had prompted one great power, the United States, to intervene in this conflict under the banner of the United Nations to preserve South Korean independence. A few months later, a second and resurgent country, China, was about to intervene in the conflict as well. But in October 1950, something more than a historical attachment to a satellite kingdom swayed Communist China to act preemptively and strike at the imperialist United States.

Mao Zedong, the leader of the newly established People's Republic of China, believed that China should fight the United States in Korea rather than wait until American and UN forces advanced into China from that neighboring country. He reasoned that it was better to fight them over there, on ground of China's choosing, than to wait until they moved on his capital of Beijing. The mountainous terrain in northern Korea would slow down a mechanized army. The opposite was the case should US armored columns reach the open plains in front of Beijing. If this advance came to pass, the principal city of the new Communist state would be virtually defenseless, sure to fall to enemy forces, and Mao's revolution would be over. No, the American aggression had to be stopped in Korea before China faced an insolvable military situation in China itself. Preemption was a matter of national security and for this reason Mao's intervention in Korea rested on the moral high ground of self-defense.

Vital Chinese interests were at stake long before a US advance could threaten Beijing. In Manchuria, along the Sino-Korean border, great

---

* Chen Jian, *China's Road to the Korean War: The Making of the Sino–American Confrontation* (New York: Columbia University Press, 1994); Shu Guang Zhang, *Deterrence and Strategic Culture: Chinese–American Confrontations, 1949–1958* (Ithaca, NY: Cornell University Press, 1992).

hydraulic plants operated in support of a burgeoning Chinese industry. From a larger perspective, the entire northeast of China represented a key industrial region possessing numerous raw materials such as coal and iron. Primarily for this reason, this part of China already had been a battlefield in the recent past. Enemies ranging from Japan and Russia had used military force to control this vital area. Mao was fortunate to have regained Manchuria in the wake of the just concluded Chinese civil war. Should China hope to move forward and become a revitalized and modern state, Manchuria could not fall to an outside power again. Clearly UN forces, once they freed themselves of the fighting in North Korea, posed this risk. This economic imperative dictated a Chinese preemptive attack to forestall a UN invasion seeking the domination of Manchuria.

Acting preemptively in defense of China became all the more crucial once Kim Il-sung, the Communist leader of North Korea, launched his attack south leading to American intervention on the Korean peninsula. Should North Korean efforts to spread communism to South Korea fail, and should North Korea subsequently face an invasion by American and South Korean forces, the Chinese at a minimum wished to preserve a Communist state in North Korea. Mao did not want to see a brother socialist nation fall, particularly one serving as a buffer zone on China's border. Mao also believed he could hardly act otherwise. North Korea had aided the Chinese revolution. Many of its soldiers had fought in Mao's army, the People's Liberation Army (PLA), during China's civil war, and the North Koreans had offered PLA soldiers supplies and transportation when available. This support had significantly aided Mao's cause of liberating and uniting China under his leadership. For China to now extend protection to North Korea was a matter of repaying a debt, of expressing gratitude.

For this reason, from the earliest days of the conflict, Mao exhorted his comrades to prepare China for war in Korea. If the North Koreans successfully overran South Korea, then China could relax its vigil. But with almost immediate American intervention in the Korean War, a defeat of North Korean forces was possible but unacceptable and China would have to be prepared to assist its brother nation. When the fighting stalemated in the south near the city of Pusan in August 1950, Mao and his generals correctly judged that an amphibious attack by UN forces was to be expected and most likely at Inchon, a port far to the rear of the North Korean army fighting in the south. In fact, such an attack did occur on September 15, 1950. But Mao's warnings of the North Korean vulnerability to a counterstroke from the sea went unheeded, and the American offensive was successful and immediately changed the course of the war. Even if North Korea was unprepared for this shift in the fortunes of war, Mao had made sure China was prepared. He redoubled his efforts to launch a Chinese advance into North Korea. As the American forces approached the 38th parallel only a few weeks after landing at Inchon, Mao's armies were ready to intervene and meet this threat.

Mao believed in the need for a preemptive attack for another reason. An American victory in Korea would embolden them and spark more advances in Asia. Turning from Korea, the United States would unleash Chiang Kai-shek, the leader of Nationalist China on Taiwan, to directly threaten the Chinese mainland, or the Americans would support French forces in Vietnam to foster a southern threat to China as well. In short, imperialist forces under American command could encircle the PRC and strike China from multiple directions. An ineffectual Chinese response to such an attack was inevitable given that it would have to defend three fronts at once. This weakness would encourage the Americans and they would accelerate their military action against China, from the outright invasion of Chinese territory via Korea, to the bombing and then occupation of key Chinese cities along its vulnerable coastline. A strong showing by the PRC in Korea would stop this unfavorable scenario in its tracks. Blunted in Korea, the Americans would be less likely to allow Chiang to try a risky sea-borne operation from Taiwan directed at the Chinese mainland. A threat far to the south was serious but far away from Beijing and therefore a more manageable threat than would be a successful attack from Korea or opposite Taiwan. In sum, a preemptive stand in Korea allowed the PRC to plan defensive battles on only two fronts, not three, increasing the chance of a successful defense of China.

Securing the defenses of China was only part of Mao's goals. He also considered his role as a sponsor of international communism. China actively sought to export its revolution on the three fronts threatened by the Americans: Korea, Taiwan, and Indochina. This rationale placed Mao at the forefront of the communist struggle against imperialism in Asia, and he understood that such a position would inevitably lead to conflict with the United States. Early on, Mao desired an alliance with the USSR to deter possible American aggression and he started down this road on June 30, 1949, when he announced China's "leaning to one side" policy. In a world divided between the progressive forces of communism and the reactionary forces of capitalism, China would back the USSR. In return, its Communist brother would offer China reconstruction aid and military protection. China could trust the USSR. All other European nations had a history of imperialism in China. But Russia, having purged itself of such a legacy and now advancing under the banner of socialism, could be invited into China without fear of sacrificing China's national integrity. This belief gained credence with Mao due to Stalin's assurances that the Asian landmass would be left to the PRC to ensure that communism did spread in the region.

Stalin's willingness to turn over this "eastern revolution" to China demonstrated a certain trust in his new partner and Mao welcomed the opportunity to prove his communist mettle.* Furthermore, both countries agreed that the USSR remained the leading progressive force on the international stage. It was a partnership where each party understood its role. This arrangement became formal when the countries signed an alliance on February 14, 1950, with military guarantees of mutual support. Mao's preemptive strike in Korea at the end of that year demonstrated his commitment to this alliance. His intervention amounted to a defense of the communist revolution, a critical goal to achieve since Korea was too important a region to lose in the fight on behalf of international communism.

Ultimately, Mao concluded that a preemptive strike gave China its only opportunity to manage the negative situation certain to arise from American military success in Korea. But it was still a battle Mao did not want to fight. Perhaps a series of diplomatic warnings issued by the PRC to other nations would make it clear to the United States that China no longer was a sleeping giant helpless before their machinations. If necessary, China would resist foreign domination with military force prior to the enemy arriving on Chinese soil. Hopefully, in the face of these overt threats by China, the president of the United States, Harry Truman, would call off the UN invasion of North Korea and not allow his armies to move past the line of demarcation between the two Koreas, the 38th parallel. By using diplomacy, Mao believed he would not have to resort to this step at all.

The warnings appeared very clear indeed. On September 24, 1950, the Chinese complained to UN headquarters that American planes had bombed Chinese territory in Manchuria and protested the additional American "intervention" and "aggression" in Taiwan and Korea respectively. In response, American officials admitted that the attack in Manchuria had occurred and that the United States was willing to pay any damages. Unsatisfied, the PRC soon upped its rhetoric. On September 30, Zhou Enlai, a close confident of Mao, in a speech commemorating the first anniversary of the founding of Communist China, stated that "the Chinese people absolutely will not tolerate foreign aggression nor will they supinely tolerate seeing their neighbors being savagely invaded by imperialists." Zhou also said in this speech that if the North Koreans were pushed back to the Manchurian border, China would "fight outside her borders and not wait for the enemy to come inside." This speech seemed strong evidence that Chinese leaders were willing to fight preemptively in Korea. Zhou followed

---

* Chen, *China's Road to the Korean War*, 74.

up his more general warning of Chinese intervention with an explicit threat of the use of force. On October 3, he told India's ambassador to China, K.M. Panikkar, that if "UN Armed Forces crossed the 38th Parallel China would send troops across [the] frontier [to] participate in [the] defense [of] North Korea." Surely such statements would be enough to stop the United States from advancing past the 38th parallel and threatening China by occupying North Korea.*

While China made it clear that it would intervene in the conflict to resist a UN advance in Korea, the United States dismissed these warnings. Large Chinese troop concentrations did not escape the notice of American intelligence. However, US intelligence personnel questioned the purpose and capability of these troops. Chinese divisions already were in Korea, maybe some 50,000–70,000 strong, but these units consisted of Korean nationals, so they were not considered Chinese but Korean divisions that the PRC had returned to North Korea. The 500,000 or so Chinese troops massing along the Sino-Korean border could be discounted as a sign of Chinese willingness to enter the conflict as well. Many of these soldiers were ex-Nationalist troops and therefore of dubious loyalty to Mao's regime. Most were ill-trained and poorly equipped, so they would not fight well. Given the limitations, they could only be used as regional forces needed to police Manchuria. This view that these soldiers were there for internal defense matched US intelligence assumptions that the PRC faced far too much disruption at home to risk war in Korea.

There also were cautionary statements from PRC officials. For instance, on September 25, Chu Teh, commander of the People's Liberation Army, stated that China would not become involved in a "world war" at this time. For this reason, Chu said that Chinese troops would not be sent into Korea, although China remained sympathetic to the Korean people and would give them other forms of aid. In regards to India, American officials questioned the credibility of Panikkar because he had shown "distinct communist leanings and anti-American feelings in the past." Even in India his reports were suspect. American officials believed China was using Panikkar to bluff the United States into not crossing the 38th parallel to advance into North Korea. For those having to make the decision whether or not to invade the communist country, such an advance was now more palatable given that UN forces were unlikely to meet Chinese resistance in Korea.

---

* These quotes, as well as US intelligence estimates and the assessments by diplomatic personnel on the following page, are taken from Chapter 4 of my master's thesis, "Gauging Enemy Intentions." See Matthew J. Flynn, "The Decision to Cross the 38th Parallel" (master's thesis, San Diego State University, 1996).

The American dismissal of these Chinese warnings must have convinced Mao that war in Korea fit a larger pattern of foreign aggression directed at China. Korea was a proven gateway to China. Japan had defeated Chinese forces there in 1894, leaving the island nation in control of Korea. Japan then seized Manchuria in the early 1930s, and continued to advance, occupying Beijing and large areas of southern China. Mao had just won a long war enabling China to reconstitute itself and he was not going to allow an international effort under the guise of the United Nations to occupy Korea and repeat this same process of advancing in the north via Korea resulting in a Chinese national crisis.

That the United States led this new threat made the situation in Korea even worse. While posing as a friend to China in the past, the record of recent US aggression at China's expense laid this fiction to rest. First, the United States had done little to support China in its death struggle against Japan. Only after Japan attacked the United States, thereby drawing that nation into World War II, did the US government accelerate its aid to China. If this practicality was understandable—the United States hoped to avoid war with Japan—once in the struggle, how this aid was distributed by the Roosevelt administration was inexcusable. America supported Chiang, Mao's mortal enemy. The attempt by several US diplomats to send aid to the Chinese Communists during World War II was dismissed by Mao as an aberration. More typical was what occurred at the end of World War II. In the closing stages of the war, two Marine divisions landed at the port of Tianjin and advanced and occupied Beijing. Tianjin had served past invaders in like capacity. Added to the old fear of the capital's vulnerability was the ease with which the Americans rapidly reached Beijing from that port city. With Japan defeated, the American forces did not stay long in the capital, a welcomed development but one offset by an increasing US propensity to support Chiang in the ensuing Chinese civil war. Aid continued to pour in and arm the Nationalist military forces. American airpower intervened at times to give Chiang an edge, as it did in 1945 and 1946 when US planes airlifted Nationalist troops to northern China, to Manchuria, this to inhibit the advance of Mao's army in the area. To Mao it was clear the United States was an enemy of the Chinese Communist Party (CCP) and it was very probable the United States was an enemy of China as well, given its military activities there over the past ten years.

US military activities in Asia were not confined to China alone. In 1945, US forces arrived in Korea and established the southern state. They withdrew in 1947, but left the puppet nation of South Korea under the control of Syngman Rhee. A return to defend their client state in 1950 surprised Mao in that the struggle against American imperialism came to China's doorstep sooner than he anticipated. Given the ideological differences between China and the United States, a showdown was inevitable, but Mao had assumed the United States was too weak militarily both to defend Europe and to engage in adventurism in Asia, so he had believed that war between China and America would not come for many years. That the American "imperialists" acted otherwise and looked to humble Chinese power by fighting in Korea merely convinced Mao that the United States had nothing but contempt for China. This arrogance added to an already clear track record: the United States possessed a keen interest in the Asian mainland and such interference in Korea closely mirrored past aggression by Japan. If China had not fought, or was unable to fight, successfully in the past, Mao was determined that this would not be the case in 1950. To avoid the humiliation of foreign domination, China would have to fight in Korea and to fight there on favorable terms meant launching a preemptive attack.

In 1950, however, Mao did not wish to go to war. China was devastated after thirty-plus years of conflict and in no position to continue fighting. Looking to focus on rehabilitation at home, war was a last resort. With this in mind, the PLA, an institution that had done so much to win the war, now took center stage in the rebuilding of China. The army turned out in great numbers to help peasants raise crops, reclaim lands for planting, and perform other tasks that promised to speed China's economic recovery after so many years of war and bloodshed. Together, the army and the people would form an unbeatable combination for the Communists by acting as a force of liberation. Industry received as much attention from Mao as he sought to industrialize China with a dynamic proletariat. As a result of this shift of emphasis, output would grow, product quality improve, and worker contentment rise to unprecedented levels of satisfaction with the end of low wages, long hours, and miserable working conditions. Communism in China promised rapid industrialization, but CCP leaders would accomplish this end without exploiting workers. Next Mao strove to overcome China's longstanding problem of national unity. The question remained, just what were the Communists going to do with the country's many non-Chinese populations? The PRC's news outlets loudly broadcast that the government would give "minority" Chinese their freedom. In response, the "liberated" peoples, such as the Manchurians in the north, the Moslem peoples in Sinking to the west, the Tibetans to the southwest, and the people of Taiwan if that island fell to Mao, would begin to enjoy the benefits of the Communist system. In return, they would extend their gracious support to the new regime. The political unrest afflicting China would end as a PRC ascendancy ushered in a new period of national unity. A war would only spoil the objective of achieving these ambitious goals and healing China. But the fight loomed anyway given American intransigence, so preemption would serve China best since the war would occur in Korea. In this way a reprieve could be won at home and Mao still could rebuild China even if forced to fight an unwanted war.

The Attack

After the UN counterstroke at Inchon on September 15, 1950, North Korean resistance collapsed and UN forces stood poised to overrun the country and establish a unified Korea hostile to the PRC. From this base, the UN command could threaten China. Considering this security risk unacceptable, Mao believed he had no choice but to act. Fortunately, he had been preparing for this eventuality since the beginning of the conflict and now his foresight paid off. By October, some 600,000 PRC soldiers were ready to enter North Korea, under the command of Peng Dehuai, a tough and trusted officer. More forces were available should they be needed. The attacking force included some of his best armies, transferred from positions opposite Taiwan where they had been preparing to attack that island. Officially, he labeled the intervening force the Chinese People's Volunteers (CPV). In this way, the PRC was not at war in Korea and the USSR would not have to exercise its security agreement with China and also be drawn into the fray. With the forces deployed and Stalin seemingly in support, all appeared to be ready.

Despite the foresight, Mao's plans immediately ran into problems. On the eve of the crossing, Stalin informed him that he would get no air cover from the USSR. This development forced Mao to reconvene the Politburo and again review the decision to go to war in Korea. Many of those present opposed intervention, arguing that without air cover, Chinese soldiers would be too exposed to enemy firepower and suffer tremendously. It already was a formidable task, taking on a superpower like the United States when Chinese armies were lacking all the modern weapons of war. To do so without air cover appeared suicidal. This resistance within the Communist inner circle prompted Mao to do his best to gain support for intervention. He repeated his worries of UN attacks into China, of a loss of prestige for socialism, and of the need for China to seize the initiative in defending itself. A war in Korea served all of these purposes. More than that, he argued forcefully that US firepower could not match the PRC foot soldier because of his dedication to the ideological struggle at hand. The ability of socialism to tap this human reservoir would spell the difference in the coming battle and would do so in China's favor. Soviet air cover meant little for this reason alone. With Mao's decision obviously made, the senior leaders of the PRC relented and agreed to war. Chinese forces crossed the Yalu River on October 19, 1950, and moved into positions in the mountainous terrain of North Korea.

Chinese military intervention in Korea then became a reality at the end of October as elements of two PRC armies successfully engaged the two wings of the advancing UN forces. On October 25, 1950, Chinese forces attacked the South Korean (ROK) 6th Division of the Eighth Army at Onjong, a village 30 miles from the Chinese border in the western portion of northern Korea. Even with a hasty retreat, much of that ROK division was destroyed in a matter of days. A short time later it was the Americans' turn. On the night of November 1, Chinese forces attacked the 1st Cavalry Division at Unsan, just 10 miles southwest of the ROK 6th Division at Onjong. At least one battalion of this division shared the fate of the Korean division and was cut off and destroyed. The rest of the 1st Cavalry remained intact but Chinese pressure forced it back below the Ch'ongch'on River. Soon the entire Eighth Army retreated to the safety of defensive positions along the river.

On the eastern half of the Korean Peninsula, the American X Corps fared much better than did the Eighth Army when Chinese forces first intervened. On October 26, Chinese resistance halted the advance of the ROK 3rd Division toward the Chosin Reservoir. Elements of the 1st Marine Division reinforced this ROK unit on November 1 and the advance continued, the Marines eventually reaching the base of the reservoir on November 10. The other American division of X Corps, the 7th, supported the advance of the ROK Capital Division. This ROK division was at the forefront of the UN advance, streaking forward to capture the port city of Songjin on the far northeast coast of Korea. Neither the 7th Division nor the ROK Capital Division encountered any Chinese opposition. Moreover, at the end of October, the X Corps had not suffered any Chinese attacks of significance. The X Corps, however, like the Eighth Army, could confirm the presence of a new enemy in Korea, the Chinese Communists. And like the Eighth Army, X Corps was spread out and vulnerable to attack.

Then the Chinese attacks ceased. The Americans, confused but undaunted, resumed the advance with the Eighth Army operating on the western half of the peninsula, the X Corps on the eastern half. At the end of November, the Chinese struck again and overwhelmed many South Korean and American units. A Chinese attack destroyed the entire ROK II Corps, leaving the right flank of the Eighth Army exposed and vulnerable to attack. The American 24th Division, in the lead along the west coast of Korea, was hastily withdrawn. This time X Corps shared the fate of Eighth Army and was heavily counterattacked by Chinese forces. The 1st Marine Division, attempting to advance northwest from the Chosan Reservoir, was stopped by heavy Chinese resistance. This was on November 27. By the next day, the Chinese had isolated two regiments of this division. There could be no mistaking Chinese intervention at this point.

For the Chinese, things went as anticipated and they achieved complete surprise when they did attack. In a short time, the UN command faced a crisis. MacArthur sent a message to the Joint Chiefs of Staff in Washington DC stating, "We face an entirely new war" with the Chinese objective the "complete destruction of all United Nations forces in Korea."* This goal was within the reach of the Chinese as the renewed advance of UN forces had exposed MacArthur's command to complete defeat. Spread out and now deployed in isolated columns, the only course of action was to withdraw the forces of both the Eighth Army and the X Corps as fast as possible. Whether or not the ensuing retreat was a rout or an orderly withdrawal is unclear. What is clear is that the Chinese were on the attack and in position to inflict a major and humiliating defeat on the UN forces in Korea.

Chinese intervention was so successful that Mao expanded Chinese operations into a general offensive. He now hoped to drive UN forces from South Korea altogether. This step meant Chinese armies advanced south and soon reached the 38th parallel themselves. Mao did not hesitate to order the advance to continue. Seoul fell in the first week of January 1951. At this point, however, the offensive waned. The path south had taken a great toll on the Chinese soldiers. Combat losses had been heavy, and UN firepower had made a great impact. Supply became a problem as Mao's soldiers moved further away from China. The antiquated system of support had great difficulty moving food, ammunition, and medicine long distances, and what logistical support the Chinese possessed came under steady UN air attack. Exhaustion and increased UN resistance meant the Chinese offensive stalled in mid-January 1951.

After the Chinese offensive came to halt, it was now the turn of the UN command to take the next step in the Korean War. A new UN commander, General Matthew Ridgeway, launched an offensive in January. His primary aim was to inflict the maximum amount of casualties on the Chinese forces, and in this end he succeeded. In a month UN forces again reached the 38th parallel. This time around, however, Washington halted the attack, content to leave the peninsula divided between North and South Korea. The fighting did not abate, however. With Korea now a key point of conflict in the Cold War, battles won here served as a measure of ascendancy in the overall

---

* A frequently quoted statement. See again my master's thesis, "The Decision to Cross the 38th Parallel," 90; and William Stueck, *The Korean War: An International History* (Princeton, NJ: Princeton University Press, 1995), 119.

struggle of communism versus imperialism. The bloodshed continued for over two years before all parties wearied of this yardstick. Mercifully the combatants declared an armistice on July 27, 1953, and an uneasy truce descended on the peninsula that still exists today.

Success

By the measure of the duration of the conflict, preemption failed. Mao had hoped for a short war but he lost this gamble and the end result in Korea was a deadly war stalemated along the 38th parallel. Stalemate meant an increased risk to China's security as the Americans hinted at the use of atomic weapons against China to force an end to the fighting. A new American president, Dwight D. Eisenhower, openly sanctioned this option. Mao's bravado that he did not fear a nuclear threat was put to the test, and Mao relented at the peace table to avoid pushing the "paper tiger" further. He also had to consider the state of his own forces. The hardships of exposure to weather, a lack of food, and the punishing military attacks by UN artillery and air power against PRC soldiers in Korea had taken a great toll. If Mao could express satisfaction that his soldiers had met the US army on the battlefield and performed admirably, the losses they had suffered in the process were enormous. Should a clash occur on less favorable terrain, would not the losses escalate to prohibitive levels? The fighting in Korea certainly had created some doubt as to whether Mao could trade lives endlessly in the name of defending China. Mao had tested what Shu Guang Zhang labeled in *Mao's Military Romanticism* his romantic notions about the Chinese soldier, and a rational view would dictate that the Chinese soldier could not withstand a war with the west, given western technological advantages.* It was possible that the west might be encouraged by this discovery and attack China. In this respect, Mao had put Chinese security at greater risk by fighting in Korea.

Mao seemed not to notice or to care. Success in Korea in terms of engaging the military might of the United States, and in Mao's view confirming its limited capabilities of impacting China, emboldened him to act more forcefully elsewhere in the very near future. After all, Korea was but one front where the PRC felt it needed to engage imperialist forces. In 1954, a year after the armistice in Korea, Mao refocused his attention on Taiwan and confronted Chiang by shelling two small islands close to mainland China that served as outposts for the defense of the Republic of China. Once again this brash move brought the intervention of the United

---

* Zhang, *Mao's Military Romanticism: China and the Korean War, 1950–1953* (Lawrence, KS: University Press of Kansas, 1995), 10–11.

States and initiated a war of nerves that prompted the United States to declare its willingness to use nuclear weapons to defend Taiwan from a PRC invasion. Mao again altered course before the crisis reached a point where these weapons were used. In this respect, he backed away from a confrontation, meaning that he really did fear American military power. This conclusion has to be true to a great extent. But the additional point to consider is that with intervention in Korea, Mao had seized the initiative in the Cold War. His actions that created a crisis in the Taiwan Straits on two occasions, 1954 and again in 1958, merely spoke to learning the lesson of Korea: that it was better to dictate the crisis points of a Cold War that produced so many crisis points. The war in Korea after PRC involvement created a certain momentum for him and Mao did not wish to lose it. In this way, China could avoid being caught on a three-front war over Korea, Taiwan, and Indochina. By this measure, preemption in Korea was successful since it gained Mao the initiative, allowing him to pick his battlefields.

He was only partly successful. Korea and Taiwan remained hotspots that required Chinese attention, and Vietnam erupted into a war involving the United States though not China directly. China watched as US support of non-communist South Vietnam once again brought a large American army near China's border, this time in the south. A three-front war had become a reality, even if two of those fronts were relatively quiescent and the other remained a front in which China was not directly involved. Curiously enough, Mao's response was to open more battlefronts. China soon found itself involved in border clashes with India in 1962, and then with its erstwhile ally, the USSR in 1969. The home front also had to be listed as a battlefront since Mao embarked on radical new experiments to modernize China, such as the Great Leap Forward and the Cultural Revolution. These events had multiple causes, but one factor had to be the Korean conflict that strained Chinese relations with the USSR, overly burdened the home front, and created a bravado that circumscribed Mao's freedom of action. After 1950, because of "successful" intervention in Korea, Mao found himself trying to prove the value of the Communist state of China time after time. But China buckled under his efforts to do just this and preemption exacted a heavy toll indeed.

Preemption did have its clear successes. The war in Korea undoubtedly prevented a possible UN ground attack into China from this direction. Even should this attack never have been considered by UN commanders, Chinese intervention so surprised US leaders that they took great care to limit the fighting to Korea. If China now faced a limited war in Korea, so too did their enemies. The long-term results of Mao's war in Korea also point to the success of preemption. True, hostility plagued Sino–US relations for the next twenty years. But China eventually earned US recognition, won admittance to the United Nations, and took its place as a key power in the region. Indeed, Mao's stand in Korea can certainly be viewed as a first step in this direction, a reconstituting of China that made its role in world affairs prominent and one that could not be ignored. In other words, PRC intervention in Korea had put China on the road to great power status, a success that has to be attributed to Mao, at least in part, no matter the contradictory motives that included a validation of socialism as well as a restoration of the Chinese empire.

Conclusion

In Korea in 1950, Mao believed he acted in the name of self-defense because of the validity of his national security fears. No matter US protests that it had no aggressive attentions toward China, its formidable armed forces stood at the head of a sizeable international coalition advancing toward the Sino–Korean border. If US decision makers placed no credence in Chinese history, Mao did. Here was the old gateway to China that past invaders had taken to invade China. Why would this be any different in 1950? To find out, Mao issued a series of diplomatic warnings to UN forces not to threaten China by advancing past the 38th parallel to occupy North Korea. The Americans ignored these warnings and invaded North Korea anyway. The arrogance western leaders exhibited toward China by dismissing PRC threats to fight in Korea confirmed Mao's belief that a UN advance into China was likely after the successful American conquest of North Korea. Given UN belligerence, the question became how best to engage a technologically superior enemy. A preemptive strike into North Korea by Chinese forces would allow China to fight on ground of its own choosing, consisting of mountainous terrain, advantageous to PLA soldiers in that it neutralized enemy firepower by offering good cover. By fighting in Korea, PRC forces had a good chance of shielding China from invasion.

Even though consumed by the fear of a triumphant United States on his doorstep, Mao showed great restraint. He issued a series of statements warning that China would fight in Korea if the UN advanced past the 38th parallel. Even after this advance occurred, he again showed great moderation in that he allowed a UN advance past the 38th parallel as long as UN forces stopped at the waist of the peninsula, that is, short of the Chinese border. Only after UN forces continued to advance to the Chinese border did Mao order his soldiers into North Korea. This restraint was a bold gesture considering that key Chinese economic resources lay within reach of the UN advance. Mao needed the hydraulic plants near the Korean border and the resources of Manchuria to rebuild China. By waiting and risking an attack on this vital infrastructure and possibly losing these raw materials, Mao appeared willing to go to great lengths to avoid a clash with UN forces in Korea and he acted only at the last possible moment and when China had no choice but to act. Mao then broke off his initial attacks to see if UN forces would retreat or at least stop attacking. They advanced instead. Therefore, the measures he took were in self-defense, his decision to cross the Yalu River tied to ensuring China's national security.

Seizing the initiative by fighting preemptively in Korea also was essential to allow the PRC to spread the communist revolution on the Asian mainland. China looked to strike a blow for communism against either Taiwan or Indochina. Taiwan needed to be secured to complete the Chinese phase of the revolution by eliminating the last vestiges of the Nationalist regime still holding out on the island. It was a priority target for this reason. It also seemed a ripe target. The Americans had not intervened militarily on Chiang's behalf during his final days on the mainland. Nor did they appear anxious to help him defend Taiwan. In early January 1950, Truman proclaimed Taiwan part of China, strongly suggesting that the United States would not stop a PRC assault on the island. Then Secretary of State Dean Acheson omitted Taiwan from the US defense perimeter in East Asia. Committed to defending Europe and facing pressure from the international community not to intervene in an internal Chinese affair, the United States had detached itself from Chiang. Chiang was alone and a quick strike by the PRC was certain to succeed.

Indochina also was important as a proving ground of China's ability to export its revolution. Mao's close ties with Vietnam's revolutionary hero Ho Chi Minh proved that the revolution indeed was spreading, and it also underscored China's determination to lean-to-one-side and back a brother socialist nation. Furthermore, while the USSR received Ho favorably as well, it expected China to take the lead and guide his fledging government. Support of Ho would be a test of China's ability to spread communism in Asia. Moreover, hostile imperialist forces to the south of China would be an obvious threat to Chinese national security. That a significant portion of Chiang's forces had fled to this region after Mao's victory in southern China served as an added incentive; the PRC could eliminate this potential threat. Last, the failure of the Vietnamese revolution would weaken China's international prestige, highlighting the PRC's inability to advance the cause of socialism. For these reasons, Mao pledged China's full support to Ho.

When the Americans did intervene in Korea, Mao and key leaders of the PRC fretted over how best to fight on one front without leaving China vulnerable to attack on another front. They had no choice but to rearrange their priorities. Mao cancelled further preparations to attack Taiwan and moved that invasion army to the Sino–Korean border. Mao ordered his generals advising the Vietnamese to try to delay any planned Vietnamese offensive in Indochina. In something of a surprise development, Korea would be the main proving ground for the spread of the communist doctrine. Here the United States directly challenged China and Mao was determined to meet this challenge. A preemptive war in Korea would force UN forces to remain there and not allow their redeployment to China's two other fronts, Taiwan and southern China. This in turn meant the Chinese home front would be spared another round of fighting, and therefore it would be able to heal its deep wounds from past wars. This reprieve was dearly needed given the devastation China had suffered in almost three decades of warfare. Should Korea be the main front of US imperialism directed against China, Mao would be ready, armed with the moral righteousness of self-defense.

The mantle of self-defense was not absolute, however. How seriously Mao pursued diplomatic warnings is an open question. They could have served his purpose of preparing the home front for war, and so controlling the volatile situation there. The CCP leadership took deliberate and effective steps to do just this. If the army helped liberate the country, it also served as the defender of the new regime, enforcing the decree to end lawlessness in a country grown accustomed to warfare. When the PLA moved to confiscate the abundant firearms present in the cities and in the countryside after years of conflict, China's population could only hold its breath as the army became an institution used by the government to consolidate its power. Additionally, the government used employment of the new worker to further its political control of China. Once assigned to a job, employees could seldom change their occupation. They almost always found themselves confined to the city where that work took them. Only slowly did workers realize that job security and full employment bound them to the government as much as the vigilant stares of army personnel. Last, PRC ascendancy did usher in a new period of national unity for China. But Taiwan remained an obvious exception to this new nationalism, and early on the PRC faced challenges from its minority populations that did not want to be part of the new Communist state.

Mao was confident his government would overcome these challenges but they served to draw attention to the fact that the Communist regime's appeals for national unity simply represented a new chapter to an old story: a central power struggling to assert its political control of China. A Chinese population fearing renewed foreign control might respond favorably to the continued commitment to China's revolution, if for no other reason than to defend China. To this end, Mao threatened China with fears of a US invasion if the PRC did not fight in Korea. Moreover, he told his people that the PRC leadership had made every effort to avoid such a conflict but to no avail. This clever conflating of two not necessarily related ends—establishing political control at home and meeting an outside threat to China—would allow Mao to consolidate his rule. So Mao welcomed a war with the United States. Even better, while the United States posed a long-term danger to communism, it did not directly threaten China. The US menace was remote enough to make it the perfect enemy to keep the home front in check. Having convinced himself that the Americans were too weak to fight in Asia, too distracted, American intervention in Korea was a surprise to Mao. But it also presented him with an opportunity. With war on its doorstep, the Chinese nation would have to follow Mao, or face possible foreign occupation and national humiliation once again. In this way, preemption served as a political device, not as a means of self-defense.

Mao may have convinced himself that war in Korea would be in the defense of socialism, but was this the true motive? More likely, he linked Korea to Taiwan and to southern China because a communist success on each front would reconstitute a Chinese empire as much as it would vindicate the arrival of a socialist ascendancy in the world. He wanted a war that would advance the socialist revolution to return China to the splendor of its ancient past. In his own mind, these ends did not have to be exclusive of one another; on the contrary, they could feed off one another. However, the two ends could not be linked, given that his communist ideology forswore any such imperialistic act. Ultimately, Mao was tied to an ideological purpose that contradicted his sense of Chinese nationalism.

His lack of coordination with Kim and Stalin may have been due to their recognition of this underlying tone of Chinese resurgence. Kim and Stalin wished to curb this result while Mao looked to foster it. Mao stepped carefully. He made sure that when Chinese intervention came, it was preceded by calls of friendship and respect for North Korea and Kim, a clear nod to the sensitivity Koreans may have felt toward Chinese troops on their soil given the history of Chinese suzerainty in the region. In addition, Mao's armies came in under the title of Chinese People's Volunteers, a name ostensibly chosen to shield the USSR from being drawn into the war, but one also chosen to assuage North Korean fears of Chinese occupation. Mao wished to make it clear to Koreans that China did not wish to establish political control over Korea as it had in the past. Should this assurance not be offered, Mao feared that North Korean suspicions in response to the arrival of PRC forces in North Korean would produce a fall-out between the two communist states that could endanger the entire enterprise.

Mao's fears were well-founded, since before this point Kim had been less than cooperative. As he planned his attack, Kim held council with the USSR and only belatedly notified Mao of his decision to attack South Korea. Once the fighting started, Kim rebuffed the efforts of Chinese advisers to enter North Korea and observe the situation. In response, the PRC increased its diplomatic personnel, adding important military observers to keep the PRC informed as to the developments of the fighting. The obfuscation was doubly useful, appeasing the North Koreans and hiding from the Americans a Chinese military presence in Korea. But this step represented the extreme circumlocution necessary to alleviate North Korean fears of Chinese intrusion into the peninsula. In the end, North Korea allowed Chinese intervention only when having no recourse due to the UN victory at Inchon and the advance of UN forces past the 38th parallel into North Korean territory. Clearly Kim feared Chinese expansion and he relented only when facing obliteration at the hands of UN armies.

Stalin was just as cautious when dealing with Mao. The Soviet premier offered his support of Chinese intervention in Korea, but Russian assistance had distinct limits. Most importantly, Stalin did not wish to be drawn into a war against the United States. To calm this fear, Mao agreed with Stalin to label the Chinese soldiers entering Korea volunteers. Given this equivocation, China was not entering the conflict. Should the United States declare war on the PRC after encountering Chinese forces in Korea, Stalin would not feel obligated to honor his treaty obligations with China and declare war on the United States. Then, in October 1950, after Mao had given the go-ahead to Chinese forces to enter North Korea, Stalin refused to honor his pledge of air support for the CPV forces, disrupting the entire plan of Chinese intervention. This seeming betrayal required Mao to hold another Politburo meeting to again reaffirm the decision to intervene in the absence of Soviet air support. Previously, Mao had faced much opposition from within the CCP regarding his wish to send Chinese armies into Korea to face the Americans. He had succeeded in overcoming this dissent largely by emphasizing that aid from the USSR, air cover in particular, would make the task of standing up to American firepower—the key worry—a manageable endeavor. This time around, Mao again squelched opposition within communist ranks at home and successfully advocated for Chinese intervention in Korea, but thanks to Stalin's wavering on the issue of air cover, Mao had suffered much embarrassment among CCP leadership in the process.

The fact is the communist war in Korea in the name of socialism clearly had aroused suspicions among supposed allies. Mao was not above such suspicions. That he still insisted on Chinese intervention after Stalin reneged on his promise of air cover pointed to something more than an unyielding dedication to spreading the communist revolution. More than likely, he wished to assert Chinese independence from the USSR. This point became all the more probable since Stalin's foot dragging in 1950 certainly reminded Mao of the USSR's poor treatment of the Chinese Communists during the Chinese Civil War. China would no longer be held hostage to the whims of the USSR. Testing the ability of the Chinese soldier to stand up to a modern army was essential to achieving this independence of action, since the PLA would serve as the tool to reassert Chinese autonomy. A preemptive strike in Korea allowed China this opportunity by serving Mao's expansionist designs that looked to return China as a prominent actor on the world stage.

Such discord among the Communist leaders deciding Korea's fate strongly suggests that Mao viewed the spread of communism as a mere bonus to acting preemptively. In a larger sense, Mao's call for revolutionary expansion masked his aim to make China a great power in Asia. Stalin and Kim were not fooled. They recognized this concomitant result to China's patronage of the socialist revolution and looked to limit Mao's triumphs. Stalin hoped to pit the PRC against America in a war in Korea to make China dependent on the USSR. In this way, he could control Mao. Kim turned to the USSR as his chief patron to keep the Chinese at bay, reversing this position only when military necessity left him no choice. No matter the assumed communist harmony, the PRC and the Soviet Union remained rival powers using North Korea to battle for supremacy in Asia. To this list could also be added the state of North Vietnam, since Ho Chi Minh also feared Chinese expansionist designs in Southeast Asia. Mao, for his part, continued to play the role of advancing socialism in Asia and so mollify his fellow dictators. In more private moments, he dreamed of a Chinese empire. A war in Korea meant that this empire might not be that far off.

In either case, whether spreading communism or returning China to its past glory, Mao ordered Chinese intervention in Korea in the name of expanding Chinese power, not self-defense, and this goal painted him as an aggressor. The aim of protecting China certainly was achieved as well, but shielding China from attack served only as opportunity. Mao portrayed the UN presence in North Korea as an imminent threat in order to advance Chinese interests. He was an empire builder, much as the Chinese emperors who had wielded power before him. In striving for something more than protecting China, he lost the slender justification he had for preemptive war; a UN attack into China was never a certainty, only a supposition on Mao's part, one largely resting on historical precedent. In his haste to fight his enemy in Korea so he did not have to fight them in China, Mao conflated two reasons for war: self-defense and a drive for Chinese hegemony on the Asian landmass. Infatuated by what a policy of preemption could do for him, Mao hoped to reinstate an empire that he believed rightfully belonged to China. In pursuing this end, the PRC entered the ranks of aggressor nations waging war to serve interests that had little to do with self-defense and therefore little to do with a preemptive purpose for war.

CHAPTER 9

Being Everywhere at Once: Israel Defeats the Arab League, 1967

Introduction

The first wave of planes approached the target while flying very low and the pilots readied themselves to make the assault. A number of things had to unfold quickly and all of those things had to go well in order for the attack to succeed. The Israeli planes first ascended to trigger radar detection protecting the airfields. The fighters then closed in on the air base, looking for the Egyptian planes lined up next to the airfields or trying to get down the runway and into the air. They were easy victims. The first Israeli planes destroyed the aircraft attempting to take off. Successive fighters and bombers smashed the planes lined up along the runway. Success was overwhelming and largely accomplished in fifteen minutes. This scene repeated itself at nine different airfields all under attack at the same time. Israeli success in the air would be repeated on the ground, and Israel soon found itself victorious in a war that had demanded it accomplish the impossible. Outnumbered, facing numerous and intransigent enemies, the Israelis used preemption to turn the tables on their enemies. The Six Day War appeared to underscore the value of preemption in starting a war, although the totality of the military success could not dispel the more uncertain political fallout of this war. As usual, preemption may have provided the rationale for getting into a war, but it did not promise to secure a lasting success from the war.

The Six Day War was one of a series of wars the Israelis have fought against their Arab neighbors since the creation of the Jewish state in 1948. This war in 1967 occupies a key place in the history of these conflicts, given the Israeli success and the manner it was achieved—using preemption. In a matter of days, the Israelis successfully engaged and defeated five Arab states, no matter being outnumbered and facing an unfavorable strategic situation. It is hard to imagine a more complete Israeli success. At the end of the war Israel took possession of the Golan Heights in the north, mountainous terrain that separated Syria and Israel. Opposite the frontier with Jordan, the Israelis captured the West Bank, protecting the Jewish state from an attack to its center. And in the south, Israel overran the Sinai Peninsula, dealing a severe military blow to Egypt in the process. Absorbing these territorial possessions was one success. A second was achieving these objectives in just six days; Israel could not fight a long war. These successes are a testimonial to preemption, but also a reminder of the limits of "winning" such a war. This conflict in 1967 was followed by another in 1973, as Egypt attacked Israel and again brought crisis to the region. Even after the last Arab–Israeli war in 1982, the fighting has continued, assuming the form of Arab terrorism reaching into Israel and opposed by Israeli counter-measures. The 1967 conventional victory did not end Israel's struggles.

The Six Day War is universally hailed as a preemptive war and one that Israel openly labeled as such. In flattering terms, the Israelis recount their success. The Arabs offer a decidedly different view, dismissing the Israeli success as a product of aggression, not preemption. At stake is the moral high ground. Those scholars assigning preemption to Israel and doing so in favorable terms stress that Israel's goal was the preservation of the Jewish state. There was no larger purpose. This chapter assesses this claim of a morality born of using preemption as a means of self-defense, and of the absence of a hegemonic or civilizing motive in Israel's Six Day War.

The Case for Preemption

Surrounded on all sides by hostile powers, Israel faced a very bad strategic situation as it contemplated its fate in 1967. Four enemies could be found on its borders. Egypt in the south presented the most formidable opponent. Its armed forces were large and it had assumed a leadership role in fomenting antagonism toward Israel among the Arab states. Gamal Abdel Nasser, president of Egypt, was a magnetic personality who championed Arab nationalism and did so by stressing the need for the Arab states to destroy Israel. Jordan sat along Israel's eastern border. There a more timid ruler than Nasser, King Hussein, commanded an army of much more modest size than Egypt's. But Jordan's proximity to Israel made this state a threat no matter its military limitations. North of Jordan, a second great enemy of Israel lay in waiting in Syria. This state again fielded a large army and its hostility to Israel was as pronounced as that of Egypt. The threat from Syria was one that had to be taken very seriously. Finally, Lebanon appeared willing to engage Israel along its northern border. A state plagued by internal problems and one with a small army, Lebanon could be discounted as a threat to a large extent. But should it work in tandem with the other Arab states, Israel would have to assign units to defend this frontier, units needed elsewhere.

The task of defending the Jewish state was complicated by Israel's geography. It was small in size, one with a salient in its midsection leaving Israel no more than ten miles wide and inviting a thrust there that would cut the country in half. Its separate parts could then be overwhelmed by its enemies in a short period of time. A look at the map made it clear the Israelis could not await an attack. They simply could not absorb such a blow and survive. To fight defensively invited the physical destruction of the state and an enormous loss of life trying to prevent this result. Preemption would rectify this problem. Such an attack would feature an offensive thrust into the neighboring countries, sparing Israel a war on its soil. The ground would be of Israel's choosing since the initiative would lie with the Jewish state. In this way, casualties could be kept to a minimum, the prospects for success greatly enhanced.

The numbers opposing Israel were as distressing. In the months preceding the outbreak of fighting in 1967, Egypt reinforced its troops on Sinai from 30,000 soldiers to 100,000. Six full divisions and armor totaling 900 tanks now bolstered the Egyptian position nearest Israel. In the north lay another 75,000 Syrian troops and 400 tanks. Worse, this force occupied some vital high ground, the Golan Heights. Situated on this terrain, the Syrians commanded this area due to their ability to survey the surrounding countryside from this advantageous position. On the Jordanian frontier, King Hussein deployed 32,000 soldiers and 300 tanks, including his elite armored units, the 40th and the 60th Brigades. All told, over 300,000 Arab soldiers and 2,300 tanks encircled Israel. It was a formidable force, outnumbering the Israelis two to one in manpower, three to one in tanks. Nor was this tally complete. In the air, the Arabs also enjoyed a three to one advantage: over 900 Arab planes facing only 250 combat aircraft of the Israeli Air Force (IAF). Added to this were a few other states that looked to join the Arab coalition. Iraq pledged to send four brigades and another 150 tanks to Jordan. Kuwait offered an armored brigade to Egypt. Even more support was promised from Morocco, Libya, Saudi Arabia and Tunisia, all hoping to participate in the annihilation of Israel. Taken altogether, the Arab states massing their armed forces against Israel assumed such a powerful front that Israel's ability to defend itself appeared impossible.

Finally, Israel's hostile neighbors appeared unwilling to negotiate with the Jewish state. The rhetoric coming from the Arab nations was vehement and candid in its intentions. Nasser's Egypt again took the lead. Radio Cairo announced on May 16 that "All of Egypt, with her human, economic, and scientific potential, is now ready to throw herself into a general war which will put an end to Israel's threats." As Egypt reinforced Sinai, one of its generals went on a broadcast of the Voice of the Arabs and declared, "Our forces are absolutely ready to carry the battle outside Egypt's frontier."* Nasser himself put things in stark terms when he publicly stated on May 28 that, "We plan to open a general assault on Israel. This will be total war. Our basic aim is the destruction of Israel."** The Syrian public address system proclaimed Arab solidarity: "The annihilation of Israel is a necessary step for the establishment of a life of freedom and honor for the Arab people."*** Such talk could not be dismissed as mere posturing among Arab states trying to gain political clout to bully one another. These statements amounted to genuine threats to Israel. And given the apparent Arab unity and the shared purpose of destroying Israel, Israel could not hope to fracture the Arab alliance and lessen the numbers against it. It seemed an impossible situation and Arab confidence in victory in the impending clash appeared valid.

Nor did the international community seem willing to help. The United States offered only the most general assurances of Israel's security. It talked in coy diplomatic terms, the Johnson administration telling the Israelis that they would be alone only if they acted alone. This meant US opposition to an Israeli preemptive strike. Nor did the United States believe that this step would be necessary. President Johnson explained to Israel's foreign minister, Abba Eban, that Egypt could not threaten Israel militarily. The Jewish state was too strong, the Egyptian nation too weak. The Americans were confident that recent actions by Nasser were only bluster, his intent being to win a political victory at the expense of his Arab partners, not to attack Israel. The lukewarm support Johnson extended to Israel was best exhibited by his almost too eager embrace of an international show of force

---

* David Dayan, *First Strike: A Battle History of Israel's Six-Day War*, trans. Dov Ben-Abba (New York: Pitman Publishing, 1967), 4, 5.

** Eric Hammel, *Six Days in June: How Israel Won the 1967 Arab–Israeli War* (New York: Charles Scribner's Sons, 1992), 36.

*** Dayan, *First Strike*, 8.

to reopen the Straits of Tiran. This became one of Nasser's most provocative steps toward Israel since its closure amounted to a direct challenge to Israel's sovereignty by denying the Israeli port of Eilat access to outside shipping. Johnson also deferred to Congress, arguing he could do nothing on behalf of Israel without that body's approval. The United States could afford to be complacent. On the front lines of this struggle, Israel believed differently. It could not be sure the Egyptians were only playing a political game.

The Soviet Union appeared an open antagonist. It warned Israel not to attack its Arab neighbors. It then went on public record that, should Israel attack an Arab state preemptively, such an act would be considered an attack on the USSR. Israel's prime minister, Levi Eshkol, deftly insisted on Israel's right of self-defense. On May 29, as tensions reached a peak with belligerent statements from Egypt threatening Israel, the USSR declared that it would not allow outside interference in the looming war. Directed at the United States, this declaration appeared designed to prevent its Cold War rival from supporting Israel and furthered Israel's sense of isolation. The Cold War was very much an active item in the Middle East, and it worked against Israel and in favor of the Arab states that now believed they were free to attack and win an easy victory. A final warning came a few days before the outbreak of war, when the Soviet Union's foreign minister Andrei Gromyko told his Israeli counterpart not to allow his emotions to get the better of him and start a war.

The timid actions of the United Nations ended Israeli hopes of international support in stopping a war or aiding Israel if a war broke out. First, its peacekeeping element, the United Nations Emergency Force (UNEF) of 3,400 men withdrew from Sinai and the Gaza Strip under pressure from Nasser. Once the commander of that force, Major General Indar Jit Rikhye of India, evacuated Sinai after May 19, tensions escalated. The numbers of this force mattered little; what it had provided was a semblance of stability in that neither side, Egypt or Israel, wished to attack this UN presence to start hostilities. It had for this reason provided a measure of calm. The UN troops left precipitously, however, and Nasser could claim another victory of having intimidated the United Nations. This success further inflamed Arab opinion in favor of war with Israel, and it further convinced Israel of Nasser's hostile intentions. The fact was, the international community had again shown its unwillingness or inability to aid Israel. The reasons why did not matter. Israel stood alone, and it needed to act accordingly. A preemptive strike therefore gained more credence among Israeli leaders as a means—the only means—of survival.

Even in the face of this crisis, Israel tried a low-key approach, hoping nerves could be soothed and war avoided. But this effort backfired immediately. When celebrating its independence on May 15, 1967, the Israelis withheld from the parade an ostentatious display of armor as a means of calming escalating tensions. Instead, the Egyptian press declared that the Israelis had massed the missing armor on the northern front to fight Syria. The outrage was less one of Israeli aggression against a neighbor as it was more a slighting of Egyptian power. Israel needed to remember that its chief foe lay in the south. In this atmosphere of Arab one-upmanship, it was hard for Israel to determine the true intentions of its enemies. Eshkol moved cautiously, hoping to give Nasser room to win a war of words with his Arab neighbors, but allowing Israel to stay out of a real war. From the prime minister's point of view, preemption was a last resort.

In this spirit of conciliation Eshkol continued to blunder. Nasser's public relations successes quickly snowballed on him, and he soon faced mounting pressure from within his own nation and from many other Arab states to take things a step further and close the Straits of Tiran. By choking off the Israeli port of Eilat, Egypt would strike an economic and political blow against Israel, since the Israelis had long maintained that the closure of the straits to its ships meant war. But on May 21, Eshkol gave a speech that mentioned no consequences of a blockade. Nasser closed the port the following day, believing the Israelis were too afraid to fight. That same day, May 22, Eshkol spoke in moderate terms in relation to the port crisis in the Knesset chamber, Israel's legislature. He immediately faced charges of appeasement from his peers. The prime minister repeated this performance in a speech to the nation on May 28. All who listened believed his hesitations in purpose and resolve threatened national morale and emboldened the Arabs. The public feared the worst in an atmosphere of crisis where there was no government reassurance of success. A state outnumbered and surrounded by hostile powers could not afford to look weak or intimidated. Eshkol's hesitations did net a key benefit for the army. Under pressure from political opponents who believed him taxed beyond his capabilities, he yielded his post as minister of defense and allowed an army man, Moshe Dayan, to assume this position. The army now could dictate policy more directly and with less delay. The pressure to launch a preemptive attack increased.

From the point of view of the army, the arrival of Dayan came just in time. It worried that the faltering of the national civilian leadership threatened to seep into the armed forces. The Israeli Defense Force (IDF) believed it could win the pending war with a preemptive attack. But the government's delay in ordering that attack meant it did not share this confidence in the armed forces so the generals in the IDF feared a loss of troop morale. And with each passing day that the politicians frittered away, Arab strength increased and the costs of challenging this strength mounted and might soon reach a level of unacceptable losses. A preemptive strike would vindicate the confidence Israel had in its armed forces that would reward this trust by winning a great victory for the state.

Nor could the Israeli army stay on standby indefinitely. The call to arms of some 250,000 troops meant an economic standstill at home. Too many men were away from their livelihoods. Eshkol always understood this. In yet another act of conciliation, he had ordered only two brigades, 18,000 men, to be called up initially on May 17. As Egyptian rhetoric grew more inflammatory, and as the Egyptian army flooded into Sinai, the IDF wanted the Israeli government to put the state on more of a war readiness. Still Eshkol balked. The prime minister's approach had many advantages. A slow mobilization would be least disruptive to the state, calm fears of a pending war, and not tip Israel's hand to its enemies. With this last end in mind, many soldiers reported at night. Even on the eve of war, Israel kept this masquerade going, sending soldiers on leave during the day, and then recalling them that very night. It was too clever for the army. IDF commanders insisted on a deliberate act of mobilization and a deliberate act of war. Better to act decisively to maximize Israeli's military assets. This thinking, of course, furthered the push toward a preemptive strike.

Outnumbered, unclear of which enemy to face first, trying to defend an unfavorable geography, Israel was in a very vulnerable situation. How was Israel to defend itself? For the army, the answer was preemption. Preemption capitalized on two military principles, operating on interior lines and seizing the initiative. By striking first, Israel could plan to engage one enemy after the other, the most dangerous foe first. This meant the initial blow landed on Egypt. Other threats could be held in check while Israel tended to things in the south. Then, after success there, Jordan, Syria, and Lebanon would be targeted if they were foolish enough to attack. Only by seizing the initiative could this scenario unfold to Israel's satisfaction. It was the best way to address the larger numbers it faced and expect a victory.

Preemption also utilized several strengths of the Israeli armed forces. Its air force employed some advanced technology enabling it to deliver a crippling opening blow through the air. For one thing, the command and control apparatus was excellent, so numerous attacks could be launched at once. This would be imperative given the need to strike multiple targets simultaneously within one country, and to then shift the attack to a different locale altogether. In the span of hours, the Israeli air commander, Mordechai Hod, believed he could devastate several different enemies from the air. The composition of the air arm accounted for his optimism. Two excellent planes composed the strike arm in the air. The *Mirage* fighter and the fighter bomber, the *Mystère*, both French planes, were a match for any potential Arab foe. Additionally, the *Mirage* dropped special ordnance, the rocket-boosted dibber bomb, one that buried itself in the ground prior to detonating. A series of explosions from a dibber bomb made taking off nearly impossible, so great were the craters on the runway. This weapon was ideal for rendering airfields inoperable. Best of all, Israel possessed a large number of highly trained and confident pilots. They understood they were a key element of defense. As one saying went, "Israel's best defense is in the skies over Cairo."* The pilots relished this confidence in their abilities. As an elite force, they embraced their role as the lead element of a preemptive strike.

The ground forces were outstanding as well for many reasons. They too benefited from a command and control structure that enabled rapid advances and attacks. This ability, of course, was essential given Israel's determination to assume the offensive and not wait to be attacked. Once unleashed, the armored units of the IDF expected to launch a series of rapid thrusts that would seek out weak spots, disrupt enemy opposition, and achieve its objectives swiftly. The weapons themselves were not the greatest source of comfort. Many tanks, the American *Super Sherman*, or the British-made *Centurion*, were well armored vehicles, but they did face comparable opposition from the tanks the Soviets had supplied to the Syrians and the Egyptians. Tanks such as the T-54 and T-55 were a match for the Israeli weapons. Once again, the great trust of the high command lay in the personnel. Israel's armored warriors were an outstanding force, experienced in mobile warfare, confident in the direction they received from their commanders along the entire chain of command. The IDF believed it could rely on its armored force to end a conflict quickly provided it acted preemptively.

No matter the public fumbling on the part of the Eshkol government, the IDF looked forward with confidence to a preemptive attack. It only needed to get the order. The IDF assumed a week was all that would be necessary. It was an extraordinary thing. A small power in terms of size, population, and military strength, Israel measured victory in the forthcoming war in terms of a few days despite the larger size of the armies arrayed against it. This result, this absolutely essential outcome, was to be the consequence of acting preemptively. It was a weighty matter to place in the hands of a military organization of a state. Such optimism had been uttered before for a variety of reasons by commanders in past wars who had seldom met the rosy predictions of the architects of that war. Israel now entered history as yet another state willing to take the risk of going to war because it believed it could act in preemptive fashion and win a short

---

*Hammel, *Six Days in June*, 125.

conflict. The summer of 1967 represented a key moment for Israel and for the value of preemption as a strategy.

The Attack

The Israeli attack worked to perfection. On June 5, 1967, starting at 7:45 am Israeli time and attacking in successive waves, the IAF targeted nine airfields in Sinai and Egypt. The timing was intentional, aimed at catching the Egyptian planes at a key moment of vulnerability. The protective air cover had returned to base, the high command deeming an Israeli attack unlikely at that late hour. The low approach of the invaders to evade radar detection was purposely abandoned just prior to arriving over the airfields. That way the Egyptians did receive warning of the attack, but only in time to start their planes and scramble their pilots. The Israelis now had infrared targets for their missiles and the attack in all likelihood killed the pilots as well as destroying the planes. Virtually unopposed, the Israeli planes struck the Egyptian aircraft on the ground and dropped dibber bombs on the airfields. Few planes rose to meet the attackers. A haphazard ground to air defense did little to impede the assault. In three hours, the Egyptian air force suffered total defeat. Israel destroyed some 300 aircraft in these initial raids. Additional raids throughout the day inflicted further losses.

The IDF soon expanded its attack. In response to artillery fire and air raids coming from Jordan, eight Israeli planes arrived over the main Jordanian airfield in the afternoon of June 5. In a matter of minutes, the Jordanian air force was destroyed. The Israelis suffered no losses. The air attack was then extended to Syrian and Iraqi air space after both nations launched air raids against Israel. The result was the same: negligible opposition and extensive losses sustained by the Arab states. The first leg of Israel's preemptive attack had succeeded.

Israel's ground war erupted in the south almost at the same time as the air war. The success here was as dramatic as in the air. Three armored columns struck in Sinai and a rapid breakthrough allowed each force to operate in the Egyptian rear. By early afternoon on the first day, the IAF joined its ground force to speed the attack. Surprise was complete, and the fast moving armored units spread additional havoc. Cut off and demoralized, the Egyptians offered little effective resistance. Two days later, the Israelis arrived in force along the Suez Canal having overrun all of Sinai including the Gaza Strip. Thousands of Egyptian prisoners were in their hands and much equipment had been destroyed or captured.

With its chief foe bloodied in the south, Israel now looked to its other battlefronts. Israel overran the West Bank as quickly as it did Sinai. This attack started in earnest a day after the Israeli assault on Egypt's positions.

Soldiers of what was designated Central Command were given the task of taking this ground including Jerusalem, where fighting erupted in response to Jordanian artillery fire as well as small arms fire. A multi-pronged advance by tanks and motorized infantry led the attack, aided by Israeli units from the front facing Syria. The Jordanian army of 35,000 men was no match for this assault, and the frontier along the Jordan River was secured by Wednesday evening, three days after the outbreak of the fighting. The cost to Israel had been light. It sustained less than a hundred fatalities in an attacking force of 40,000 troops. Jordan suffered disaster, losing over 8,000 soldiers killed or wounded and much equipment as well.

It remained for one more important goal to be accomplished before the Israelis could claim complete success, and that was the defeat of Syrian armed forces. Syria, however, represented a formidable foe since its soldiers were dug in along the Golan Heights. A special force received this assignment commanded by David Eleazar. It contained the usual mix of tanks and mobile infantry, as well as a heavier component of artillery. The air arm again contributed significantly, since this attack commenced on Friday morning, June 9, a delay that allowed Israeli air assets to become available. The assault was not as swift as had been the case elsewhere. The fighting here proved difficult and focused on the Syrian strongpoint of Tel Fahar. The Israelis suffered a hundred casualties but this ground was taken by the late afternoon. Its capture enabled the Israelis to advance virtually unimpeded the next day, so demoralized were the Syrians with the loss of this position.

The Israeli success in the north completed the last phase of the Six Day War. Lebanon wisely stayed out of the fighting. The other Arab nations agreed to a cease-fire on June 10. They had little choice. Defeated, they feared renewed Israeli attacks that they could not stop. Humiliated, the prospect of sustaining further damage at the hands of Israel unsteadied many an Arab leader. This war had to come to an end. How to explain this defeat would come later. It was clear there was a need to limit the damage now. Israel agreed to the peace as well since it had achieved its goals: the Arab armies had been badly damaged and key defensive terrain was now in Israeli hands. Also, more fighting was not an option. The IAF had performed magnificently, but pilot fatigue and the need to refurbish much of its aircraft now limited its ability. The ground forces were in similar shape, worn out after the intense fighting. Israel had suffered close to a thousand dead and 4,500 wounded. Arab losses totaled over 10,000. This tally in favor of Israel and the enhanced security gained from the land taken during the offensive all spoke to the success of the Israeli preemptive attack initiating the Six Day War.

Success

Israel achieved the impossible in 1967. In just six days, using a combination of air power and ground forces, multiple enemies were chastened on several different fronts. As was needed, the Israelis rapidly defeated a foe that greatly outnumbered them. In the process, Israel came into possession of territory that added to the state's security. Syria lost control of the Golan Heights in the north. Jordan forfeited the West Bank and east Jerusalem. Egypt surrendered the Sinai Peninsula. These areas went far to curing Israel's vulnerable geography. The mountainous terrain in the north curbed any Syrian threat from that direction. The bulge that impaled Israel in its center was gone. To the south, a buffer zone distanced Egypt from Israel. In the Six Day War, Israel achieved a measure of security in such dramatic fashion that it did not believe its enemies would threaten the Jewish state any time soon for fear of a similar result. By this measure, it was a very successful preemptive war.

This rosy picture was a short-term assessment, however. The long-term view was not as flattering. Additional wars with the Arab states followed the one in 1967. Arab harassment of Israel continued unabated after the Six Day War. In fact it increased, particularly on the Egyptian front. So a key reason for Israel to fight this war proved illusionary since additional land did not end the terrorist threat posed by guerrillas infiltrating the country. This continued violence ensured that a new war erupted. Israel again fell into a period of crisis in 1973, as Egypt resumed its open belligerence toward Israel and attacked with great effect. So the success of 1967 bought Israel only six years of security. In 1973, a desperate defense and a tremendous amount of aid from the United States staved off disaster. Of course, the Sinai Peninsula proved its value; the Egyptian offensive might have done much more damage had it had less ground to cover. But the idea that war could win Israel security was tested in 1973, and it was less reassuring than it had been in 1967. Nevertheless, this posture remained an Israeli staple. A fifth Arab–Israeli war erupted in 1982, this time with the Israelis on the offensive, attacking Lebanon to end terrorist infiltration into Israel via that northern frontier. Military success came swiftly, and Israel soon controlled a good portion of southern Lebanon. But just as quickly, the IDF found itself waging a counter-insurgency war that proved a limited success. After many years, the Israelis withdrew, inviting Arab claims of victory in expelling them.

The recurrent wars featuring an always impressive display of Israeli conventional arms belied the purpose of the wars. The immediate aim was the preservation of the Jewish state, and Israel did achieve this goal. Still, security was more elusive. A handful of infiltrators could enter Israel and kill its citizens no matter the efforts of the IDF. This fact manifested itself throughout the history of the modern state of Israel. The Israeli raid into Jordan that preceded the Six Day War had been an attempt to stop this infiltration. Later on, the Israeli reprisals in the north against Lebanon attempted to achieve the same end. The Jewish state could tell itself that additional territory would end this problem, but even this success did not prove to be a solution. Terrorism did not stop after 1967, hence the war in 1982. It seems that preemption had met its match in the form of terrorism.

To stop terrorism, Israel had few good options; military force and the expansion of its borders might have been the best option. But the reality was this security was incomplete, perhaps impossible, no matter the wars fought by the IDF and no matter the success of these wars. Such a conclusion was discouraging in the extreme. Still, Israel pursued preemption as an essential part of its military operations. Preemption further validated the Israeli reliance on using military force to solve its security problems. A closer look revealed that military force produced limited returns in so far as generating this security. The 1982 air strike against an Iraqi nuclear facility proved again Israel's willingness to strike first, to use its military arm for this purpose, and to achieve immediate success with this option. Yet, today, Iran, a nation openly hostile and threatening to Israel, commands the attention of the international community with its claims of developing nuclear capability. Preemption as practiced by Israel appears only a temporary corrective to the long-term security problems plaguing the Middle East. The Six Day War was the most spectacular success of Israel's preemptive wars. But in retrospect, it was only one stop of many along Israel's path to complete security, a journey that continues.

Conclusion

In 1967, Israel faced an unprecedented threat to its security. Surrounded on all sides by hostile foes, defending a state that was too small to give ground and mount a defense in depth, its geographic vulnerability underscored its untenable strategic position. Yet to act offensively carried great risks. The IDF was outnumbered by its enemies in every category. Inferior in tanks, planes, and soldiers, even offensive action promised little success. The odds were simply too great. Since the Arab states appeared to be acting in unprecedented unity, sharing the common purpose of destroying the Jewish state, Israel could not expect to fragment the opposition. It would have to attack on one front and then another. Preemption offered this opportunity and represented the only course of action.

The international community did little to assuage Israeli fears. The United Nations offered no guarantees of Israel's national integrity. It then withdrew its peacekeepers from the Sinai Peninsula, a key point of friction between Israel and Egypt. While not strong in numbers, the mere presence of this force had deterred hostilities in this area since neither side, Israel or Egypt, wanted to attack the UN flag. Privately, the United States expressed sympathy as to the plight of Israel, but offered nothing concrete in discussions with Israeli diplomats or in terms of public guarantees. American hesitations during the crisis over Egypt's closure of the Straits of Tiran convinced Israel it could not rely on the United States. The USSR, the other Cold War power, assumed an overtly hostile position, siding with the Arab states against Israel. Israel was on its own in the summer of 1967. If it were to survive, it would have to devise its own solution.

One step it took was to try and allow the increasing Arab bluster to go unpunished. Provocations directed at Israel from the competing Arab states could mean an effort by Arab statesmen to win political points at home or among the broader Arab community. Israel was only a convenient sounding board, not an imminent target. Nasser was the chief practitioner of this strategy and he was the most successful, although the Egyptian leader faced a stiff challenge from Syria. Israel could endure the insults and hollow threats that did not merit a war. The trick was to be sure and gauge when the rhetoric ended and the threat of invasion became real. This analysis would be an imperfect science at best and an error could mean dire consequences for Israel. Its prime minister, Eshkol, soon found this out. By keeping the celebration of the Israeli independence day muted, and in offering a series of fumbling speeches in government chambers and to the public, he did not calm a push to war but stirred passions further. Nasser felt so confident of Israel's unwillingness to fight that he closed the Straits of Tiran, a clear threat to Israel's security. Still Eshkol held out hope of conciliation with the Arab states. War should be the last recourse, and he moved slowly and reluctantly down this path.

The Israeli military did not share his outlook. It demanded action and pointed out several valid reasons why this should be the case. Once Nasser closed the straits, there could be no denying that hostilities were imminent. Delay merely harmed Israel's chances of defending itself. The armed forces were confident of success, but the lack of confidence illustrated by the government in the IDF's ability to fight a war threatened to weaken the morale of the soldiers. Delay also served to strengthen the enemy, as it brought its superior numbers into play and allowed them to assume stronger defensive positions. A preemptive strike could soon be too expensive to contemplate. The converse was as unwelcomed. To have to defend the state by meeting an attack on Israeli soil blasphemed the entire military strategy of the IDF. And delay produced consequences at home that impacted the army. Public morale sagged and fears of defeatism rose.

In this atmosphere, soldiers might not report for duty or the army might suffer a loss of morale. Prolonging the crisis also meant exacerbating the limits of the mobilization system. The state could not stand in readiness indefinitely. Nor did a piecemeal mobilization do any good since Israel could not fight effectively at less than full strength. The war must be quick and a maximum show of force ensured this end.

The army made a persuasive case that the time to act preemptively had come. It could meet its defensive obligations on multiple fronts only by seizing the initiative. In this way, Israel determined the flow of the fighting. Egypt could be dealt a crippling blow in the air and on the ground. The Egyptian armed forces were close by and vulnerable to a rapid Israeli attack. This blow could be delivered in a matter of days if not hours. In the meantime, a holding action on the other fronts could be successful until military assets were freed up to then attack additional enemies, if necessary. Proximity again made for a tempting target, this time the victim being Jordan. Its army certainly presented less of a challenge than did the larger and better-equipped Egyptian forces, and its presence in the West Bank made a quick and decisive battle possible. More difficult was the prospect of engaging the Syrians along the Golan Heights. The Syrian army was large, well equipped with armor and artillery, and occupied defensive high ground. Yet, once the IDF displayed its military prowess here, Lebanon would be cowed into not fighting at all. And of course, after one state and then another was engaged and its armed forces defeated, Israel would gain possession of key defensive territory, ensuring its security for the future.

The IDF believed it could accomplish this end once given the go-ahead. Preemption not only offered a favorable solution to the bleak strategic situation Israel faced, but it played to that nation's strengths. Experience with sophisticated command and control operations and a large number of highly trained and motivated pilots made the air force an outstanding military asset. Crippling an opposing air arm was a strong possibility. This result would protect Israel from air attack; the air force could then support a ground attack. The army benefited from a similar command structure and high morale. Its weapons were also very good. When deployed as a rapid strike force, the armored troops could move swiftly and overrun territory in a short period of time. In total, it was an army designed for attack and, in reality, designed for preemptive warfare. Surprise and the determination to wield maximum destructive power from the first moment of war made the IDF a formidable presence on the battlefield.

Given this view, it is easy to see why Israel looked to preemption as its only chance of success. It was an exciting prospect: the defeat of all enemies in a single whirlwind campaign that cost Israel little but cost its neighbors a great deal in loss of prestige, land, and material. Only preemption could deliver this end and, with it, lasting Israeli security. Key terrain would come into Israel's possession and help it safeguard its borders. Possession of the Golan Heights shielded the northern frontier from an attack by Syria. The West Bank eliminated the bulge in the center of the state that made defense so hard to contemplate. The Israeli flag on the Sinai Peninsula kept the Egyptians at bay. No longer would its geography be a liability to Israel. Additionally, a great military victory would extend beyond the tangible realignment of its borders. Israel would have put the Arab world on notice that the Jewish state was a deadly foe and a permanent fixture in the Middle East. The days of insecurity would come to an end and the advent of living side-by-side without open hostilities could now be contemplated by all sides. It was a tremendous gain from a preemptive military strike.

Israel may have been convinced that it was necessary to act preemptively to defend itself, but other factors called this conclusion into question. Foremost in this regard was the Israeli inclination to exaggerate the forces arrayed against it. Arab unity was a myth, a truth recognized in the Arab world as well as in Israel. It was a great fiction that four of these states could act in unison, all the while inviting additional Arab states to send forces that would deploy on the territory of a rival, as was the case with Iraqi forces in Jordan. The political posturing that characterized the alliance of Syria and Egypt made this point clear. Declared Arab hatred of Israel merely served as a device to rally Arab support to one Arab state or another, but unity hardly was a result of winning such a competition. The Palestinians also served this purpose, Syria backing the terror arm of this group, Egypt sponsoring an entire division of PLO fighters in Sinai. The support extended to this group also won one state or another prestige in fighting for the Arab cause. There is no doubt the anti-Israeli rhetoric increased in the late spring and early summer of 1967. Nor is there doubt that military deployments by Syria and Egypt menaced Israel's borders. But there was great doubt that the ultimate Arab objective was a war with Israel, no matter the public declaration of these states in welcoming this outcome. With no Israeli action, the tensions may have remained just that, heated outbursts designed to appease a restless Arab nationalism that was never more than a feeling easily assuaged by such bluster.

Israel's tendency to exaggerate the threat it faced from its Arab neighbors was apparent in another area. The Arab armed forces were hardly as formidable as they appeared. The Syrian army was poorly led. Its main purpose was safeguarding whatever regime had managed to seize power. Loyalty to party became a virtue, and therefore poor military leadership a mainstay of its army. All it was capable of was harassment in the form of the shelling it dispensed from fortified positions on the Golan Heights. This activity was a problem, deadly at times, but it did not exceed the category of harassment. Nor did Syria mass large forces on the heights since an offensive into Israeli territory from there would have to enter a valley devoid of cover. Crossing this killing zone was simply beyond Syrian capabilities. Israel understood these weaknesses and limitations to an offensive. So sure were they that they could hold the Syrians at bay in the unlikely event that Syria did attack, that forces from Northern Command responsible for blocking any Syrian incursion into Israel assisted with the attack on the West Bank on the first day of the offensive. As expected, there was no major Syrian assault and the Israelis easily repulsed a few weak probing efforts. After both Egypt and Jordan had been defeated, only then did the Israelis mount an attack in the north. When they did, two days were enough to overrun the Golan Heights, the rapidity of the attack raising questions as to its necessity at all. Clearly the Six Day War served the purpose of allowing Israel to seize some coveted terrain, in this case the Golan Heights, and this aggressive purpose explained the Israeli offensive against Syria.

The armies of Lebanon and Jordan also suffered from internal political problems much as Syria endured. Given their small size, the nepotism that beset the officer corps, and the low morale of the soldiers, these states hardly posed a threat to Israel. In Lebanon, its prime minister had to threaten the military commander in order to get him to take action in the Six Day War. This latter individual understood the military folly of engaging the Israelis in any way, and did not do so. In Jordan, King Hussein visited his army on the eve of battle and prophesied defeat. His real struggle was to ensure that Jordan remained a viable state in the aftermath of this defeat, preferably with Hussein still in charge. How he was to survive the loss of the West Bank, Israel's clear objective in provoking a fight with Jordan, became Hussein's obsession.

Finally, Egypt suffered from similar weaknesses, no matter a larger and well-equipped army. Field Marshal Abdel Hakim Amer maintained a rivalry with Nasser, despite the fact that they were close friends. Power plays between these two men undid the Egyptian military effort. Most telling, the air force did little to prepare to resist a preemptive strike, despite suffering such a disaster in 1956. Nothing had been changed to protect the aircraft on the ground, a key failing of Amer. Yet Nasser dared not remove him from command for fear of the political fallout. In fact, he promoted him and Egyptian aircraft lay vulnerable in 1967 as they did in 1956. The suspicion at the top end of command was infectious. On the eve of battle in 1967, a divisional commander in Sinai fired all his subordinates and failed to replace them. This situation played to Israeli strengths and accentuated Egyptian weaknesses. The consequence was that the Egyptian soldier would be prostrate before Israeli attacks. No wonder the Israeli troops could look forward to "dip[ping] their hands in the Suez Canal" in a matter of days.* Clearly a war served the aggressive purpose of Israel in pushing its border to the Suez Canal, since an Egyptian attack on Israel was hardly possible.

In 1967, it would appear that Israel gambled everything on a preemptive strike. But it was not much of a gamble. The IDF was confident of victory. It understood the weaknesses of its enemies and the strengths of the Israeli armed forces. The politicians may have dithered, but the soldiers did not. Morale in the army was never a problem. The commanders knew this. They merely used the threat of a loss of morale to bully the government into sanctioning a preemptive attack. That the Israeli public appeared to have lost its nerve merely played into the military's hands. A dramatic and decisive attack was now needed to prop up the home front, they argued. The IDF stood ready to answer this call.

Nor were the provocations against Israel as one-sided as Israel claimed. The Syrian border was a good example. Flare-ups were constant, but one Israeli general estimated that Israeli settlers provoked the Syrians into shooting at them at least half of the time. Moshe Dayan, one of Israel's most famous soldiers, put this number at 80 percent.** These border incidents served the greater purpose of attaining land for settlement and building the Jewish state. The settlers, in fact, were hardly defenseless farmers. They were volunteers chosen because of their extreme nationalist beliefs. They would challenge and push the Syrians into an incident. The Israeli government would have to respond, and the IDF would have to attack.

The most telling incident came on April 7, 1967, when the Syrians sent some 200 shells into Israel, killing a number of settlers. The Israelis countered with a ground attack supported by air power. In response, the Syrians made an open alliance with Egypt. The same sequence had repeated itself along the Jordanian frontier. Israel launched an attack into Jordan on November 13, 1966, in response to yet another terrorist raid on Israel coming from Jordan. The Israeli attack was on a large scale, tanks and half-tracks penetrating Jordan's defenses and destroying a town in retribution. A clash between IDF forces and Jordanian soldiers erupted and turned the incident into more of an invasion. The Israelis withdrew that same day, but the damage was done. First, the Arabs claimed a victory. Second, King Hussein believed he had no recourse but to make friends with Egypt.

---

* See photo caption in Jeremy Bowen, *Six Days: How the 1967 War Shaped the Middle East* (London: Simon & Schuster, 2003).

** Ibid. 20.

This agreement was finalized on May 30, 1967. If Israel faced an unprecedented threat from a new-found Arab unity in 1967, the Israelis had created it for the most part with their aggressive raids.

The exaggerations of the threat to Israeli security continued in every area. By closing the Straits of Tiran and preventing shipping from leaving or entering Israel from the port of Eilat, Nasser hardly struck a severe economic blow at Israel. Other means of import and export were available for non-Israeli carriers including transit through the Suez Canal to Israel's Mediterranean ports. Israel insisted on its right to use the waterway via Eilat, and defending this political goal drove the country to war, not an imperative to protect its economic lifeline. The crisis over the straits was yet another excuse to launch a war Israel was confident of winning and to do so to increase its territory, not to defend itself. Here was a war in the name of aggression, not self-defense.

Israel was not as isolated internationally as it claimed either. Two days into the war, Israel attacked a US ship by air and sea, the *Liberty*, killing thirty-four American sailors. Israel apologized for what it called a mistake. The captain of the ship, and many other observers, did not believe the apology. They were convinced it was a deliberate attack to prevent the United States, a neutral power, from acquiring intelligence about the conflict. Such ruthlessness was perhaps not surprising; Israel was fighting for its survival, and a Holocaust mentality of taking any steps to ensure that survival took hold. But the risk of alienating the Cold War superpower that supported it was an extraordinary step to take. The strain was not eased until 1973. But in the arena of international relations, the Cold War served a key function of keeping the United States in step with Israel, since both anti-communist powers opposed the USSR. Preemption in 1967 tested this beneficial dynamic. But Israel reasoned correctly that it would never be alone given the Cold War setting, no matter that its actions included an attack on a US warship.

Altogether, the sum did not make sense given the parts. Preemption required that Israel engage multiple enemies on multiple fronts. Outnumbered and facing strategic dilemmas of unpleasant dimensions, such an attack appeared a desperate gamble. When a further factor was calculated, that the Israelis could not fight for a long period of time given the disruption that a call to arms posed to the home front, the Six Day War of 1967 was a step toward national disaster. Everything now relied on a quick war lasting only a matter of days. The defense of the state required it. However, since the weakness of its foes was well known, and given that the Israelis had provoked much of the opposition it faced, the preemptive strike in 1967 takes on the appearance less of a desperate gamble than it does of a desired war with an expected favorable result. The Israeli leadership believed it could defeat its foes in a matter of days. The superiority of the IDF to the military forces of its enemies assured this outcome. This war was a war of aggression, designed to secure land that solidified the state of Israel. To achieve this end, Israel flaunted international cooperation, pushed its uneasy neighbors into threatening Israel, and chose war at a time of its choosing. Preemption was a tool of opportunity, not one of necessity born of desperation.

Such a judgment casts too critical a light on preemption. To suggest that Israel unnecessarily seized an opportunity to cripple already weak states on its borders is a claim that does not hold up under close analysis. As Tom Segev reveals in his recent book, *1967: Israel, the War and the Year that Transformed the Middle East*, Israel had no plans to extend the war beyond the Egyptian front to Jordan. Israeli officials considered "grabbing some territory" in the West Bank but not Jerusalem.* Such a step they dismissed as counter-productive since it would galvanize Palestinian nationalism and lead Palestinian radicals to commit more terrorist attacks against Israel. Instead, the IDF planned to hold firm on this front. This pre-war planning gave way in the face of the euphoria of success on the battlefield, and King Hussein's provocative actions. Only then did Israel broaden the war to include all of the West Bank. This thinking also raised questions about the Israeli attack on Syria: was this necessary or more Israeli opportunism, in this case to grab the Golan Heights? In the view offered by Segev and others, the Israeli government succumbed to temptation, seizing upon Syrian air raids as a pretext for full-scale war. But this failing is a far cry from seeking battle on many fronts to expand Israeli power. Opportunity may have spurred Israel to fight on additional fronts, but only to validate the preemptive purpose of the attack to begin with—to defend Israel.

When assessing the imminent threat coming from the Arab states, Israel's need to error on the side of caution and attack made preemption a necessity. The task of understanding the true motive behind the declared Arab intention to destroy Israel, and the deliberate steps of provocation on the part of Egypt and Syria that escalated tensions, limited Israel's choices. The Israeli state was simply too small and its geography too disadvantageous for it to wait to be attacked. Yet the Eshkol government risked this end, offering several acts of conciliation to try and ease tensions and allow the crisis to pass without war. These efforts only galvanized Arab belligerence, prompting Nasser to cut off shipping to Eilat, for example. The port may not have been essential to Israel's economic survival, but it was a crucial benchmark of Israeli deterrence. Challenged in this most basic area of

---

*Tom Segev, *1967: Israel, the War and the Year That Transformed the Middle East*, trans. Jessica Cohen (New York: Metropolitan Books, 2007), 300, 344–345.

security, it is not a surprise that the Israelis extended the war to other fronts. It is a wonder that the Israelis delayed their preemptive attack as long as they did. That it then acted ruthlessly in waging this war, such as with the attack on the American ship the *Liberty*, spoke more to the need to win this war at any cost than it did a deliberate effort to defy the international community and win a war of aggression. On balance, it is fair to say that the Israel offensive in 1967 remained an act of self-defense and therefore gained the moral blessing of a preemptive attack.

CHAPTER 10

A Dangerous Simplicity:
The American Preemptive
War in Iraq, 2003

Introduction

A few Iraqis used some ropes to try to bring down the statue of the now-deposed ruler Saddam Hussein, located in the center of Baghdad. The monument held firm. Some observant US soldiers offered a hand. Soon pulleys and machinery were in place and the statue fell over. It was a moment of exhilaration, Iraqis and Americans working together to erase a symbol of tyranny that had victimized both countries and they did so in view of the world since the event was broadcast live. More importantly, it appeared a vindication of the new American policy of preemption, a result all the more poignant given the lingering memory of the terrorist attacks on the United States on September 11, 2001. This jubilation would be short-lived, however. The Americans soon discovered that Hussein's supposed contacts with al Qaeda were fiction and his stockpiles of weapons of mass destruction non-existent. The ties to 9/11 did not exist. Such discoveries undercut the reasoning behind preemption. The remaining American justification for invading Iraq—to spread democracy in the Middle East—also fell short of sustaining the rationale of a preemptive strike. Even those Iraqis who rejoiced at the end of Hussein's rule of Iraq and welcomed democracy could not but notice the bitter in the sweet: a western power had toppled the regime in a matter of weeks. This success was as humiliating to Arab identity as it was a tribute to American military power. It seemed that only the Americans could make sense of the necessity of preemption, and then only with great difficulty. It was not a good start to building the new Iraq. Nor were things to get better.

The 2003 Gulf War capped a thirteen-year period of conflict between the United States and Iraq. Saddam Hussein, president of the country since 1979, had attacked Kuwait in August 1990, ending the friendly ties between the United States and Iraq. President George H.W. Bush created a powerful international coalition that drove Hussein's army from that neighboring state in a brief war lasting less than six weeks. In the aftermath of this conflict, Hussein managed to remain in control of a now greatly weakened Iraq, despite US efforts to foster internal revolts to depose the regime. An uneasy standoff ensued, with American and coalition forces enforcing no-fly zones in northern and southern Iraq, and Hussein successfully countering these steps with increasing brutality at home and frequent public bluster directed abroad. He remained in power; the Americans remained committed to curtailing his authority. The ensuing containment of Hussein lasted for just over 10 years, jarred from place by the terrorist attacks on American soil on 9/11. A new American president, the former president's son, George W. Bush, acted to remove Hussein from power with a preemptive strike on March 17, 2003, deeming his regime an ally of terror and a threat to the American homeland. While successful in deposing Hussein, the Bush administration failed to stabilize the country since an insurgency arose after Hussein's defeat and contested the American occupation. It was an entirely new war marking the beginning of a new phase of conflict between the United States and Iraq.

The current war in Iraq has lasted over four years. Over this period of time, American support for the war has greatly diminished. Not surprisingly, the Bush doctrine of preemption has come under fire as well and for a number of reasons. The absence of weapons of mass destruction in Iraq and the inability of the administration to tie Saddam Hussein to the terrorist attack on 9/11 suggest the invasion was unnecessary. Charges of poor reconstruction planning also dog the administration; the insurgency was of its own creation. Inconsistency plagues the administration as well since it appears ready to deal with the threats posed by Iran and North Korea through diplomacy and economic sanctions, and not military force. Still, no matter the mistakes that even the president acknowledges have been made, he counters his detractors by pointing to the end of Hussein's oppression and the advance of democracy in the Middle East. Preemption worked and it works. A close examination of the purpose of the Bush preemptive doctrine will allow us to determine to what extent Bush has indeed set American foreign policy on a profitable new path to confront the threat of terrorism, or to what extent he has sent the United States on a walk in the footsteps of aggression.

The Case for Preemption

A preemptive policy on the part of the United States grew out of the tragedy of the terrorist attacks on September 11, 2001. In the wake of 9/11, Bush, appointed to the presidency by the US Supreme Court in December 2000, announced his response to those seeking to harm Americans. The United States would hold accountable nations that harbored terrorists just as much as it held accountable the perpetrators of the attacks themselves. "Either you are with us, or you are with the terrorists," the president warned in a speech before a joint session of Congress nine days after the attacks.[1] Americans signalled their support of the coming "war against terrorism" as the president's approval rating shot up to 86 percent, this from 51 percent before the attacks.[2] Much of this support may have been merely a visceral reaction to the 9/11 attacks but it did not matter. So emboldened, the president now got to work crafting his new foreign policy for America that made preemption the cornerstone of the Bush war on terror.

To guard against such attacks in the future, Bush argued that the nation had to strike before an attack could reach American shores. A foreign policy of restraint, that of containment and deterrence, so prevalent during the fifty-year period of the Cold War, was obsolete in the new century. The United States had to change its foreign policy orientation to protect itself. Foremost in this regard he advocated a willingness to engage enemies in preemptive war, that is, attack them before that foe could harm the United States. To wait invited attacks from terrorists willing to use weapons that would inflict far greater losses than that seen on 9/11.

The policy of preemption developed in two steps. First came the articulation of the policy in a series of presidential statements over an eleven-month period. In November 2001 in Warsaw, Poland, while attending a conference on fighting terrorism, the president repeated his willingness to strike preemptively, stating, "We will not wait for the authors of mass murder to gain the weapons of mass destruction. We act now, because we must lift this dark threat from our age and save generations to come." The need to defend civilization from the evil of terrorism was the US mission.[3] Four months into the new year, before an audience of cadets at the Virginia Military Institute, he restated his warning that nations must choose: "They are with us, or they're with the terrorists."[4] The benefit of standing with the United States was that the inevitable US victory would mean a better world for millions of people.

On June 1, 2002, Bush took a big step forward in putting a face on his intention to drastically reshape the orientation of US foreign policy when he addressed an audience of West Point graduates. He praised past US efforts to remain on the defensive using containment and deterrence.

He then called attention to the new age ushered in with the 9/11 attacks and the need for new thinking. The United States must act first to forestall potential aggression directed against it. Only in this way could America disrupt the looming attacks planned by rogue individuals non-aligned to a state but effectively using such entities as cover. The logic harkened back to the president's statements made in the wake of the terrorist attacks on 9/11 that countries either stood with the United States or were assumed to be acting against it. To deter any threat coming from these hostile nations, the president declared that the United States must "be ready for preemptive action when necessary to defend our liberty and to defend our lives."

The president continued, adding a second key element to preemption. If preemption departed from the Cold War foreign policy of the United States in that America would not hesitate to strike militarily, it bore a strong similarity to that war in another way. The circumstances governing the two conflicts were different, but not the morality that lay at the heart of the policy of deterrence and containment as well as preemption. After 9/11, Bush said that the United States faced "a conflict between good and evil," and the president would meet this challenge to preserve American civilization, indeed world civilization. In sum, a strong sense of history guided this new American policy, and this history validated the option now employed. The United States would not wait until attacked. To delay invited wars of epic proportion, much as had been the case in World War II. Indeed, if US policy was different, the stakes were the same. America now embarked on a new policy, but one that bore the trademark of US policy since its founding, a moral purpose that advanced the interests of the world.[5]

This aim became official policy when the administration wrapped up the evolution of its thinking regarding preemptive strikes with the release of its National Security Strategy report in September 2002. This report formally stated the Bush policy of preemption in the larger context of planning for achieving American security in the post-9/11 world.[6] Gone were the days where the United States faced enemies defined by nation-states fearing retaliation should they launch an attack. Now shadowy operators shielded themselves behind regimes officially disowning the presence of terrorist groups. In this way both opponents hoped for a reprieve from attack. With the demise of the "risk-adverse adversary" came the end of the reticence of such enemies in using weapons of mass destruction. While these weapons also had characterized the Cold War era, these arms in the hands of states always had been what the administration termed "weapons of last resort." These weapons were now the weapons of choice of terrorists and the threat posed by rogue individuals willing to commit acts of terrorism all the greater. Moreover, these terrorists could strike at any time and to great effect. To neutralize these threats and protect itself, America reserved the right to take "anticipatory action." The report categorically stated that "the United States will, if necessary, act preemptively."

The brazen endorsement of US unilateralism registered internationally across a broad spectrum. Secretary of State Colin Powell, acting as the moderate in the administration, tried to calm public fears of what might be perceived as the provocative nature of the policy when he told reporters that the United States had opted for preemption before. He cited two occasions in 1989 as examples, once in the Philippines when US air strikes bolstered the Filipino government and allowed it to withstand a coup attempt, and once in Panama when, according to Powell, the United States invaded this country to protect American lives. The president was now merely restating the right to do it again to both assure the international community that he would be acting lawfully should he order such an attack, and to warn potential foes of the consequences of further attacks on America. Additionally, Powell's very small-scale examples of preemption reassured the international community that the United States would employ an appropriate response to the terror threats it faced. In other words, preemption was not a license for the United States to invade anywhere it wished.[7]

Moreover, Bush did not act alone. Congress soon authorized the attack and did so in bipartisan fashion in October 2002. The final vote was 296 to 133 in the House, and 77 to 23 in the Senate. Twenty-nine Senate Democrats and eighty-one House Democrats voted for it. Only one Senate Republican and six Republican representatives voted against it. Bush now had the backing of Congress. The resolution read in part that the president could use the armed forces of the United States "as he determines to be necessary and appropriate in order to (1) defend the national security of the United States against the continuing threat posed by Iraq; and (2) enforce all relevant United Nations Security Council Resolutions regarding Iraq." The president signed the resolution on October 16, 2002, underscoring his newfound authority by commenting that, "the views and goals of the Congress, as expressed in H.J. Res. 114 and previous congressional resolutions and enactments, and those of the President are the same."[8] At least in the context of the workings of the US government, Bush accurately summed up the significance of the document. Congress, in effect, had approved military preemption.

Now came the second part of the reorientation of US foreign policy as envisioned by the Bush administration, and that was to find a proving ground for preemption. The president and his advisers drew confidence from the American experience in Afghanistan. The United States had attacked this nation on October 7, 2001, targeting Osama Bin Laden, the assumed mastermind of the 9/11 attacks who operated in that country with the approval of the Taliban regime. Bin Laden ultimately escaped capture in the mountains of Tora Bora, but the other purpose of the attack on Afghanistan had succeeded. US Special Forces backed an existing group in Afghanistan opposing the Taliban, the Northern Alliance, and forced that government from power by December 2001. US military force had quickly imposed itself on Afghanistan and in dramatic fashion. Better, the US military had achieved this end with limited numbers of US troops on the ground, avoiding the risk of deploying US soldiers in a quagmire in this south Asian country. With but a handful of American forces the administration had defeated a regime in unfavorable terrain and in an area of the world that challenged American logistical support. It was a clear US success and one that signaled to the world the earnestness behind President Bush's warning to nations that "Either you are with us, or you are with the terrorists." Those that stood against the United States would be and could be dealt with in harsh fashion.

The US military operations in Afghanistan came before the official implementation of the preemption policy. However, emboldened by apparent success in Afghanistan, the administration singled out other nations for preemptive action because it believed they continued to shield terrorist networks. In his State of the Union address on January 29, 2002, the president identified three states as representing the foremost threat to the security of the United States. North Korea, Iran, and Iraq all sought weapons of mass destruction, all fostered regional instability in their part of the world, and all backed terrorism in some way or another. In the new age of the post-9/11 world, this "axis of evil" represented a threat that could not be ignored. Most egregiously, each state could arm terrorist organizations with nuclear weapons or other weapons of mass destruction and these groups could then attack the United States clandestinely achieving surprise and causing great harm to the US homeland. The risk they posed was a potential tragedy far greater than what had happened on 9/11. Only one thing could prevent these attacks and that was to stop them before they occurred. "I will not wait on events, while dangers gather," Bush said. Preemption was a necessity born of the unique reality of the twenty-first century.[9]

Of these three states, the administration decided that Iraq would be the first target of the new policy of preemption. A twenty-five-page National Intelligence Estimate released to the public by the CIA in October 2002 addressed Iraq's weapons capabilities and unequivocally stated that weapons of mass destruction lay within Hussein's grasp.[10] Bush and key members of his team, vice president Dick Cheney in particular, voiced fears that any weapons of mass destruction produced in Iraq could find their way into the hands of terrorists who would not hesitate to use them against the United States. Furthermore, they charged that Iraq's president, Saddam Hussein, had a history of sympathy, if not outright alliance, with various terrorist organizations, in particular al Qaeda, the group associated with the 9/11 attacks. Finally, given Hussein's mercurial personality, his demagoguery when trying to assume a key leadership role in the Arab world, and his abusive measures to remain in control of his own country, this was more than enough for him to be regarded as a dangerous man. In the eyes of the Bush administration, he was evil. It was a combination that Bush decided made Hussein such a great danger that he had to be dealt with as soon as possible. That occasion was March 19, 2003.

A larger geo-political concern voiced by a new element of the political right, the neo-conservatives, reinforced this logic that Iraq had to be neutralized by an American attack. Their belief in the ability of the United States to shape the new era came from an expansive view of American power. The United States had defeated the USSR in a lengthy and costly war, and now stood as the preeminent power in the world. In the Middle East, Iraqi intransigence suggested there were limits to this newly won power. If such defiance had had to be accepted in the Cold War era given the threat of nuclear war with the USSR, this was not the case in the 1990s or thereafter. The United States could act with impunity to ensure its security. The United States needed only to take advantage of its power, not remain mired in old thinking that dictated caution where none was needed. As always, the United States did not act selfishly when it did project its power in the world. When it made war, it did so to spread democracy, and in this way it liberated millions of people demanding the right of self-rule. This moral purpose, teamed with unprecedented American power, required that the United States unleash its military to remake the world so it was free of evil. The preceding century had seen a hesitant American nation reluctantly pulled into wars perpetrated by those harboring evil designs. The new century would be different in that wars would be perpetrated by those spreading hope.[11]

The grandiose thinking reinforced the desire to attack Iraq because it represented a key test of the neo-conservative world view. Paul Wolfowitz, now deputy secretary of defense in the second Bush administration, laid the blueprint for meeting this challenge in a report he circulated in 1991 within the first Bush administration. The timing meant everything. Authored long before 9/11, the report, a bi-annual study titled, in this case, the *Defense Planning Guidance for the Fiscal Years 1994–1999*, targeted US allies as the chief obstacle to American preeminence in world affairs, not Iraq. Should the United States fail to keep nuclear weapons from falling into the hands of Iraq or North Korea, nations such as Germany and Japan would feel the need to rearm to protect themselves. They would then compete with the United States and challenge a US-dictated "world order" in the post-Cold War era. This twisted reasoning grouped Iraq and North Korea together with longstanding friendly nations as "potential competitors." To deter this threat, the report called for the United States to act unilaterally against Iraq or North Korea to secure American hegemony in world affairs and so protect American interests, and to act preemptively if necessary. There was to be only one dominant military power, the United States, and its leaders "must maintain the mechanisms for deterring potential competitors from even aspiring to a larger regional or global role." In this light, preemption was not a right of self-defense, but a deliberate effort to assert an American hegemony globally. American civilization would reign and the world would heed its call.[12] Hussein was but a small step forward in this direction.

If this American ascendancy appeared to neo-conservatives to be a natural result of the unfolding American experiment, to the leaders and peoples of other nations it was no more than American imperialism. In fact, this report, when leaked to the *New York Times,* created such uproar that President George H. W. Bush ordered it rewritten by Cheney, then secretary of defense, and Powell, the acting Chairman of the Joint Chiefs of Staff. It reemerged a month later stripped of claims of unilateral military action to assure US hegemony. Instead, the document used language designed to assure nations that the United States would continue to seek out friends to form alliances and work multilaterally. There would be no preemptive strikes by the United States.[13]

This reaction from within Republican ranks was a clear setback to neo-conservative ambitions. More disappointment followed. Forced to the sidelines during the Clinton presidency, they could do no more than offer policy recommendations to the sitting president. They repeated the call for preemption against Iraq in an open letter to President Clinton in 1998 from the neo-conservative think thank, Project for a New American Century (PNAC).[14] They rejected the Clinton policy of containment, of isolating Hussein in the hopes of a coup within Iraq removing the dictator, and of imposing economic sanctions on Iraq in the belief that this step would force Hussein's compliance with the UN demands of disarmament so Iraq could again enter the international community. Ample evidence spoke to the failure of this policy. Hussein appeared firmly in control long after surviving his most vulnerable period of March 1991, just after UN forces had expelled him from Kuwait and Hussein had faced rebellions in northern and southern Iraq. No coup materialized. The almost daily skirmishes that occurred over a number of years between UN aircraft enforcing the no-fly zone over the country and Iraqi air defense assets contesting this international presence, underscored the regime's defiance of the international community, not a willingness to rejoin it. Moreover, America's allies were threatening to end economic sanctions imposed on Iraq to force a regime change. Undaunted, Saddam continued to obstruct UN weapon inspectors trying to verify that Iraq had destroyed its weapons of mass destruction.

Signers such as Wolfowitz, Don Rumsfeld, later secretary of defense under George W. Bush, and Richard Armitage, who would serve as deputy secretary of state under Colin Powell, urged an American attack on Iraq to protect American interests in the Middle East. The refreshing candor of stating a policy that looked to secure oil resources as the foremost reason for military intervention in the region amplified the shocking nature of the idea of unilateral military action against Iraq. Accept a more difficult path and lead, they pleaded. Recognizing the difficulty of moving US policy away from a marriage with multilateralism, the letter offered good news even in this respect. A US-led preemptive attack would validate UN authority by holding Hussein accountable for defying the UN mandates the international community had imposed upon Iraq though this body. A unilateral action would actually restore credibility to the multilateral body of the United Nations. It was a win-win situation. Clinton did not change policy, however. Worse, neo-conservatives believed the Clinton policy of containment perpetuated the security risk posed by Iraq, making it more likely that Hussein could export weapons of mass destruction. Decisive action would end this risk once and for all, but it was clearly not forthcoming from Clinton. Should they be given the chance, neo-conservatives told themselves they would act differently.

In so rebuking Clinton, neo-conservatives forgot their agreement with or contribution to Clinton's containment policy. Many members of the 2000 Bush administration had been on the scene when the international coalition defeated Iraq in 1991. At this time, to a man they stressed the need for caution and they shrank from advocating the US occupation of Iraq. The potential of guerrilla war was too great, they argued. Cheney was the most explicit, appearing on *This Week with David Brinkley* on April 7, 1991, and stating: "I think for us to get American military personnel involved in a civil war inside Iraq would literally be a quagmire. Once we got to Baghdad, what would we do? Who would we put in power? What kind of government would we have? Would it be a Sunni government, a Shi'a government, a Kurdish government? Would it be secular, along the lines of the Ba'ath Party? Would [it] be fundamentalist Islamic?" These questions pointed to the impossibility of the task. "I do not think the United States wants to have U.S. military forces accept casualties and accept the responsibility of trying to govern Iraq. I think it makes no sense at all," Cheney said.[15] UN forces left Iraqi territory intact, and Saddam reestablished his grip on the country.

To many observers at the time of the First Gulf War, the United States had failed to complete its mission and topple Hussein. Wolfowitz, then undersecretary of defense for policy, refuted these charges publicly by stressing the limits of American power to transform Iraq. "No one can read about what's going on there without feeling a great sense of sympathy for what's going on," he told the press, "But that doesn't mean it is in our power to straighten it out." He listed modest goals. "If we could identify a democratic faction in Iraq, I think we'd look at it differently. In a way, I think we will settle for something way short of democracy. If it's just a country that can treat its people decently and not attack its neighbors, it would be great progress," he said.[16] According to this logic, Hussein's removal by a US invasion led to uncertain outcomes that did not necessarily promise democracy and testified to the limits of American power.

President George H. W. Bush offered repeated denunciations of such a step because he was determined not to involve the United States in another Vietnam-type conflict. At one point he said, "All along, I have said that the United States is not going to intervene militarily in Iraq's internal affairs and risk being drawn into a Vietnam-style quagmire." No matter the brutality of the measures Hussein employed to hold onto power, the president stood by his decision. He continued, saying, "This remains the case. Nor will we become an occupying power with U.S. troops patrolling the streets of Baghdad."[17] He also took steps to reassure world leaders that the United States had no intention of occupying Iraq. To Soviet leader Mikhail Gorbachev, Bush offered assurances that there would be no permanent American ground force in Iraq and that the United States had no interest in intervening in an Iraqi civil war or in dismembering the country. As America helped channel aid to beleaguered Kurdish refugees, Bush told Turkey's president, Turgut Özal, that any American military presence was temporary because "I don't want the U.S. to become bogged down in a civil war in Iraq."[18]

As late as 1998 the ex-president adamantly defended his position by casting the decision not to invade Iraq in its broadest strategic terms. He wrote, "Going in and occupying Iraq, thus unilaterally exceeding the United Nations' mandate, would have destroyed the precedent of international response to aggression that we hoped to establish." Moreover, Bush stressed the obvious problem raised by such a move: "We would have been forced to occupy Baghdad and, in effect, rule Iraq." This made no sense because it further weakened the US position internationally. "The coalition would instantly have collapsed, the Arabs deserting it in anger and other allies pulling out as well," Bush said. He then stressed the interminable nature of such an occupation, commenting, "Under those circumstances, there was no viable 'exit strategy' we could see." He summed up his view by writing, "Had we gone the invasion route, the United States could conceivably still be an occupying power in a bitterly hostile land."[19] His assessment spoke to the dangers of an unstable Iraq capable of consuming any force that tried to tame the country.

In 2003, as neo-conservatives geared up for the invasion of Iraq, they forgot such caution. It might never have been there. Wolfowitz might have held the line during the first Bush administration and mouthed his support of a policy of refraining from attacking Iraq and removing Hussein in 1991, but he did so reluctantly. The report he authored in 1991 spoke to his real policy view of a willingness to use US military power to ensure a US dominance of world affairs. Iraq remained a key stepping stone to this end at that time and right up to 2003. Cheney also may have still understood the risks in attacking Iraq, but when he spoke publicly he voiced optimism of a quick campaign; his private comments are still unclear. In 2003, he opted for the invasion anyway given the danger he believed Iraq posed to the United States. Any rogue element possessing weapons of mass destruction posed an imminent threat. To wait for such attacks to unfold was unthinkable given the magnitude of the destruction they could inflict. If the United States responded with military overkill in terms of countering a potential attack on America, such was the necessity of the new kind of war. Ron Suskind labeled this Cheney logic the "one percent doctrine," a resolve to act and meet even a slight possibility of a threat to the United States with military force.[20] The president concurred. After 9/11, the rationale of America protecting itself with unilateral military action now seemed clear, even vindicated. The United States had the power to do this; it now must possess the will.

Preemption, as the Bush administration defined it, matched the neo-conservative desire to use the American military abroad to secure its interests. They saw no contradiction in offering repeated assurances of a US willingness to work within the international community prefaced by the bold statement that America would act unilaterally to protect itself. Neither did the president. Here was a flexible response to a changed world, a sign of a willingness on the part of the United States to work within the norms of the international community but also a willingness to make tough decisions and go it alone if necessary. But such a mandate as presented in the 2002 National Security Strategy report possessed deep roots that spoke to the more foreboding aims of this American plan of action. The ascendancy of neo-conservative thinking within the administration, best seen in the preemptive policy, raised the specter of American aggression as the driving rationale behind the attack on Iraq. In a very real way, preemption was no more than a means to this end.

With fears of a messy occupation either forgotten or ignored, all that was needed on the administration's part was a compliant general willing to overturn the Powell doctrine of resorting to military force only when enjoying overwhelming numbers and only when that mission possessed a clear exit strategy. The neo-conservatives found such a man in General Tommy Franks. Under prodding from the administration, Franks reduced the planned strike force of half a million soldiers to 100,000. His plan now satisfied Rumsfeld, who had made plain his desire for an attack with troops totaling something in the order of 150,000. The president and his key advisers embraced the plan at a Camp David meeting in September 2002. There, Powell offered a dissenting voice, insisting on a larger number of troops that he believed was needed, even if this demand contravened the Rumsfeld goal of streamlining the attack. In the end, Franks put his faith on what he perceived as a revolution in warfare, satisfying himself and his superiors that there would be no manpower problem given superior American firepower and mobility. On this dubious conclusion, what Franks nicknamed "shock and awe," rested the fate of operation "Iraqi Freedom."[21]

With these decisions settled, the neo-conservatives at last could undertake their long-awaited invasion of Iraq, and they voiced great optimism of success. Cheney assured Tim Russert of *Meet the Press*, in an interview on the eve of war, that given the brutality of Saddam Hussein, "things have gotten so bad inside Iraq, from the standpoint of the Iraqi people, my belief is we will, in fact, be greeted as liberators." William Kristol, chairman of the Project for the New American Century, offered a representative statement when he said in testimony before the Senate Foreign Relations Committee as it debated the merits of an attack on Iraq, "American and alliance forces will be welcomed in Baghdad as liberators." An Iraqi exile uttered the most famous remark given its bitter reverberation in the face of the insurgency that was to come. Scholar Kanan Makiya told Bush personally that, "People will greet the [American] troops with sweets and flowers."[22] Bush was elated, recognizing that such a greeting would serve as a ringing endorsement of preemption in the hands of the United States.

The international community disagreed. When Powell stood before the United Nations during the final preparations for war, he argued that an attack on Iraq was legal in the name of preemption. In a presentation given on February 5, 2003, Powell did his best to convince this world body that it had to act to disarm Iraq.[23] However, with the level of threat uncertain, few nations saw things his way. No matter Powell's appeal to the United

Nations, the Security Council rejected his argument and the United States did not gain UN approval for an attack on Iraq. Defeat before the United Nations was so certain that the US did not even ask for a vote on the issue. Instead, Bush demanded that the United Nations pass a resolution calling for Iraq to immediately disarm or be disarmed by force. He made this announcement on March 16, 2003, during a summit held on Portugal's Azores islands in the Atlantic Ocean. Standing alongside the prime ministers of Britain and Spain, the president said that the United States and its "friends" would act to enforce existing UN Security Council Resolution 1441 from November 8, 2002, that sought to disarm Iraq of its weapons of mass destruction. The mandate had proved unenforceable within three months after Iraq had used troops to interfere with weapons inspectors. The administration argued that its policy of preemption validated the United Nations by enforcing this resolution, not that it defied this body's authority by acting unilaterally. In other words, by holding Hussein accountable, preemption secured the US goal of eliminating a threat while serving the interests of the international community. It was a fitting scene, the American president and but two supporters declaring that "tomorrow is a moment of truth for the world."[24] If this rhetoric overstated things a bit, Bush's comment was exact in at least one respect. As things would turn out, the US-led invasion of Iraq would prove a moment of truth for the Bush policy of preemption.

The Attack

On March 17, 2003, President Bush gave Hussein forty-eight hours to leave Iraq to avoid hostilities. The deadline came and went with no response from the Iraqi president. The attack started by air on March 19. The ground offensive followed two days later, preceded by special forces that seized Iraqi oilfields and prepared the battlefield for invasion. On March 22, President Bush announced that Operation Iraqi Freedom had begun, and its goal was "to disarm Iraq of weapons of mass destruction, to end Saddam Hussein's support for terrorism, and to free the Iraqi people."[25] The US-led assault on Iraq began with this moral claim appealing to self-defense as a reason for preemptive war with the added civilizational goal of freeing Iraq from tyranny.

The US-led attack on Iraq was not a surprise. The Iraqis observed the US buildup in Kuwait and waited. This was the first of many difficulties the invasion force had to overcome. Another problem arose when Turkey refused the US access to Turkish soil despite a US offer of $6 billion in aid. This setback deprived Franks of a northern attack route and of an entire division, the 4th US infantry division that was to attack from this direction. Instead, the attack would come strictly from Kuwait, the expected avenue of advance. No matter these restrictions, the attack would go forward. If anything, the one-dimensional axis of advance helped obscure the limited number of troops available to make the attack. Hopefully, Iraq resistance would crumple so precipitously that the Americans could advance with ease. Stout resistance might test the conclusion that more troops were unnecessary.

Franks decided on an assault that was simplistic in the extreme, a two-pronged attack from Kuwait. The US Marines spearheaded one arm of the advance, while the US 3rd Infantry Division composed the other. The small British contingent expected to join the "Coalition of the Willing" would attack and seize the largest southern city, Basra. All told, it was an army numbering but 140,000 soldiers and marines. Almost twice that number of Iraqis, some 300,000 soldiers, opposed the offensive. But, if limited in size, the invasion force possessed tremendous mobility and, when teamed with air assets, it had at its disposal an incredible amount of firepower. Thanks to these two assets, the compact nature of the force did little to impair its offensive capability, much as Franks had envisioned, and as the American army soon proved.

An initial breakthrough was immediate and the advance rapid. Iraqi resistance crumbled, and the assaulting forces now looked to secure key landmarks to make certain that natural obstacles did not aid the Iraqis by giving scattered units a chance to recover and form a defensive front. Bridges over both the Euphrates and Tigris Rivers became key objectives, and for the most part, fast-moving American assault teams did reach these areas before effective Iraqi resistance could take shape. This is the rosy picture offered in books written in a matter of months after the attack. Distinguished scholars such as Williamson Murray and Robert H. Scales, in *The Iraq War: A Military History*, and John Keegan, in *The Iraq War*, presented a view of the offensive as a race across the desert guided by a sound plan that led to success.[26] From the very start of the attack, however, Franks dealt with problems that undermined this view, including, most seriously, weighing the decision to remove a corps commander leading one arm of the attack on Baghdad. This man, Lt. General William A. Wallace, told reporters that he would have to delay the push forward until he could eliminate the *fedayeen* stoutly resisting the advance on the capital.[27] These irregular fighters threatened the supply links to the capital and since there were not enough troops to both advance and safeguard the important lines of communication, Wallace looked to halt and shore up his rear. Franks ordered Wallace forward to the capital and Wallace obeyed. But as a result, Franks ignored a main component of the insurgency that was to plague US occupation forces after the war officially ended. Had he had more troops, perhaps Franks could have maintained the momentum of his advance and blunted potential irregular resistance.

No matter these problems, by early April, the invasion force approached the outskirts of Baghdad more or less according to plan and without suffering a major loss or setback. The invasion now faced the most difficult challenge of the two-week-old attack. As US forces approached Baghdad, American commanders worried that Hussein might use chemical or biological weapons to defend his capital. When this possibility did not occur, American commanders still worried about a Stalingrad-type battle where US soldiers would be drawn into a costly struggle in the city itself. Should this happen, the good news up to this point would be completely overshadowed by the high casualties expected in a deadly fight in the Iraqi capital. The US military dealt with this problem in a manner characteristic of the planning of the campaign to this point, an aggressive, even reckless, plan of action. A combat team raced into the city, successfully reaching the center after drawing much fire but only sustaining light casualties. This action was repeated a second time with similar results. Stiff opposition failed to materialize and resistance in the city ended abruptly. Nothing symbolized this achievement more than the hundreds of Iraqis who turned to US military personnel to help them topple the enormous statue of Hussein located near the center of the city in Firdos Square. This spectacle was seen throughout the world and trumpeted the great American success.

Not content to reap this award of seizing the Iraqi capital and deposing Hussein, the Bush administration opted to cap the outstanding US military performance in Iraq with a formal declaration of victory on May 1, 2003. Ferried in a war plane to the deck of a carrier, the president congratulated the US military on a job well done. True, Hussein was not captured but he was on the run. The US preemptive attack had achieved its primary goal of deposing the dictator, and so it was a success. Even better, Iraq would no longer serve as a safe harbor for al Qaeda or as a supplier of weapons of mass destruction. The president warned that the war against terrorism was not over, but he offered the good news that the tide had turned. Civilized nations could rest assured that America had carried the world standard of freedom, planted it in Iraq, and struck a blow for human liberty by defeating evil.[28] The Iraqi campaign had proven that preemption had not invalidated American benevolence when making war.

The full ramifications of the attack were only just beginning to make themselves felt, however. The president's declaration of success came as Iraq clearly faced a void of authority marked by looting and violence. Here were the seeds of the guerrilla resistance that were to challenge the US claim of victory. The unsettling nature of the "victory" in Iraq echoed well outside the bounds of that country. The US military action in Iraq had strained longstanding friendships with European nations, Germany and France in particular. And how Iraq would prove a decisive contribution to the war on terror remained unclear, a problem amplified with each passing day no weapons of mass destruction were found. A US preemptive strike in Iraq now faced a different measure of success, one all the more difficult to determine should an endless war take hold there. In short, it was not at all clear that the tide had turned in the war against terror. The complications inherent in the attack now came to the foreground and with them came a new understanding of the meaning of this preemptive strike.

Success

The Bush rationale for preemption broke down immediately in the aftermath of the attack. Despite the efforts of three separate search teams, weapons of mass destruction were never found. This included efforts by Hans Blitz of the United Nations, and another by the Iraq Survey Group headed first by David Kay and then by Charles Duelfer. Kay and Duelfer were able to do their work after the country had been liberated, that is, after Hussein was deposed and when these inspectors had a free hand to scour the country. They found nothing, resulting in pleas from the president for US citizens to be patient. Iraq was the size of California, he reminded Americans. His more adamant defenders offered the absurd notion that Hussein had moved his stockpile of weapons to a neighboring country such as Syria. The spectacle of hundreds of thousands of warheads, just one of the assumed weapons cache in Hussein's possession, being moved without detection by US intelligence was too fantastic to be believed. The search finally ended on September 30, 2004, with the publication of the Duelfer Report, the investigators admitting, that for whatever reasons, they had found nothing.[29] It was a crushing setback to the preemptive rationale for the attack on Iraq.

Nor could the administration establish links between Hussein and al Qaeda. American fears that Hussein would pass weapons to this terrorist group had justified the US invasion as self-defense. But a number of intelligence reports had cast doubt on this connection prior to war, given the animosity between al Qaeda and Hussein.[30] US intelligence prior to the March 2003 invasion had followed what they characterized as a sporadic relationship between Iraqi nationals and members of al Qaeda, since the analysts either could not substantiate the evidence of contacts or doubted it altogether.[31] And incredibly, a CIA report also explained any contacts as an effort by Iraqi agents to infiltrate and disrupt or control al Qaeda, possibly to shield Iraq from attacks by that terrorist organization.[32]

No evidence changed this picture once US forces controlled the country. Shorn of a discovery of weapons of mass destruction and of a discovery of ties to al Qaeda, the invasion of Iraq quickly lost its most compelling reasons for action, deflating the euphoria of having removed Hussein with a lightning stroke. Since Iraq did not pose a threat to the United States, here was a devastating blow to the preemption strategy.

Inconsistencies in the administration's application of preemption again questioned the necessity for a military attack on Iraq. Bush continues to argue publicly that Iran and North Korea, the other members of the "axis of evil," remain threats to US security. But to face them, the administration has pursued means other than a preemptive military attack. The US policy at present is to contain Iran, although given the proximity of the American army in Iraq to Iran, the administration offers more bluster towards that state, refusing to rule out the use of military force against it. More galling is the administration's insistence on using a regional power such as China to restrain North Korea, while relying on the United Nations to control Iran's nuclear ambitions. These options of courting neighbors in the Middle East and securing UN authority for the attack on Iraq had been cast to the side by the administration when weighing its decision to invade Iraq. It may well be that Iraq was the most dangerous of the three states in the "axis of evil." But by seeking to contain these other states with actions short of military force, the administration suggested that the nation had not needed to resort to preemptive military action in the case of Iraq.

Preemption failed another benchmark of success because the American invasion of that country created more problems than it solved. Hussein certainly fell from power, a fact registered with his execution by the American-created government of Iraq just after Christmas 2006. However, the insurgency now engulfing US forces in the country has created a host of new security threats. Chief among them is that Iraq indeed assumes a key role in the war on terror, even if it did not sponsor al Qaeda before the US invasion. A 2006 National Intelligence Estimate (NIE) report concluded that the threat of terrorist attacks had increased after the US invasion of Iraq because there was now a large number of battle-hardened, radical Muslim fighters who had trained in Iraq and looked for opportunities to strike the West. A subsequent report a year later confirmed this threat, that it came principally from al Qaeda, and that it included potential attacks on the US homeland.[33] Perhaps there can be no greater condemnation of the policy of preemption than recognizing that it created more enemies who are now pitted against the United States in the war on terror. The president's response is to cling to another attempt at a public rallying call. Better to wage this war in Iraq than on American soil, he asserts. These frequent statements indicate that the president may not have grasped the failure of preemption as it applies to Iraq. While Bush's insistence that Iraq is the center-front to the war on terror does appear more compelling in light of the 2006 and 2007 NIE reports, the president overlooks the obvious conclusion that he created this front on terror where none existed before. Preemption is supposed to eliminate threats, not create them as occurred in Iraq. By this measure, the US invasion of Iraq was a tremendous failure.

This shifting of position to justify the US invasion of Iraq has continued and revolved around redefining the imminent nature of the threat facing the United States. In the wake of the failure to find weapons of mass destruction, Bush adjusted the objective of the attack, publicly stating that the *intent* to develop weapons of mass destruction was enough cause to strike Iraq preemptively and wage a moral war in Iraq. This statement put the administration in the wrong again, this time fighting an illegal preventive war in Iraq since intent did not constitute an imminent threat. Four years later the administration still struggles with understanding this key to preemption. Condoleezza Rice, a trusted Bush confidant now serving as secretary of state, put this failure in plain view in April 2007 when she said the question about the imminence of the threat was not "if somebody is going to strike tomorrow." "It's whether you believe you're in a stronger position today to deal with the threat, or whether you're going to be in a stronger position tomorrow."[34] Here was an argument in favor of preventive war, not preemption, since, according to Rice, Iraq posed a potential threat, not an imminent one. In so arguing, the administration abdicated the moral high ground, probably without realizing that in their public statements lay the stated failure of preemption.

Conclusion

President Bush argued that a preemptive policy was the best course of action to follow given the advent of the terrorist threat in the post-9/11 world. American fears that Iraqi leader Saddam Hussein would pass weapons of mass destruction to al Qaeda, the terrorist group responsible for the 9/11 attacks, justified a preemptive US invasion of that country in the name of self-defense. In so acting, the administration made clear its belief that terrorist attacks are repelled best by resorting to American invasions of enemy states harboring terrorists or rogue states possibly arming terrorists. The Bush administration also realized that preemptive war might not appear to the US public as self-defense. Rather, Americans would believe the United States had departed from its Cold War policy of deterrence and containment and assumed the offensive. Establishing the morality of a preemptive attack was therefore of paramount importance for it provided a direct tie to America's notion of using force only in self-defense. To do this, the administration asserted a belief in the righteousness of its cause as a means to blunt further terrorist attacks on the United States. It also declared that any invasion represented a benevolent gesture by the United States in that it would free beleaguered peoples from oppression. This moral stand on both accounts compelled US military action and Iraq appeared the perfect test-case for this new rationale of US foreign policy. Defeating Hussein's regime would make it clear that the United States could fight preemptively and still occupy the moral high ground.

The strategy of preemption meant the United States had to break from its tradition of going to war only in response to aggression. As the president repeatedly said, it was time to make some hard choices. One of these was that the United States would have to attack another country that the United States believed posed a threat to it. This approach would be an imperfect science and some mistakes might be made. The intelligence fiasco that preceded the 2003 Iraq war spoke to such risks. But the strategy of preemption, Cheney's "one percent doctrine," had to be followed to protect the country from terrorism, and the intelligence had certainly raised suspicion of such a threat. Moreover, even if the United States was attacking, the morality of American foreign policy would remain intact because the administration did not find its morality in the act of preemption. Rather, it found its morality in the purpose of preemption, in the assumed superiority of American democracy that would be transplanted to the targeted country. For this reason, the United States could act preemptively and be assured of the moral certitude of its actions.

The administration always maintained that military force was the best course of action for the United States to take in Iraq, given the looming threat that country posed; that danger had to be faced as soon as possible. That this was not the case, that Iraq was without weapons of mass destruction, was known with certainty only after the invasion. Moreover, other options had been tried short of military force, such as diplomacy and economic sanctions. Containment was deemed unsatisfactory by the Bush administration. There also had been a remarkable audacity on the part of Hussein to give the impression that he had a weapons capacity he did not possess. The obfuscation so often practiced by the Iraqis fostered acute fears of Iraqi-sponsored terrorism on the part of US leaders. For his foolhardiness, Hussein paid dearly by provoking a US attack. This generous view of the US motives for acting preemptively certainly has to be true to some extent and carries with it the much needed larger point that the moral arguments behind the invasion remain intact. This line of argument assumes that the administration was misled by US intelligence as to the danger Iraq posed to the United States homeland, and that the administration did not doctor the record to warrant an invasion of Iraq. The Iraq offensive was not aggression but a mistake. In this way, the virtue believed inherent in American foreign policy remains intact.

Before acting preemptively, the administration had covered its legal bases both abroad and at home. The United States operated within the confines of the United Nations since the US attack on Iraq matched the definition of preemption as accepted by that body. Article 51 of the UN Charter allows states to take defensive measures and attack another nation as long as the threat is an imminent one and as long as the response is appropriate to the threat. Members of the Bush administration understood the difficulty of determining what constituted an "appropriate," preemptive attack in response to terrorism perpetrated by organizations only sometimes enjoying state support, but eliminating such threats was absolutely necessary. In the face of such an imminent threat, the United States unleashed an appropriate response to neutralize Iraq. To act otherwise in the age of terror was irresponsible. The administration did more than this by invading Iraq. It also gave some much-needed backbone to an institution that mired itself in protocol at the expense of action. The numerous sanctions in place against Iraq had gone largely ignored. Now the United States brought this transgressor state to account by enforcing the sanctions on behalf of the United Nations.

Additionally, Bush had the approbation of Congress. The Senate and House had voted in favor of allowing Bush to conduct his preemptive policy. Consequently, the president did not act alone. Congress had authorized the attack, and had done so in bipartisan fashion. By clearing the offensive with the United Nations and Congress, there had been no rush to war, as the president insisted. The president had acted responsibly abroad and at home. What more could he have done?

When Iraqi resistance collapsed precipitously, neo-conservative thinking appeared to have been vindicated. American military power was impressive, destroying a formidable foe in just two weeks and at little cost: only 138 Americans killed. Also, the civilian side had been spared the worst in terms of the numbers killed and in terms of the destruction of infrastructure. This last area had been kept intact as much as possible in order to speed the rebuilding of the country. By discovering the will to use American power, to act in place of the international community that refused to act, the United States had eliminated a dangerous regime. This act of good on the world stage was evidence of American sponsorship of justice, not an invasion evidencing US aggression.

That things turned out so differently in Iraq belied the moral reasoning the administration gave for using preemption. With no weapons found and no ties to al Qaeda, the moral justification for preemption faded since Iraq did not pose a threat to the US homeland. Bush laid this error in threat perception at the feet of the intelligence community. Less clear was how the administration handled the volume of information generated on the topic. The October 2002 report it made public was but a condensed version of a classified ninety-page report that offered a much more thorough review of Iraq's weapons programs and voiced grave concerns that the threats were not credible. Even a cursory comparison of the two NIE reports makes it clear that this issue was thoroughly examined by the intelligence community and that much disagreement arose over Iraq's weapons capabilities.[35] In pointing to a single, abridged intelligence report that expressed unanimity of opinion and therefore served as the basis of his decision, Bush, and his administration, exposed themselves as overly simplistic or, worse, as prevaricators willingly doctoring the intelligence to justify the strike on Iraq. These two ugly choices meant that the US attack on Iraq in 2003 lacked any mantle of self-defense, a fact sufficient to undo any legitimate motive for a preemptive invasion, including Cheney's "one percent doctrine." Operation Iraqi Freedom was not preemption at all but took an unsettling step toward aggression.

Besides blaming the intelligence community, the president hoped to cope with this policy failure by arguing that Hussein had had the *intent* to build these weapons, and so the dictator was indeed a grave danger to the international community and he had to be neutralized. In so arguing, the administration equated preemption and preventative attacks. But these two terms are very different. Preemption allows a country facing imminent attack to take effective and necessary measures to defend itself. Preventive war is something else altogether. In opting for this strategy, an attacker lays waste to an enemy that, if given time, would possibly attack it. The distinction between these terms was important because the morality of the US attack on Iraq lay in the balance. Preemption enjoys the sanction of the international community. Preventative war, on the other hand, does not, given the ability of such logic to underwrite an attack by any nation anywhere at any time.[36] While the president and his neo-conservative supporters could tell themselves they aided the world in acting preemptively in Iraq and removing Hussein from power, the attack came under the category of preventive war. That this was the case knocked another pillar from the Bush argument of preemption as self-defense. Preemption would be a new policy for the United States, but one cast in the shadow of aggression.

The deep roots of preemption suggested another motive that weakened the moral stand of the United States. A drive to achieve US supremacy in world affairs drove the neo-conservative embrace of preemption long before the 9/11 attacks. Wolfowitz's efforts from within the first Bush administration testify to this fact. So too does the letter-writing campaign of the newly created Project for a New American Century. In each case, the unilateral design of the proposed policy and the preferred use of military force in achieving the desired end of US dominance gained the members of this organization few supporters; even Republican partisans considered them reckless. However, this view changed in the wake of 9/11. Caution was ignored and a defense of America now seemed best served by a unilateral offensive that utilized the great military power of the United States. Preemption was a matter of self-defense, the advance of American power a blessing for the world. Bush allowed the neo-conservative thinking of defending American interests by taking preemptive military steps to ensure American hegemony in the world to hijack the American people's legitimate call for effective self-defense in an age of terror. These two aims needed to be mutually exclusive to ensure the moral purpose of the administration in crafting a new foreign policy. If the Bush administration understood the distinction, we do not know about it. In another example of simplistic thinking, it conflated the two ideas publicly so that, once again, preemption challenged the morality supposedly driving American foreign policy.

This self-righteous myopia always shrouded the reasoning of those seeking to attack Iraq within the administration, and while they embraced the term of preemption, they rushed into a war to secure US hegemony that cast the United States as an aggressor in Iraq. The hegemony was apparent in the unilateralism of the invasion since the United Nations did not approve the attack. The United States did not even put a resolution in favor of its war in Iraq to a vote, given the certainty of its defeat. This defeat underscored the futility of Powell's efforts before the United Nations, his errors in threat perception enumerated in a fashion that Powell later referred to as "painful" and as a permanent "blot" on his record.[37] The United Nations also vigorously contested Bush's use of existing UN sanctions as justification of the invasion of Iraq. Hegemony was apparent in the inappropriate use of force—the world's foremost military power inflicting a hammer blow on a much weaker state to occupy that country and stop its "threat" to America. Such defiance of the international will and the excessive show of force both bear the hallmarks of aggression and, for this reason, cast the US preemptive strike against Iraq in an unfavorable light. This outcome stressed the difficulty of sustaining the moral purpose of the US decision to attack Iraq.

Only a civilizational purpose was needed to complete the hallmarks of aggression, and Bush provided that as well. The notion that Hussein was an evil man stood as the lone justification for the military attack, but it was enough for the administration to insist that the moral purpose of American foreign policy remained intact. For Bush, preemption enabled the United States to confront an ideology of hatred with the best weapon possible, freedom. But the moral cause Bush found in preemption actually served as a justification for aggression. When it attacked Iraq, the United States acted to defend civilization, an all-embracing term but one clearly resting on western norms of elections to secure representative government and a material prosperity derived from open trade markets. In sum, the world had to become like the United States. Those resisting this end Bush classified as evil. The moral vision offered in preemption never went past these general terms that justified the imposition of the US will on the world. Consequently, the administration did not see a need to differentiate between preemption in the name of self-defense and preemption in the name of US world hegemony. In their eyes, the second category did not exist. A single morality underlay a single policy. Americans practiced the correct form of morality, one that best fit the world. US preemptive war merely returned rogue nations to the brotherhood of civilized nations, or stymied those radicals seeking to destroy the best system.

The simplicity of thought endemic in the Bush administration's conduct of Iraq policy undid the morality of preemption. The most telling point here was the brevity of the argument in favor of preemption. One can only hope the administration had given this strategy more attention in private than it did in public—the president's four, key speeches. The biggest problem of simplicity when concocting the policy of preemption and selecting Iraq as the first target was that, in its own fumbling way, the administration accepted the neo-conservative argument that the United States had to use its military preemptively. Bush ignored the hegemonic purpose of this policy in favor of waging war to save civilization. Even if attacking first, the justness of the cause imbued the policy with a moral standing. So the new approach was grounded in an old morality always associated with US policy. But preemption in Iraq did represent a drastic departure in US foreign policy. What is new was that in its war in Iraq, the United States acted as an aggressor nation because it pursued an assumed universal good. Unfortunately, like Bush, most Americans continue to view preemption as a policy that features the only morality, and therefore justifies war, no matter the historical context that belies this belief.

Endnotes

1. George W. Bush, "Address to a Joint Session of Congress and the American People," White House Press Release, September 20, 2001, http://www.whitehouse.gov/news/releases/2001/09/20010920-8.html.

2. Michael Genovese, "George W. Bush and Presidential Leadership: the Un-Hidden Hand Presidency of George W. Bush," chap. 10 in *Striking First: The Preventive War Doctrine and the Reshaping of US Foreign Policy* (Basingstoke: Palgrave Macmillan, 2004), 142.

3. George W. Bush, "Remarks by the President to the Warsaw Conference on Combating Terrorism," November 6, 2001, Office of International Information Programs, US Department of State, http://usinfo.state.gov.

4. George W. Bush at the Virginia Military Institute, "President Outlines War Effort," White House Press Release, April 17, 2002, http://www.whitehouse.gov/news/releases/2002/04/20020417-1.html.

5. George W. Bush, "President Bush Delivers Graduation Speech at West Point," White House Press Release, June 1, 2002, http://www.whitehouse.gov/news/releases/2002/06/20020601-3.html.

6. United States, White House Office of Homeland Security, "The National Security Strategy of the United States of America," September 2002, http://www.whitehouse.go/nsc.html.

7. Threats and Responses: Perspectives, "Colin L. Powell; Juggling the Demands of Diplomacy and a Different Kind of War," *New York Times*, September 8, 2002.

8. The House voted on the resolution on October 10, 2002, the Senate did the same on October 11, 2002. Final Version, "Joint Resolution to Authorize the Use of United States Armed Forces Against Iraq," H.J. Res.114.ENR, October 11, 2002, Library of Congress, http://thomas.loc.gov/cgi-bin/query/C?c107:./temp/~c107kMxe1X. Bush's comments when signing the resolution are found at "Statement by the President," White House Press Release, October 16, 2002, http://www.whitehouse.gov/news/releases/2002/10/20021016-11.html. Congressional voting record for the Senate is found at, "Use of Force – Passage," *CQ Weekly Online* (October 11, 2002), http://library.cqpress.com.ezproxy1.lib.asu.edu/cqweekly/floorvote107-54579000. Congressional voting record for the House is found at, "Use of Force – Passage," *CQ Weekly Online* (October 10, 2002), http://library.cqpress.com.ezproxy1.lib.asu.edu/cqweekly/floorvote107-54400000.

9. George W. Bush, "The President's State of the Union Address," White House Press Release, January 29, 2002, http://www.whitehouse.gov/news/releases/2002/01/20020129-11.html.

10. "Iraq's Weapons of Mass Destruction Programs," Report, Central Intelligence Agency, CIA WEB Page, October 2002, https://www.cia.gov/library/reports/general-reports-1/iraq_wmd/Iraq_Oct_2002.htm#01".

11. James Mann, *Rise of the Vulcans: The History of Bush's War Cabinet* (New York: Viking, 2004), XII, XV, 194-195, 246. See also Ivo H. Daalder and James M. Lindsay, *America Unbound: The Bush Revolution in Foreign Policy* (Washington, DC: Brookings Institution Press, 2003), 17-34.

12. The document remains classified. The *New York Times* published lengthy excerpts and this is where the quotations come from. See "Excerpts from Pentagon's Plan: 'Prevent the Re-Emergence of a New Rival,'" *New York Times*, March 8, 1992. And see Patrick E. Tyler, "US Strategy Plan Calls for Insuring No Rivals Develop," *New York Times*, March 8, 1992. The George H. Bush Presidential Library, College Station, Texas (GHBLCSTX), has not made this document available.

13. Dick Cheney, "Defense Strategy for the 1990s: the Regional Defense Strategy," January 1993, http://www.informationclearinghouse.info/pdf/naarpr_Defense.pdf. The *New York Times* offered its analysis of this new report. See Patrick E. Tyler, "Pentagon Drops Goal of Blocking New Superpowers," *New York Times*, May 23, 1992.

14. Letter, The Project for the New American Century to President William Clinton, January 26, 1998, http://www.newamericancentury.org/iraqclintonletter.htm.

15. Transcript, "Secretary of Defense Richard Cheney," *This Week with David Brinkley*, ABC News, April 7, 1991.

16. Martin Walker, "US Fights Shy of Joining in Iraq Civil War," *Guardian*, March 28, 1991.

17. George H. Bush, "Remarks on Assistance for Iraqi Refugees and a News Conference," April 16, 1991; GHBLCSTX, http://bushlibrary.tamu.edu/research/papers/1991/91041608.html

18. Letter from President Bush to President Gorbachev, April 17, 1991, National Security Council, Richard Hass Files, [Iraq] Working Files—April 1991 [1 of 2] [OA/ID CF01584], Bush Presidential Records: White House Staff and Office Files, GHBLCSTX; Memorandum of Telephone Conversation with President Özal of Turkey, April 20, 1991, National Security Council, Richard Hass Files, [Iraq] Working Files—April 1991 [2 of 2] [OA/ID CF01584], Bush Presidential Records: White House Staff and Office Files, GHBLCSTX.

19. George Bush and Brent Scowcroft, *A World Transformed* (New York: Alfred A. Knopf, 1998), 489.

20. Ron Suskind, *The One Percent Doctrine: Deep Inside America's Pursuit of Its Enemies Since 9/11* (New York: Simon & Schuster, 2006), 150–151.

21. Tommy Franks, *American Soldier: General Tommy Franks*, with Malcolm McConnell (New York: HarperCollins, 2004), 394–395, 415–416.

22. Transcript, "Vice President Dick Cheney Discusses a Possible War with Iraq," *Meet the Press*, NBC News, March 16, 2003. William Kristol, testimony before the Senate Foreign Relations Committee, Senate Hearing 107-417: *What's Next in the War on Terrorism*, 107th Congress, 2nd session, February 7, 2002. Kanan Makiya's statement is in George Packer's book, *The Assassins' Gate: America in Iraq* (New York: Farrar, Straus and Giroux, 2005), 97–98.

23. Colin Powell, "US Secretary of State Colin Powell addresses the UN Security Council," Transcript, White House Release, February 5, 2003, http://www.whitehouse.gov/news/releases/2003/02/20030205-1.html.

24. "President Bush: Monday 'Moment of Truth' for World on Iraq," White House Press Release, March 16, 2003, http://www.whitehouse.gov/news/releases/2003/03/20030316-3.html.

25. George W. Bush, "President Discusses Beginning of Operation Iraqi Freedom," President's Radio Address, White House Press Release, March 22, 2003, http://www.whitehouse.gov/news/releases/2003/03/20030322.html

26. Williamson Murray and Robert H. Scales, Jr., *The Iraq War: A Military History* (Cambridge, MA: The Belknap Press of Harvard University Press, 2003); John Keegan, *The Iraq War* (New York: Alfred A. Knopf, 2004).

27. Michael R. Gordon and Bernard E. Trainor, "Dash to Baghdad Left Top US Generals Divided," *New York Times*, March 13, 2006. See also Michael R. Gordon and General Bernard E. Trainor, *Cobra II: The Inside Story of the Invasion and Occupation of Iraq* (New York: Pantheon Books, 2006), 261, 282, 307–308. In the book, the US military's concern over *fedayeen* attacks reached the overall commander of the ground attack, Lieutenant General David McKiernan.

28. George W. Bush, "President Bush Announces Major Combat Operations in Iraq Have Ended," Remarks by the President from the *USS Abraham Lincoln* at Sea Off the Coast of San Diego, California, White House Press Release, May 1, 2003, http://www.whitehouse.gov/news/releases/2003/05/20030501-15.html.

29. Comprehensive Report of the Special Advisor to the DCI on Iraq's WMD, 3 vols., September 30, 2004, University of Michigan Library, Documents Center, http://www.lib.umich.edu/govdocs/duelfer.html.

30. Senate Report, *Prewar Intelligence Estimates about Postwar Iraq Together with Additional Views*, 110th Congress, 1st session, 2007, Committee on Intelligence, Select Senate Rept, Appendix C: Overview of Other Intelligence Assessments on Postwar Iraq, 92–105.

31. "Iraq and al-Qa'ida: Interpreting a Murky Relationship," Report, Central Intelligence Agency, June 21, 2002, Press Release, Carl Levin, Senate Foreign Relations Committee, "Levin Releases Newly Declassified Intelligence Documents on Iraq–al Qaeda Relationship," http://levin.senate.gov/newsroom/release.cfm?id=236440. And "Iraqi Support for Terrorism," Report, Central Intelligence Agency, January 29, 2003, Press Release, Carl Levin, Senate Foreign Relations Committee, "Levin Releases Newly Declassified Intelligence Documents on Iraq–al Qaeda Relationship," http://levin.senate.gov/newsroom/release.cfm?id=236440.

32. "Iraq and al-Qa'ida: Interpreting a Murky Relationship," Report, Central Intelligence Agency, June 21, 2002, Press Release, Carl Levin, Senate Foreign Relations Committee, "Levin Releases Newly Declassified Intelligence Documents on Iraq-al Qaeda Relationship," http://levin.senate.gov/newsroom/release.cfm?id=236440, page 3.

33. For the 2006 NIE report, see Declassified Key Judgments of the National Intelligence Estimate, "Trends in Global Terrorism: Implications for the United States," Office of the Director of National Intelligence, April 2006, http://www.dni.gov/press_releases/Declassified_NIE_Key_Judgments.pdf. For the 2007 NIE report, see National Intelligence Estimate, "The Terrorist Threat to the US Homeland," Office of the Director of National Intelligence, July 19, 2007, http://dni.gov/press_releases/20070717_release.pdf.

34. Katherine Shrader, "Tenet Memoir Draws Heat from Key Players," *Associated Press*, April 29, 2007.

35. Only a portion of the October 2002, NIE, "Iraq's Continuing Programs for Weapons of Mass Destruction," the "Key Judgments" section of eight pages, is available to the public. This occurred in July 2003. Senator Carl Levin did release one additional page—heavily redacted— from this NIE in April 2005. See "Iraq's Continuing Programs for Weapons of Mass Destruction," National Intelligence Estimate, October 2, 2002, Press Release, Carl Levin,

Senate Foreign Relations Committee, "Levin Releases Newly Declassified Intelligence Documents on Iraq–al Qaeda Relationship," http://levin.senate.gov/newsroom/release.cfm?id=236440. The entire report of 96 pages was declassified in June 2004, but so heavily redacted that its release added nothing of importance. This NIE, in effect, remains classified. For the abridged report released by the CIA, see "Iraq's Weapons of Mass Destruction Programs," Report, Central Intelligence Agency, CIA WEB Page, October 2002, https://www.cia.gov/library/reports/general-reports-1/iraq_wmd/Iraq_Oct_2002.htm#01". Analysts Jessica T. Matthews, George Perkovich, and Joseph Cirincione of the Carnegie Endowment for International Peace compared the "key judgments" section of the NIE to the released CIA report, citing over a dozen instances in which important qualifiers applied to intelligence judgments in the NIE were dropped from the CIA white paper. See *WMD in Iraq: Evidence and Implications*, Carnegie Endowment for International Peace, January 2004. For a complete discussion of this process see also John Prados, *Hoodwinked: The Documents that Reveal How Bush Sold Us a War* (New York: New York Press, 2004). See the National Security Archive for all released versions of the documentation at http://www.gwu.edu/~nsarchiv/NSAEBB/NSAEBB129/. I cover this ground in detail in a paper entitled, "Intelligence Failure: Iraq, 2003, Korea, 1950" (paper presented at the North–South Divide and International Studies, International Studies Association, San Diego, CA, March 2006).

36. The US Department of Defense does not clearly condemn preventive war. See DOD "Dictionary of Military Terms," which defines preemptive attack in familiar terms, as "An attack initiated on the basis of incontrovertible evidence that an enemy attack is imminent." Preventive war it defines as, "A war initiated in the belief that military conflict, while not imminent, is inevitable, and that to delay would involve greater risk." The caution that is lost in this definition of preventive war is trying to forestall nations from launching attacks on the basis of a threat lurking in the undefined future.

37. See the interview of Powell by Barbara Walters on ABC's *20/20*, September 9, 2005.

Conclusion—Preemptive Doctrine: The Weight of History, Limited Returns

Introduction

Central to the Bush preemptive doctrine was the belief that the United States had to change its foreign policy orientation to protect itself in the new age of terrorism. Foremost in this regard was a willingness—a need— to engage an enemy in preemptive war, that is, before that foe could strike the United States. A foreign policy of restraint, that of containment and deterrence, so prevalent during the almost fifty-year period of the Cold War, was obsolete in the new century. However, Bush claimed that even if the United States acted preemptively, it could maintain the moral compass that had driven US policy during the Cold War. This claim is severely challenged by the case studies offered in this book. The first part of this chapter indicates how too often the United States appears to walk in the footsteps of some of the most notorious aggressors in history, losing the moral high ground along the way. The second part of this chapter reveals how the American struggles in Iraq follow the pattern of limited returns and historical failure present in the case studies. Clearly, the usefulness of a preemptive policy is questionable and a policy change is in order. In looking for a better application of preemption, the goal is not to endorse military action as the foremost component of international policy, but to place it in a context that does not deny its utility or its necessity at times. Even with this allowance, another aim is to critique the Bush policy in the hope that this will lessen the incidence of future wars founded on preemption.

The Weight of History

Injecting morality into war is always problematic. One rarely wishes to furnish a valid reason for starting or waging a war. An exploration of preemption does take us down this road, however, since the question becomes, is there a moral ground to start a war? The answer is "yes," but only in the most exceptional circumstances. This is good news since a brake is still applied to war. But the Bush doctrine of preemption has expanded the possible reasons to go to war preemptively, and therefore offers more answers to the question of when it is moral to start a war. The brake has been released and the task now is to rein in the apparent American enthusiasm for war to mitigate disastrous consequences for the United States and for other nations.

Only two belligerents can claim the moral high ground that is inherent in preemption when it is strictly defined as taking defensive measures and attacking another nation as long as the threat is an imminent one and as long as the response is appropriate to the threat. The Confederacy during the American Civil War looked to fight a war sooner than later, convinced that conflict was inevitable due to the ponderous presence of its hostile neighbor. Why not decide the timing of that war? Delay accomplished nothing; if anything, the disparity in strength between North and South would increase over time, and Southern defeat would be certain. Similarly, Israel during the Six Day War launched its very successful preemptive strike after concluding that a war with its neighbors was imminent, and that this struggle of arms would go badly for them should they wait to be attacked. Delay imperiled the security of the young and surrounded nation of Israel. The self-defensive nature of these preemptive attacks was underscored by the lack of territorial expansion of either state. The attack on Fort Sumter that started the Civil War regained "Southern" territory. Later on, the South did employ an offensive-defensive strategy, invading the North on two occasions but only to preserve the integrity of the Southern states as a new nation. There would be no conquest of Northern territory. Israel also went on the offensive but it did so to preserve its borders, not to expand into neighboring states. The territory it took possession of arguably did this very well. The cases for self-defense were complete, given the belief of each state that war was imminent and the response was an appropriate one.

The moral high ground is not as absolute as one might believe, however. The South, even while acting in accordance with a strict definition of preemption, and therefore garnering the moral high ground even as it started the Civil War, fought this war, at least in part, to preserve slavery. Try as they might, Southerners could not escape the contradiction of claiming the moral high ground by initiating a conflict that protected the immorality of slavery. The South's arguments that slavery was somehow a "good" were legion but ineffectual. Its belief that it fought a war to protect itself from oppression while enslaving millions spoke to the absurdity underlying "the cause." However, the South is secure in the knowledge that preemption did match the definition that awarded that state the moral high ground for starting the Civil War. So the South was unique in launching a war on moral grounds for immoral ends.

Israel stands alone as the only state to enjoy the morality of launching a preemptive strike in self-defense and of fighting a moral war. The morality of starting a war that was already coming appears to clash with the aftermath of the war that left the Jewish state in control of the Golan Heights, the West Bank, the Gaza Strip, and the Sinai Peninsula. This territorial expansion impinges on the morality of a war of self-defense. This is the case in a narrow sense. But the land taken by Israel was too limited to support a charge of aggression. Israel held this key terrain to defend the state from future attacks. To single out this land as evidence of a desire for hegemony, and therefore of a war of aggression that belied the morality of preemption, misses the point. Clearly there was no civilizational motive on the part of Israel, only that of survival and survival in as minimal a form as possible. This is small consolation to a Palestinian population denied a homeland. Still, Israel's military success in 1967 makes it the lone example of a state enjoying the moral high ground of preemption in a conventional war setting.

The other nations considered in this book cannot match this strict definition of preemption. They normally would be considered aggressors and have no moral high ground to stand on. However, the Bush preemption doctrine is so extreme that it makes past examples of aggression appear to be acts of preemption, gaining the moral high ground of self-defense as the Bush Doctrine defines it. But the territorial expansion of these states through military means undermines their claim to justifiable self-defense. This limitation is good news, save for the fact that the logic that expansion invalidates arguments in favor of preemption also undermines Bush's arguments of enacting a moral preemptive policy as well.

Bonaparte's wars in Europe ushered in a period of conflict so turbulent and violent that his name hangs on the era. To view the Napoleonic Wars as preemption, as occurring as a means of self-defense, is to extend a kind reprieve to Bonaparte. His personal ambition and affinity for making war are excused. It is only possible to think favorably of Bonaparte's war motives and behavior by contrasting them with Bush's call for taking no chances on future attacks by terrorists against the United States. In similar vein,

Bonaparte felt that he had to use force against neighboring states heeding England's call to make war on France. Each war from 1805 and after fits this rationale. But where lay the motive of self-defense in the expansion of French power? Certainly French armies moved beyond the "natural boundaries" of France when reaching Moscow and Madrid. This was hardly defensive, no matter what benefit Bonaparte believed French conquest imparted to its new "citizens." There is no morality here, just naked aggression, that is, until compared to the Bush doctrine that sanctioned military expansion as a preemptive attack in the name of national security.

Japan's war with Russia in 1904–1905 is unique in that Japan did not try to achieve the moral high ground by acting preemptively. The surprise attack at Port Arthur was intended to secure a military advantage, nothing more. The containment of the Russian fleet would allow Japan to occupy Korea and secure a key foothold in Manchuria, all the while curtailing Russian power in the region. In this way, Japan's war against Russia represented an effort by Japan to secure a hegemonic position in Asia. The military benefit Japan sought by acting preemptively contrasts with the Bush policy that did not seek a tactical military advantage when attacking Iraq. But in like fashion, one can overlook the hegemony inherent in the Japanese plans in Asia in 1904, much as Bush overlooked this result in his attack in 2003. In this sense, the Bush use of preemption offers Japan the moral high ground it never sought by stripping any sense of aggression from the hegemony it achieved. Or, to put it another way, Bush's careless definition of preemption gave Japan's war for hegemony a moral tinge that it had lacked.

Imperial Germany's initiation of war in 1914 is again a case where an aggressor state can be seen as acting preemptively and therefore morally according to the Bush definition. Surrounded on all sides by nations that, at a minimum, sought to rein in German power, Germany opted for war at a time of its own choosing to secure the military advantage of solving its problem of "encirclement." The subsequent war to achieve German hegemony in Europe mirrors that of the US effort to assert its global hegemony with a strike on Iraq. In similar fashion, the Bush administration enthusiastically embraced the neo-conservative push for war against Iraq and other minor states to ensure a US hegemony world-wide. In each case, the expansion of power in the name of self-defense could hardly be considered a defensive war. Therefore, preemption supports no claims of having started a moral war. Yet this is exactly the argument Bush made, allowing the German attack in 1914 to become an example of preemption, not aggression.

The Bush doctrine of preemption also offers a moral reprieve to Germany and Japan during World War II. These nations no longer acted as aggressors, but as nations defending what they considered their civilizations. Germany, suffering from a punitive peace dictated by hostile powers, again faced a suppression of its natural right as a nation to expand its borders in Europe. The consequences of its confinement exceeded the ramifications that underlay World War I, at least in the mind of one man, Adolph Hitler. Should Germany not find its rightful place as a great power, he argued, it would die. Germany's attack on Poland in 1939 was a preemptive attack to initiate a war to settle the civilizational question facing Germany, and to settle that question in its favor. Similarly, Bush claimed that America's attack on Iraq was a blow struck to defend the civilized world, a moral cause taken far beyond a nation's borders on behalf of all peoples. A civilizational norm defined by one nation and imposed on a neighboring state suddenly excused aggression as the necessary act of self-defense inherent in preemption.

The Japanese offensive in late 1941 in the Pacific is another case where a nation no longer acted aggressively when allowed to use the Bush doctrine of preemption as a measure of Japanese policy. Denied raw materials and room to expand in Asia, Japan chose to go to war against the United States because it had no choice. America was the empire's chief obstacle to securing the economic resources Japan needed if it wished to avoid national extinction. A Japanese hegemony in East Asia secured its economic lifeline and also advanced a civilizational goal of freeing Asia from colonial servitude. Bush in 2003 pursued the same rationale as Japan did in 1941. By securing oil for the United States and freeing first Iraq and then the Middle East as well, expansion served a regional dominance benefiting primarily one nation, the United States, as it combined a drive for hegemony and civilization that spoke to aggression. But Bush has acknowledged only the civilizational goal of US policy, a more palatable explanation to the American public of US actions in the Middle East. The same consideration can also be extended to Japanese actions in World War II, its economic goals that spelled aggression recast in favor of preemption as a tool to advance a civilization liberating all of Asia.

The Soviet Union's attack on Finland in the winter of 1939 appeared to be a case of clear-cut aggression given the illogic of an infinitely stronger power claiming it had to make war on its tiny neighbor in the name of self-defense. Yet the Soviets did see a threat from Finland should that nation come under the control of a foreign power looking to harm the USSR. In the turbulent world of the 1930s, such enemies abounded and Stalin believed he could not be sure which nation constituted the greatest threat to Russia. Better to act preemptively and deny Finland to any would-be predatory power. For similar reasons, Bush brought the enormous power of the United States to bear on Iraq, a weak nation that still presented a great threat to US security because it fostered unknown dangers in the new age of terrorism. Better to act preemptively than to wait and discover the destructive capabilities of a new terrorist attack. In this rationale of self-defense taken to extremes, Stalin's preemptive attack on Finland became a shrewd move on the part of a far-seeing statesman, not an overt act of aggression by a depraved dictator.

The Cold War initiated in the post-1945 era a new round of conflict that again witnessed much conventional warfare. Korea became an early focal point of such combat. In 1950, the Americans had quickly turned the tide of battle in Korea and had continued their advance into North Korea, threatening to destroy this communist state. Mao now feared a UN attack on Chinese soil. Like Bush in 2003, Mao concluded in 1950 that it was better to fight his enemies on a battlefield he selected. The motto to fight them "over there so we don't have to fight them here" captured the rationale of self-defense in this Chinese preemptive war of 1950, as well as the American preemptive war of 2003, when Bush argued that US expansion inherent in the act of self-defense constituted preemption, not aggression. Likewise, even if Chinese interests were served in Korea both in the name of defending the socialist revolution and reconstituting the Chinese empire, these acts of aggression could now be considered to hold the moral high ground Bush found in preemption.

There is one more aggressor nation to consider, and that is the United States. In 2003, President Bush launched a preemptive invasion of Iraq to defend the United States from an imminent threat. Unwilling to risk another terrorist attack on US soil, the president decided that potential threats had to be neutralized before they materialized. Iraq under Saddam Hussein was portrayed as posing such a threat due to the possibility of him using weapons of mass destruction. Confirming that Iraq did not pose this threat in the aftermath of the invasion did little to weaken the president's belief that he had acted morally. If the use of military preemption as self-defense did not hold up, the purpose of the war, defending civilization, was a moral good. This argument meant that Bush expanded US hegemony in the name of defending civilization. In the president's mind, his defense of civilization had no hegemonic implications. But he had not differentiated between these two ends. The president did not make it clear if his effort to defend civilization deviated from the neo-conservative drive to preserve US world hegemony. By fumbling the definition of preemption in this manner, the administration put the United States in mixed company with some of the worst aggressors in history who had acted "preemptively" when starting wars to achieve the moral purpose of defending civilization.

It is either this result or the sudden redemption of past figures of notorious repute. Napoleon's wars in Europe become efforts to export the

French Revolution, a civilizational gift to Europe. German and Japanese militarism spread out over a forty-year period can now be admired as examples of self-defense, the leaders of these nations launching preemptive wars to serve a hegemonic impulse that protected magnificent civilizations, cultures that would benefit the world should they spread across the globe. The civilizational conceit in US preemptive doctrine is bad enough, but the hegemonic drive is also present. Napoleon and Mao certainly aspired to achieve this goal no matter their appeals to spreading revolution. The Japanese and German civilizational mantra of World War II necessitated a hegemony that had its roots in the preemptive wars of 1905 and 1914, respectively. Stalin's war to assert Russian hegemony over Finland now bears a startling similarity to the US war in Iraq as a much smaller country defies the military might of a great power. Bush's efforts to recast this war in a favorable light, that the United States is fighting terrorists in Iraq that would otherwise be attacking the United States at home, further the US ties to this company of aggressors since Mao offered the same rationale: better to fight the Americans in Korea than in China. Preemption giving validation to such wars is unthinkable. This means that the Bush preemptive doctrine has cost US foreign policy any claim to a moral high ground since the United States can no longer be seen as defending the moral principles found in the concept of freedom that nation holds so dear. Yet even now the Bush administration cannot see the great limitation of using preemption to start conventional wars that puts the United States further in the company of aggressors.

Limited returns

Having suffered the ignominy of sharing this sordid company, one could hope the returns are great and worth the tarnishing of American foreign policy. This is not the case, however, because the nations acting pre-emptively were mostly unsuccessful, foreshadowing the limited returns of striking preemptively at Iraq. In the first place, a preemptive strike attained only a limited military advantage, the tactical benefits of such an attack seldom producing a victory in the war that the attacking nation involved itself. In the second place, many of the nations acting preemptively, like the United States in Iraq in 2003, used preemption as a reason to go to war. This preemptive purpose invariably started a war that these nations could not win. The current situation in Iraq and the historical examples presented in this book do not augur well for US success in Iraq or for the validation of Bush's preemptive doctrine.

Napoleon's lightning campaign in 1805 at first glance seems to provide a strong endorsement of preemption. Outnumbered and pressed on every front, only by attacking and being overwhelmingly successful on the battlefield could Napoleon realistically expect to triumph in this war and in that way keep his throne and defend France in the process. This argument needs careful clarification, however. By acting preemptively, Napoleon gained the military advantage of the initiative, allowing him to determine when and where the main fighting would occur. His was not a surprise attack or even a first strike that blunted a forthcoming Allied attack. In fact, the Allied offensive had already taken place; Austria had surprised Napoleon by invading France's ally Bavaria. Despite this setback, Napoleon quickly seized the initiative and this advantage netted him two great victories, one at Ulm and the other at Austerlitz, allowing him to recast preemption in his favor, at least to a point. The 1805 campaign ended well for the French, but subsequent campaigns underscored the limits of this early success. Napoleon had to repeat this performance again and again and he eventually faltered. In making preemption his reason for fighting these wars, and not using it as a tool that helped him win these struggles, Napoleon doomed himself to failure no matter how much credence— feigned or otherwise—he placed in the value of spreading the French Revolution.

The South's determination to start a war with the North in 1861 that it believed could not be avoided perhaps best exemplifies the folly of using preemption. By firing on Fort Sumter, Southern expectations of intimidating the North into inaction were far off the mark. Northern resolve hardened and Lincoln's support for using force to confront the South increased greatly. Consequently, war did erupt between the states, and in far different circumstances than envisioned by Southern leadership. The military weight of Northern material eventually ground down Confederate resistance and the South collapsed. Some heroic fighting certainly characterized the stand of the outnumbered South but this accomplishment did not change the outcome of the war which was a Northern victory. Preemption now rebounded with a vengeance since it invited the very interference from the North that the South had feared in the first place, perhaps more so given the military nature of this defeat. In the aftermath of war, the South had to endure complete military occupation. Its lone claim to mitigating total defeat was Jim Crow, the defiant stand of white culture against the new status quo of racial equality. This moral blight of racial segregation again cast a pallor on the so-called moral purpose of self-defense. For the South, preemption had started a war they could not win and ensured that it would unfold in a fashion that underscored the absurdity of acting preemptively in the first place. The war might have been coming, the South might indeed have been conquered anyway, but preemption accrued no military advantage and only sped the collapse of Southern resistance.

On the other hand, two nations appeared to start war preemptively in search of a decided military advantage. In 1904, the Japanese struck the Russian fleet at Port Arthur. Containing this force allowed Japan to land troops in Korea and China and begin a land campaign necessary to end the war. In this military sense, preemption succeeded. But by another measure, it did not. The Japanese attack damaged but three ships. This was hardly a devastating attack that destroyed Russian naval power in a single blow, an outcome that Japan needed because Russia had two fleets at its disposal and Japan only one. Japan's ability to neutralize the Russian fleet in Asia anyway stemmed from the psychological impact of the attack. The Russians never did recover from the painful realization that this Asian nation dared to challenge a western power. There is no evidence to indicate that the Japanese had hoped for this advantage from launching the torpedo boat attack. Its objective was intended in some undefined way to aid Togo in eliminating the threat from Port Arthur. This contribution became clear only as the campaign developed. The Japanese fleet did protect the discharge of ground forces on the Liaodong Peninsula, since, for whatever reasons, it kept the Russia fleet bottled up in Port Arthur. A Japanese army then forced the capitulation of the port, resulting in the capture or elimination of the Russian fleet. So the Japanese successfully prosecuted this war as intended. They never faced two Russian fleets at the same time. Instead, the Japanese enjoyed parity of numbers at sea and were confident that this situation favored them. The final and climatic battle of the war, a naval battle, Tsushima, made it clear that this was a safe assumption. However, in the battle that began the war, the preemptive strike at Port Arthur, the chief advantage to Japan was demoralizing the Russia fleet. This fortuitous and unimagined development obscured the limited return of military preemption. Preemption worked but for the wrong reasons.

Germany in World War I also looked to preemption as a means to gain a decided military advantage at the beginning of the war. The attack on France through Belgium would be so overwhelming and swift that the consequences of violating Belgian neutrality mattered little. The main drawback of the violation would be British entry in the war on the side of France, but even should this occur, German military leaders believed they could defeat France. Once the war in the west was settled, Germany could then face Russia and defeat this power as well. So success in France, and success strategically, depended on a preemptive attack in the west that allowed Germany the chance to defeat multiple enemies on multiple fronts, enemies that together could defeat her. It was a tremendous gamble, banking on the tactical advantage of turning the French flank by advancing through Belgium to forestall strategic disaster—a two-front war. It also counted on French ineptitude in defending itself. As it was, the French showed remarkable resiliency and ingenuity, both factors combining at the Battle of the Marne. France held out and the greater negative that Germany feared by striking preemptively in the west became a reality: a two-front war leading to her defeat. Preemption had led to Germany's fears of encirclement becoming real. In these two examples, the tangible gain of acting preemptively to gain a military advantage was either limited in the extreme or completely absent: Japan getting a boost in an unlikely way, not material advantage but psychological; Germany's bid for a quick war in the west failing altogether.

In World War II, Germany's reliance on preemption changed completely. Less important was the hope for a military advantage. Instead, Hitler used preemption mainly as the reason to go to war. Germany again looked to end its "encirclement" and to take its rightful place as a European power. That place was the domination of the Continent. Denied this success in World War I, Europe's encirclement of Germany had remained a problem and by the 1930s it had grown to such a concern that Germany now faced extinction as a nation. This "imminent" threat justified an effort to ensure Germany was in a stronger position in the near future than it was at present, including crippling its enemies and ending this threat with military force. Hitler's determination to embark on "conquest by installment" grew out of this preemptive purpose. Civilization depended on the outcome of this struggle, Germany acting as the custodian of the best civilization. Therefore, whatever steps were necessary must be taken, including waging a "preemptive" war.

Like Germany, Japan believed it must fight preemptively during World War II. Its preemptive purpose was twofold. First, it struck US naval forces at Pearl Harbor to gain a decided military advantage. Pearl Harbor certainly represented another Port Arthur in the overt preemptive nature of the attack: a military strike before a declaration of war. However, this time around, Japan attempted to devastate the enemy fleet in one decisive blow and inflict such material loss on the US fleet that Japan would have a free hand to expand in the Pacific. It achieved this purpose to some extent. The attack destroyed the main American battle fleet and Japanese expansion was remarkable in the first six months of the war. But the limitations of this attack are famous, including the failure to destroy the American aircraft carriers, absent from the harbor on the day of the attack. That Pearl Harbor served as a rallying point of American resistance is another significant fallout of the attack, more so perhaps given that Japanese expansion south most likely could have been undertaken without a strike at Pearl Harbor at all. What the attack did mean was that the American military response was only delayed, and that this counter-attack, when it came, would be prosecuted in a ferocious manner and to completion. Japan's defeat in World War II rested to a large degree on the limits of the military value of the preemptive attack on Pearl Harbor.

Second, Japan added a civilizational purpose to preemption as one of the reasons for war in 1941. Japan maintained that its drive for hegemony in the region was a blessing for those it liberated from western exploitation. Asian peoples would benefit from Japanese protection and Japanese culture. In exchange, Japan would receive the raw materials so vital to its livelihood. But Japan's rise to dominance in Asia would be resisted by the western powers. Japan had to meet this challenge since without these economic assets, it would perish. So, like Germany, Japan's war in 1941 was for the survival of its civilization. It was this charge of invoking preemption in the name of civilizational wars that took these two Axis nations down the path to war, and to disaster. Preemption served Germany and Japan very poorly, the hegemonic implication of the civilizational purpose of the preemptive attacks so plain as to inflame opposition, and the civilization being offered to those attacked so abhorrent that this resistance eventually became so great that both Axis powers met defeat at the hands of a large coalition.

Two more examples produce contrary results in measuring the success of preemption. In Stalin's winter offensive against Finland in 1939, he did not act preemptively to secure a military advantage. Given the relative strength of the two countries, he did not believe he needed one. Rather, preemption served as the reason to go to war. Stalin looked to forestall other nations from using Finland as a base from which to threaten the USSR. Finland saw only a push for Soviet hegemony and rejected Stalin's terms for a settlement of the dispute. In the brief war that followed, it was indeed a preponderance of Soviet strength that forced the Finns to capitulate. The aftermath of this clash spoke to the limits of Stalin's preemptive war in Finland, however. The Finns, defeated in that war, turned to Germany as an ally to oppose Stalin. The arrival of a German army on Finnish soil meant Stalin's attack had produced the very goal he wished to avoid, an enemy using Finland as a launching pad to strike the USSR. The purpose of preemption—to enhance the security of the Soviet Union—had failed, since it had created a threat where none had existed before. Such an outcome spoke to a folly on par with the South's war with the North and again advertised the limits of preemption as a reason to go to war.

Mao enjoyed more success in his preemptive attack into Korea in 1950. The Chinese army he sent across the Yalu River did enjoy a military advantage from ideal defensive terrain. This benefit was certainly needed given the great superiority in firepower of UN forces. Another military goal was achieved by fighting the enemy "over there" in Korea since Chinese troops prevented a UN advance into China. These military successes can too easily be overstated, however. First, a UN offensive into China was unlikely, meaning the PRC advance into Korea was probably unnecessary to meet this threat. Second, PRC successes on the battlefield in Korea convinced Mao of the PRC soldier's ability to stand up to western imperialism. This assurance spurred Mao to more adventurism and to more dangerous confrontations with the United States, some involving the potential use of nuclear weapons. His subsequent recklessness would appear to outweigh any benefit of having made a stand in Korea, and speaks to the limitation of military preemption, that is, until the other preemptive purpose of Chinese intervention is considered. Mao's main reason to fight preemptively in Korea was to reestablish Chinese hegemony on the Asian mainland. In this sense, he succeeded, even if at great cost in Chinese lives and in terms he could not have envisioned. After all, Chinese great power status today is a reality largely because of tolerable relations with the United States, the obdurate enemy of the 1950s. If the purpose of Chinese hegemony was well served by fighting preemptively in Korea, the limited return on Mao's use of military preemption still calls into question the value of preemption as a tool to advance foreign policy.

Finally, Israel offers the lone example of successfully using preemption since it sought a military advantage without resorting to a hegemonic or civilizational purpose. The military advantages were many, including defeating an enemy deploying superior numbers and threatening the state of Israel on multiple fronts. Acting preemptively may have been the only way to offset these disadvantages. The aftermath of this brief war left Israel in control of some key terrain, such as the Golan Heights in the northeast, the West Bank opposite Jordan, and the Sinai Peninsula in the south. These gains hardly amounted to Israeli hegemony in the region. Nor did they point to a civilizational objective. What they did was further augment Israeli defenses against future attacks. Of course these attacks have persisted, and this reality puts a limit on the Israeli success of using military preemption to make it secure. But this is a slender limitation given Israel's ability to survive as a nation in a hazardous region and during some unstable times such as the Cold War and now the increased threat of terrorism. The Israeli example in 1967 employing military preemption divorced of hegemonic or civilizational motives appears an effective policy and the best use of preemption when waging conventional war.

The Israeli example contravenes that of the United States in the Iraq War of 2003 that featured a preemptive attack divorced of any imperative to gain a military advantage, and instead advanced a declared civilizational goal with hegemonic implications. Consequently, the United States achieved none of the benefits of acting with military preemption, though they are few in number, and many of the problems of using preemption as a reason to go to war, and these are plentiful. This result has had dire consequences. US military capacity is strained by the war in Iraq and its ability to fight more preemptive wars is in question. Yet, much like the Napoleon example, the preference for military force as implementing policy appears to doom the United States to doing just this and eventually faltering. Equally harmful is the creation of a front in the war on terror in Iraq where none existed before the US invasion. Like Stalin when attacking Finland in 1939, an attack that increased Soviet security concerns, the United States now faces a greater risk from terrorism than before invading Iraq. The civilizational change the Bush administration has sought in Iraq serves US interests mainly and to such an extent that American preemptive warfare closely shadows the aggressor states of Germany and Japan. The foremost concern here is fomenting resistance to the American efforts to defeat terrorism that mirrors the resistance that defeated Nazi Germany and militarized Japan. Ultimately, Bush would have been better served with the morality found in the cause of self-defense. Such a preemptive military attack would have pushed to the side the burden of denying a reach for hegemony and the task of defining a civilizational superiority. These were the marks of aggression and could not be easily defended morally. But a military advantage was not necessary when attacking Iraq and this fact deprives the United States of any reason of having acted preemptively at all.

While this historical analysis is too late to put the brakes on any preemptive action on the part of the United States against Iraq, it clearly serves as a warning about the terrible costs of preemption in the future. The limited return on preemption has not reduced its appeal, however. It has been used in the past and now Bush uses it. There is a seductive premise here. Who would deny the right and advantage of eliminating a threat before it materialized? But preemption is a tactic of dubious moral validity and of limited utility: it did not win wars or prevent future wars. At best, preemption can serve as a small part of a grand strategy. A carefully crafted policy relying on economic and diplomatic initiatives as well as a military option, has been a hallmark of successful policy in the past. This is noticeably absent in the Bush administration. The dependency on war, justified as preemption, has harmed American interests. Allies have been alienated, possible alliances thwarted by a unilaterally acting United States. In an age demanding a global effort to stop terrorism, this error is fatal. The Bush administration adopted preemption as an expedient way to win its self-proclaimed "war on terror." The history offered here makes it clear that preemption cannot serve this policy but will actually undermine it. Maintaining a moral high ground is clearly essential in defeating terrorism. A preemptive policy as Bush defines it has no moral compass. Should preemption stand as US policy, its enemies can be expected to multiply, and its isolation increase. Clearly a new policy needs to be put in place to face the threat from international terrorism. The hard thinking remains ahead for the United States in order to craft a comprehensive strategy. If history is our guide, yielding to the temptation of preemptive war will only take the United States farther down the path of aggression and to eventual failure.

Select Bibliography

This book attempts an ambitious aim, the examination of the origins of ten wars over a two hundred-year period. The task would perhaps be impossible if the aim is narrative history, but the goal is analytical. To this end, my reading focused on the most important interpretive works related to each conflict. Many outstanding and useful narratives of these wars are not listed below, nor are many books I consulted for a better understanding of the battles, campaigns, and military strategies.

Introduction

A great number of books, book chapters, and articles informed my overall analysis of preemptive war. These include Russ Howard, "Pre-emptive Military Doctrine: No Other Choice," in *The Changing Face of Terrorism* (London: Eastern Universities Press, 2004), Robert J. Pauley, Jr. and Tom Lansford, *Strategic Preemption: US Foreign Policy and the Second Iraq War*, US Foreign Policy and Conflict in the Islamic World (Burlington, VT: Ashgate, 2005), John Lewis Gaddis, *Surprise, Security and the American Experience* (Cambridge, MA: Harvard University, 2004), Betty Glad and Chris J. Dolan, eds., *Striking First: The Preventive War Doctrine and the Reshaping of US Foreign Policy* (New York: Palgrave Macmillan, 2004), Erick Labara, *Preemptive War* (Washington, DC: Global Security Press, 2004), Michael Walzer, *Just and Unjust Wars: A Moral Argument with Historical*

Illustrations (New York: Basic Books, 1977), James Turner Johnson, *The War to Oust Saddam Hussein: Just War and the New Face of Conflict* (Lanham, MD: Rowman & Littlefield Publishers, 2005), Lyle J. Goldsetin, *Preventive Attack and Weapons of Mass Destruction: A Comparative Historical Analysis* (Stanford, CA: Stanford University Press, 2006), D. Robert Worley, *Waging Ancient War: Limits on Preemptive Force* (Carlisle, PA: Strategic Studies Institute, 2003), Alan M. Dershowitz, *Preemption: A Knife that Cuts Both Ways*, Issues of Our Time (New York: W.W. Norton, 2006), and Helen Duffy, *The "War on Terror" and the Framework of International Law* (Cambridge, UK: Cambridge University Press, 2005). All of these books are directly mentioned in the Introduction. Some additional, important books not appearing in the Introduction are stated here. In particular, the task of understanding distinctions between preemption and preventive war is addressed in *Reshaping Rogue States: Preemption, Regime Change, and US Policy Toward Iran, Iraq, and North Korea* (Cambridge, MA: The MIT Press, 2004), edited by Alexander T.J. Lennon and Camille Eiss, and *Hitting First: Preventive Force in US Security Strategy* (Pittsburgh, PA: University of Pittsburgh Press, 2006), edited by William W. Keller and Gordon R. Mitchell. The US Department of Defense, *Dictionary of Military Terms*, also defines these two terms; I used the online version at http://www.dtic.mil/doctrine/jel/doddict/. The meaning of grand strategy is perhaps best handled in Gordon A. Craig and Alexander L. George's, *Force and Statecraft: Diplomatic Problems of Our Time* (New York: Oxford University Press, 1990), and Paul Kennedy's edited volume, *Grand Strategies in War and Peace* (New Haven, CT: Yale University Press, 1991). Paul Ramsey's *The Just War: Force and Political Responsibility* (New York: Charles Scribner's Sons, 1968) is another staple on just war theory. A key study of preemptive war written before the 2003 Iraq War is Dan Reiter's article, "Exploding the Powder Keg Myth: Preemptive Wars Almost Never Happen" (*International Security* 20 (Fall 1995): 5–34).

1   The Seven Streams: Napoleon Moves on Vienna, 1805

This analysis benefited from several new studies of the 1805 campaign. Frederick C. Schneid's *Napoleon's Conquest of Europe: The War of the Third Coalition* (Westport, CT: Praeger, 2005), is the most helpful because it deals with the diplomatic, strategic, and tactical elements of the war. David Chandler's *The Campaigns of Napoleon* (New York: Macmillan, 1966), remains the most comprehensive and authoritative account of the military aspects of the wars waged by Napoleon, including the Austerlitz campaign. A military treatment of the battle in chapter form is, "Austerlitz, 1805," by Richard Holmes and published in the book, *Two Centuries of Warfare*

(London: Octopus Books, 1978). Owen Connelly's *Blundering to Glory: Napoleon's Military Campaigns* (Wilmington, NC: Scholarly Resources Inc., 1987) attempts to deflate the Napoleonic legend that grew out of battles like Austerlitz. In a book focused exclusively on Austerlitz, Robert Goetz, in *1805: Austerlitz, Napoelon and the Destruction of the Third Coalition* (London: Greenhill, 2005), tried to do this as well by focusing attention on the Austrian and Russian points of view. Much more laudatory views of Napoleon at war are easy to find, such as Henry Lachouque's, *The Anatomy of Glory*, translated by Anne S.K. Brown (New York: Hippocrene Books, Inc., 1978). The difficulty of determining Napoleon's impact on the French Revolution, and how it shaped his views, is addressed in a large amount of literature. Charles Downer Hazen, in *The French Revolution and Napoleon* (New York: Henry Holt and Company, 1917), Robert B. Holtman, in *The Napoleonic Revolution* (Philadelphia, PA: J.B. Lippincott Company, 1967), and Martyn Lyons, in *Napoleon Bonaparte and the Legacy of the French Revolution* (New York: St. Martin's Press, 1994), are three good studies. For Napoleon's impact on France, Louis Bergeron's *France Under Napoleon* (Princeton, NJ: Princeton University Press, 1981), translated by R.R. Palmer, offers perhaps the best account. The numerous biographies also split on their assessment of Napoleon. Emil Ludwig's *Napoleon* (New York: Boni & Liverright, 1926) is an older, very favorable account, Alan Schom's more recent, *Napoleon Bonaparte* (New York: HarperCollins, 1997), offers a responsible critique. Also, authors that concentrated on just a portion of Bonaparte's life contributed to this study, Robert B. Asprey's *The Rise of Napoleon Bonaparte* (New York: Basic Books, 2000) being the most useful here. Another takes a thematic approach, Steven Englund's *Napoleon: A Political Life* (New York: Scribner, 2004).

2 Preserving a Way of Life: The War Between the States, 1861

James M. McPherson's *Battle Cry of Freedom: The Civil War Era* (New York: Ballantine Books, 1988) is a critically acclaimed look at the entire Civil War and a great place to start any study of the subject. The origins of the Civil War enjoy an extensive literature. Avery O. Craven's *The Coming of the Civil War* (Chicago, IL: University of Chicago Press, 1957), and David M. Potter's *The Impending Crisis, 1848–1861* (New York: Harper & Row, 1976), represent two classic treatments of the topic. Michael F. Holt, in *The Fate of Their Country: Politicians, Slavery Extension, and the Coming of the Civil War* (New York: Hill and Wang, 2004), and Bruce Levine, in *Half Slave and Half Free: The Roots of the Civil War* (New York: Hill and Wang, 2005), are two good recent studies of the events leading to war. Also useful is Kenneth M. Stampp's collection in *The Imperiled Union: Essays on the*

Background of the Civil War (New York: Oxford University Press, 1980), another book by Craven, *The Growth of Southern Nationalism, 1848–1861* (Baton Rouge, LA: Louisiana State University Press, 1953), and Richard Current's treatment of the fall of Fort Sumter in *Lincoln and the First Shot* (Philadelphia, PA: J.B. Lippincott Company, 1963). Abraham Lincoln's important role is covered in J.G. Randall's *Lincoln the Liberal Statesman* (London: Eyre & Spottiswoode, 1947), and in biography, Stephen B. Oates' *With Malice Toward None: The Life of Abraham Lincoln* (New York: Harper & Row, 1977), and David Herbert Donald's *Lincoln* (New York: Simon & Schuster, 1995), being two of the best. A famed treatment of the fighting that characterized the Civil War is presented by Russell F. Weigley in *The American Way of War: A History of United States Military Strategy and Policy* (Bloomington, IN: Indiana University Press, 1973). McPherson's *Battle Cry of Freedom* closes with a discussion of why the South lost the war, a topic that is the focus of the book, *Why the South Lost the Civil War*, authored by Richard E. Beringer, Herman Hattaway, Archer Jones, and William N. Still, Jr. (Athens, GA: University of Georgia Press, 1986).

3   Imperial Hegemony: The Russo–Japanese War, 1904–1905

A number of good books examine the war in detail, such as Richard Connaughton's *Rising Sun and Tumbling Bear: Russia's War with Japan* (London: Cassell, 2003), David Walder's *The Short Victorious War: The Russo–Japanese Conflict, 1905–1905* (New York: Harper & Row, 1973), Denis Warner and Peggy Warner's *The Tide at Sunrise: A History of the Russo–Japanese War, 1904–1905* (New York: Charterhouse, 1974), and J.N. Westwood's *Russia Against Japan, 1904–1905: A New Look at the Russo–Japanese War* (Basingstoke: Macmillan, 1982). The origins of the conflict are the topic of Ian Nish's book, *The Origins of the Russo–Japanese War* (London: Longman, 1985). John Albert White also addresses the subject of the origins of the war in *The Diplomacy of the Russo–Japanese War* (Princeton, NJ: Princeton University Press, 1964). The same ground is covered in a recent book that seeks to assess the global impact of this regional war, *The Russo–Japanese War in Global Perspective: World War Zero* (Boston: Brill, 2005), edited by John W. Steinberg, Bruce W. Menning, David Schimmelpenninck Van Der Oye, David Wolfe, and Shinji Yokote. In *Toward the Rising Sun: Russian Ideologies of Empire and the Path to War with Japan* (DeKalb, IL: Northern Illinois Press, 2001), Van Der Oye looks at the origins of the conflict from the Russian perspective. The role of the Japanese elite in deciding the war and its interaction with the home front is best covered in *The Japanese Oligarchy and the Russo–Japanese War* (New York: Columbia University Press, 1970), by Shumpei Okamoto. Several books focus on the American efforts at ending this conflict, among them Raymond A. Esthus in *Double Eagle and Rising Sun: The Russians and Japanese at Portsmouth in 1905* (Durham, NC: Duke University Press, 1988). The "sneak" attack on Port Author is the topic of William H. Honan's chapter, "Port Author: the First Pearl Harbor," in *"Fire When Ready, Gridley!": Great Naval Stories from Manila Bay to Vietnam,* ed. William H. Honan (New York: St. Martin's Press, 1993).

4 Trapped into War: Imperial Germany and the Great War in Europe, 1914

Books addressing the origins of World War I are numerous and many are very good. A few are James Joll, *The Origins of the First World War* (London: Longman, 1992), Laurence Lafore, *The Long Fuse: An Interpretation of the Origins of World War I* (New York: J.B. Lippincott Company, 1971), and John H. Maurer, *The Outbreak of the First World War: Strategic Planning, Crisis Decision Making, and Deterrence Failure* (Westport, CT: Praeger, 1995). A recent examination of the roots of the conflict is an edited volume by Richard F. Hamilton and Holger H. Herwig, *The Origins of World War I* (Cambridge, UK: Cambridge University Press, 2003). Some famous accounts of the war include Fritz Fischer's extremely influential work, *Germany's Aims in the First World War,* trans. (New York: W.W. Norton, 1967). Barbara W. Tuchman in *The Guns of August* (New York: Macmillan, 1962) offers a famous narrative of the outbreak of war and the opening stages of the conflict. There are some useful aids for dealing with a very complicated history and historiography, such as Gordon Martel's *The Origins of the First World War* (Harlow, Essex: Pearson, 2003), Neil M. Heyman's *World War I* (Westport, CT: Greenwood Press, 1997), and James L. Stokesbury's overview of the war, *A Short History of World War I* (New York: William Morrow and Company, 1981). Other books address the complicated historiography of the origins of the war. John W. Langdon, in *July 1914: The Long Debate, 1918–199* (New York: Oxford University Press, 1991), is very good on this point. Gregor Schollgen's *Escape Into War? The Foreign Policy of Imperial Germany* (Oxford: Berg, 1990), covers this ground from the German perspective. Gordon A. Craig, in *Germany, 1866–1945* (New York: Oxford University Press, 1978), offers an incisive overview of German history.

5 A Question of Survival: National Socialism takes Germany to War, 1939

Gerhard L. Weinberg and H.P. Willmott provide important overviews of the war in *A World at Arms* (New York: Cambridge University Press, 1994), and *The Great Crusade* (New York: The Free Press, 1989). The most comprehensive treatment of the events involving Germany, Hitler, and the outbreak of World War II is another book by Weinberg, his original two-volume work now republished in a single text and entitled *Hitler's Foreign Policy: The Road to World War II, 1933–1939* (New York: Enigma Books, 2005). As would be expected, a number of books trace the origins of the conflict. Most important in this regard is A.J.P. Taylor's, *The Origins of the Second World War* (New York: Atheneum, 1962), a book that challenged the view of the war as a moral crusade to stop Hitler so prevalent in the 1950s. Scholars have continued to examine the roots of the war, striving for a "dispassionate" and "objective" treatment of the topic. British authors have dominated this effort, such as P.M.H. Bell's *The Origins of the Second World War in Europe* (London: Longman, 1997), Richard Overy's *The Road to War* (with Andrew Wheatcroft) (London: Penguin Books, 1999), and Victor Rothwell's *Origins of the Second World War* (Manchester: Manchester University Press, 2001). Gordon Martel's edited work, *Origins of the Second World War Reconsidered: The A.J.P. Taylor Debate After Twenty-five Years* (Boston: Allen & Unwin, 1986), returns to the questions raised by Taylor. An important study that goes beyond a focus on the origins of the war to determining Hitler's war aims is Norman Rich's *Hitler's War Aims: Ideology, the Nazi State, and the Course of Expansion* (New York: W.W. Norton, 1973). Rothwell broadens this view to include all of the major powers, including Germany, in *War Aims in the Second World War: The War Aims of the Major Belligerents, 1939–45* (Edinburgh: Edinburgh University Press, 2005).

6 Choosing Enemies: Japan Accepts the US Challenge for War, 1941

Gerhard L. Weinberg and H.P. Willmott again provide useful overviews of the war in *A World at Arms* (New York: Cambridge University Press, 1994), and *The Great Crusade* (New York: the Free Press, 1989). Japanese policy leading to war is covered in a wide range of books. Japanese determination to use military force to achieve economic self-sufficiency received comprehensive treatment in Michael A. Barnhart's *Japan Prepares for Total War* (Ithaca, NY: Cornell University Press, 1987). Stephen E. Pelz, in *Race to Pearl Harbor* (Cambridge, MA: Harvard University Press, 1974), focuses on the naval race as the key cause of war between Japan and the United States. Other useful looks at the Japanese decision for war include Sumio Hatano and Sadao Asada's essay, "The Japanese Decision to Move South," in *Paths to War* (London: Macmillan, 1989). A series of books entitled *Japan's Road to the Pacific War*, edited by James William Morley and based on the translation of Japanese scholarship, is also valuable, in particular the volume entitled, *The Fateful Choice: Japan's Advance into Southeast Asia, 1939–1941* (New York: Columbia University Press, 1980). Just as valuable is the study *Pearl Harbor as History: Japanese-American Relations, 1931–1941* (New York: Columbia University Press, 1973), edited by Dorothy Borg and Shumpei Okamoto. The deep roots of Japanese economic imperialism are the topic of W.G. Beasley's *Japanese Imperialism, 1894–1945* (Oxford: Clarendon Press, 1987). General Tojo's role is best covered in Robert J. C. Butow's *Tojo and the Coming of War* (Princeton, NJ: Princeton University Press, 1961). There are also useful insights into Japanese motives in *Threshold of War: Franklin D. Roosevelt and American Entry into World War II* (New York: Oxford University Press, 1988), by Waldo Heinrichs. Herbert Feis's *The Road to Pearl Harbor: The Coming of the War Between the United States and Japan* (Princeton, NJ: Princeton University Press, 1950), and Akira Iriye's *The Origins of the Second World War in Asia and the Pacific* (London: Longman, 1987), are two more important studies on this topic. Iriye also provides a useful compilation of documents in *Pearl Harbor and the Coming of the Pacific War: A Brief History with Documents and Essays* (Boston, MA: Bedford/St. Martin's, 1999).

7 The Soviet Monroe Doctrine: The Russo–Finnish Winter War of 1939

A number of writers examine the roots of this war, largely emphasizing the Finnish perspective. See Max Jakobson, *Finland Survived: An Account of the Finnish–Soviet Winter War, 1939–1940* (Helsinki: The Otava Publishing Company, 1961), and Anthony F. Upton, *Finland, 1939–1940* (Newark, NJ: University of Delaware Press, 1974). Väinö Tanner's *The Winter War: Finland Against Russia, 1939–1940* (Stanford, CA: Stanford University Press, 1950) does this same thing from the point of view of the former foreign minister of Finland during the war years. The war in a broader context is featured in several books, among them Leonard C. Lundin's *Finland in the Second World War* (Bloomington, IN: Indiana University Press, 1957), H.M. Tillotson's *Finland at Peace and War* (Wilby, Norwich: Michael Russell, 1996), and Olli Vehviläinen, *Finland in the Second World War: Between Germany and Russia* (New York: Palgrave, 2002), translated by Gerard McAlester. The Russian point of view is best captured in Carl Van Dyke's *The Soviet Invasion of Finland, 1939–1940* (London: Frank Cass, 1997). Allen F. Chew, in *The White Death: The Epic of the Soviet–Finnish Winter War* (East Lansing. MI: Michigan State University Press, 1971), and William R. Trotter, in *A Frozen Hell: The Russo–Finnish Winter War of 1939–1940* (Chapel Hill, NC: Algonquin Books of Chapel Hill, 1991), offer good accounts of the fighting. German motives in this theater of action are covered in Earl F. Ziemke's *The German Northern Theater of Operations, 1940–1945* (Washington, DC: US Government Printing Office, Department of the Army Pamphlet 20–271, 1959).

8 Fighting on Ground of its Own Choosing: The PRC Opts for War in Korea, 1950

The earliest treatment of Communist China's decision to enter the Korean War is Allen S. Whiting's *China Crosses the Yalu: The Decision to Enter the Korean War* (New York: Macmillan, 1960). Since that time, scholars have greatly complicated the picture and done so from multiple perspectives. The most comprehensive treatment from the point of view of the PRC is Chen Jian's *China's Road to the Korean War: The Making of the Sino–American Confrontation* (New York: Columbia University Press, 1994). For the American view, see William Stueck's account of the American role in the UN advance into North Korea in *The Road to Confrontation: American Policy Toward China and Korea, 1947–1950* (Chapel Hill, NC: University of North Carolina Press, 1981), and more specialized, James I. Matray's article, "Truman's Plan for Victory: National Self-Determination and the Thirty-Eighth Parallel Decision in Korea," *Journal of American History* 66, no. 2 (September 1979): 314–333. Other studies broaden the emphasis to include more Cold War context. Two books are particularly good in this regard, one being Shu Guang Zhang's *Deterrence and Strategic Culture: Chinese–American Confrontations, 1949–1958* (Ithaca, NY: Cornell University Press, 1992), the other again by Stueck, *The Korean War: An International History* (Princeton, NJ: Princeton University Press, 1995). Mao Zedong's role is best covered in a second book by Zhang, *Mao's Military Romanticism: China and the Korean War, 1950–1953* (Lawrence, KS: University Press of Kansas, 1995), and in a book written by Sergei Goncharov, John W. Lewis, and Xue Litai entitled, *Uncertain Partners: Stalin, Mao, and the Korean War* (Stanford, CA: Stanford University Press, 1993). Russell Spurr, in *Enter the Dragon: China's Undeclared War Against the US in Korea, 1950–1951* (New York: Newmarket Press, 1988), tracks some of the tensions present in the relationship between the PRC and North Korea early in the war. My master's thesis is the best treatment of the issue of trying to avoid war between the United States and the PRC due to a UN decision to stop at the waist of the peninsula. See Matthew J. Flynn, "The Decision to Cross the 38th Parallel" (master's thesis, San Diego State University, 1996).

9 Being Everywhere at Once: Israel Defeats the Arab League, 1967

The most recent treatment of the Six Day War is Tom Segev's *1967: Israel, the War, and the Year that Transformed the Middle East*, trans. Jessica Cohen (New York: Metropolitan Books, 2007). Books written in the immediate aftermath of the war include David Dayan, *Strike First! A Battle History of Israel's Six-Day War*, trans. Dov Ben-Abba (New York: Pitman Publishing, 1967), David Kimche and Dan Bawly, *The Sandstorm: The Arab–Israeli War of June 1967: Prelude and Aftermath* (New York: Stein and Day, 1968), and Walter Laqueur, *The Road to Jerusalem: The Origins of the Arab–Israeli Conflict, 1967* (New York: Macmillan, 1968). The Kimche and Laqueur works strive for objectivity, something that is lost for the most part in the numerous studies that have been written since 1968. See Jeremy Bowen's *Six Days: How the 1967 War Shaped the Middle East* (London: Simon & Schuster, 2003), Eric Hammel's *Six Days in June: How Israel Won the 1967 Arab–Israeli War* (New York: Charles Scribner's Sons, 1992), Donald Neff's *Warriors for Jerusalem: The Six Days that Changed the Middle East* (New York: Linden Press/Simon & Schuster, 1984), and Michael B. Oren's *Six Days of War: June 1967 and the Making of the Modern Middle East* (Oxford: Oxford University Press, 2002). The key role of the IDF is best covered in Martin Van Creveld, *The Sword and the Olive: A Critical History of the Israeli Defense Force* (New York: Public Affairs, 1998). The difficulty of determining Israel's success from the Six Day War is the subject of Colonel Trevor N. Dupuy's *Elusive Victory: The Arab–Israeli Wars, 1947–1974* (New York: Harper & Row, 1978), and George W. Gawrych's *The Albatross of Decisive Victory: War and Policy Between Egypt and Israel in the 1967 and 1973 Arab–Israeli War* (Westport, CT: Greenwood Press, 2000). A book edited by Ibrahim Abu-Lughod and entitled, *The Arab–Israeli Confrontation of June 1967: An Arab Perspective* (Evanston, IL: Northwestern University Press, 1970), is one of the few books in English offering the Arab point of view.

10 A Dangerous Simplicity: The American Preemptive War in Iraq, 2003

This chapter utilized primary sources as well as secondary literature.

For primary documentation, I drew on limited materials at the George Bush Library, College Station, Texas. See Presidential Records: White House Staff and Office Files, National Security Council, Richard Haass Files:

– Minutes for DC Meetings on Gulf [1 of 2] [OA/ID CF01585] 3 pages (2 are withdrawal)

- Minutes for DC Meetings on Gulf [2 of 2] [OA/ID CF01585] 4 pages (3 are withdrawal)
- NSC Meeting 4/30/91 Meeting 4/30/91 [OA/ID CF00873] 1 withdrawal sheet
- NSC/DC Meeting 5/21/91 Gulf Security [OA/ID CF00873] 1 withdrawal sheet
- NSC/DC Meeting 7/12/91 Iraq [OA/ID CF00873] 1 withdrawal sheet
- Iraq Working Files – March 1991 [1 of 2] [OA/ID CF01585] 17 pages
- Iraq Working Files – March 1991 [2 of 2] [OA/ID CF01585] 6 pages
- [Iraq] Working Files – April 1991 [1 of 2] [OA/ID CF01584] 31 pages
- [Iraq] Working Files – April 1991 [2 of 2] [OA/ID CF01584] 12 pages
- Iraq Working Files – May 1991 [1 of 2] [OA/ID CF01585] 22 pages
- Iraq Working Files – May 1991 [2 of 2] [OA/ID CF01585] 49 pages

A number of websites also provided documentation I utilized in this chapter. In addition to the US government's official websites for the White House, Congress, CIA, Department of State, and Department of Defense, individual Members of Congress listed documentation related to the Iraq War on their own websites. Most useful is Carl Levin's web page, http://levin.senate.gov/newsroom/release.cfm?id=236440.

A number of additional websites also made available documentation related to the 2003 Iraq War. The National Security Archive at George Washington University is an important source. See http://www.gwu.edu/~nsarchiv/. The CCNY Libraries Reference and Research page offers "Government Views of Iraq," a list striving to be comprehensive regarding US government releases of documentation related to the Iraq War. See http://www.ccny.cuny.edu/library/Divisions/Government/Iraqbib.html. The University of Michigan Documents Center offers "The Iraq War Debate—2002–2007." See http://www.lib.umich.edu/govdocs/iraqwar.html. Dartmouth College Library US Government Documents offers, "War with Iraq: Primary Sources Related to the War with Iraq." See http://www.dartmouth.edu/~govdocs/iraq.htm.

The Iraq War of 2003 already has generated an extensive literature. The origins of the war are the most extensively covered to this point. Justifications of a war in Iraq before the invasion came from Bush partisans such as Lawrence F. Kaplan and William Kristol, *The War in Iraq: Saddam's Tyranny and America's Mission* (San Francisco, CA: Encounter Books, 2003), and Kenneth M. Pollack, *The Threatening Storm: The Case for Invading Iraq* (New York: Random House, 2002). Journalists and analysts at think tanks who provided treatments of the origins of the war after it occurred are overwhelmingly critical of the decision to go to war in Iraq, and include James Bamford, *A Pretext for War: 9/11, Iraq, and the Abuse of America's*

Intelligence Agencies (New York: Doubleday, 2004), Ivo H. Daalder and James M. Lindsay, *America Unbound: The Bush Revolution in Foreign Policy* (Washington, DC: Brookings Institution Press, 2003), Todd S. Purdum, *A Time of Our Choosing: America's War in Iraq* (New York: Times Books, 2003), and Jeffrey Record, *Dark Victory: America's Second War Against Iraq* (Annapolis, MD: Naval Institute Press, 2004). Betty Glad and Chris J. Dolan, the editors of *Striking First: The Preventive War Doctrine and the Reshaping of US Foreign Policy* (New York: Palgrave Macmillan, 2004), focus this discussion of the administration's decisions for war in Iraq on the origins of the Bush doctrine of preemption. For a close examination of President George W. Bush and the Iraq War, including much about the origins of the war, see the three books by Bob Woodward, *Bush at War* (New York: Simon & Schuster, 2002), *Plan of Attack* (New York: Simon & Schuster, 2004), and *State of Denial* (New York: Simon & Schuster, 2006). The rise of the neo-conservatives to power is the topic of James Mann's *Rise of the Vulcans: The History of Bush's War Cabinet* (New York: Viking, 2004). The roles of other important figures such as George H.W. Bush, Vice President Richard Cheney, and Tommy Franks are examined in George Bush and Brent Scowcroft, *A World Transformed* (New York: Alfred A. Knopf, 1998), Ron Suskind, *The One Percent Doctrine: Deep Inside America's Pursuit of Its Enemies Since 9/11* (New York: Simon & Schuster, 2006), and Tommy Franks, *American Soldier: General Tommy Franks*, with Malcolm McConnell (New York: HarperCollins, 2004). To this point, the best military history that covers the origins of the war and the invasion is Michael R. Gordon and General Bernard E. Trainor, *Cobra II: The Inside Story of the Invasion and Occupation of Iraq* (New York: Pantheon Books, 2006). John Keegan's *The Iraq War* (New York: Alfred A. Knopf, 2004), and Williamson Murray and Robert H. Scales, Jr.'s *The Iraq War: A Military History* (Cambridge, MA: The Belknap Press of Harvard University Press, 2003) are limited studies but still useful. A picture of an inept reconstruction of Iraq appears in George Packer's *The Assassins' Gate: America in Iraq* (New York: Farrar, Straus and Giroux, 2005). The intelligence debate is best covered in Jessica T. Matthews, George Perkovich, and Joseph Cirincione, *WMD in Iraq: Evidence and Implications*, Carnegie Endowment for International Peace, January 2004, and John Prados, *Hoodwinked: The Documents that Reveal How Bush Sold Us a War* (New York: New York Press, 2004).

Index

Collateral Damage
Americans, Noncombatant Immunity, and Atrocity After World War II

"A valuable and timely contribution to examining one of the most serious and enduring dilemmas of the contemporary world."

Akira Iriye, author of *Global Community: The Role of International Organizations in the Making of the Contemporary World*

"An arresting and moving study, which demonstrates how hard it is, in modern warfare, for even the best-intentioned leaders to avoid barbarous cruelty to innocent civilians."

Ernest R. May, co-author of *Thinking in Time: The Uses of History for Decision-Makers*

"Sahr Conway-Lanz's *Collateral Damage* explores in an extraordinarily insightful manner the ways in which Americans in the Cold War era sought to reconcile the brutal nature of modern warfare with humane values. That alone would make it an important contribution to our understanding of modern international relations, but it has the added virtue of illuminating present day-concerns–a sure sign of historical writing at its finest."

Frank Ninkovich, author of *The Wilsonian Century: U.S. Foreign Policy since 1900*

"Collateral damage" is a military term for the inadvertent casualties and destruction inflicted on civilians in the course of military operations. In *Collateral Damage: Americans, Noncombatant Immunity, and Atrocity after World War II*, Sahr Conway-Lanz chronicles the history of America's attempt to reconcile the ideal of sparing civilians with the reality that modern warfare results in the killing of innocent people. Drawing on policymakers' responses to the issues raised by the atrocities of World War II and the use of the atomic bomb, as well as the ongoing debate by the American public and the media as the Korean War developed, Conway-Lanz provides a comprehensive examination of modern American discourse on the topic of civilian casualties and provides a fascinating look at the development of what is now commonly known as collateral damage.

ISBN 10: 0–415–97828–9 (hbk)
ISBN 10: 0–415–97829–7 (pbk)
ISBN 13: 978–0–415–97828–6 (hbk)
ISBN 13: 978–0–415–97829–3 (pbk)

The American Culture of War
A History of US Military Force from World War II to Operation Iraqi Freedom

"*The American Culture of War* is a first-rate study that asks big questions and provides answers that are of value to American and non-American scholars alike. It makes a major contribution to the developing cultural approach to military history."
Jeremy Black, author of *Introducing Military History*

"Lewis combines a powerful argument with a detailed critique of U.S. strategy since World War II as overly dependent on technology, and shows how these have eroded two traditional American moral concepts: the equal value of every human life and the universal civic responsibility to defend the country."
Dennis Showalter, author of *Patton and Rommel: Men Of War in the 20th Century*

"*The American Culture of War* is a striking and magisterial tour de force. Combining the hard-headed realism and moral indignation of a professional soldier with the keen analytical outlook of a trained historian, Adrian Lewis exposes the political in-fighting, intellectual follies, cultural arrogance, media ignorance, inter-service rivalries, and changes in the national mood that have repeatedly caused the United States to wage its most recent wars in ways that play to its weaknesses rather than its strengths. *The American Culture of War* should be mandatory reading for policy-makers, military leaders, students of military history, and all Americans with the slightest interest in national security."
Gregory J. W. Urwin, co-author of *The United States Infantry: An Illustrated History, 1775–1918*

The American Culture of War presents a sweeping critical examination of every major American war since 1941: World War II, Korea, Vietnam, and the First and Second Persian Gulf Wars. As he carefully considers the myriad cultural forces that surrounded each military engagement, Adrian R. Lewis offers an original, provocative look at the motives people and governments used to wage war, the discord among military personnel, the flawed political policies that guided military strategy, and the civilian perceptions that characterized each conflict. With each chapter similarly structured to allow the reader to draw parallels between the wars, Lewis deftly traces the evolution of U.S. military strategy since the Second World War. Timely, incisive, and comprehensive, *The American Culture of War* is a unique and invaluable survey of over sixty years of American military history.

ISBN 10: 0–415–97976–5 (hbk)
ISBN 10: 0–415–97975–7 (pbk)
ISBN 13: 978–0–415–97976–4 (hbk)
ISBN 13: 978–0–415–97975–7 (pbk)

Introduction to Global Military History
1750 to the Present Day

"Excellent. It integrates the land, sea and maritime aspects of conflict and strikes a reasonable balance between the context and the events of the history of war and conflict."
> Stanley Carpenter, Professor of Strategy and Policy, US Naval War College, Newport, Rhode Island

"An excellent stimulus to thought and to further study . . . very good on the theoretical underpinning of military history, the distinction between wars and battles and the necessity of examining strategy in the political context."
> Daniel Todman, Lecturer in Modern History, Queen Mary University of London

"The analysis is at a high level . . . an impressive book. The focus on Asia is a significant improvement over its competitors."
> Michael S. Neiberg, Professor of History, United States Airforce Academy

This lucid account of military developments around the modern world begins with the American War of Independence and the French Revolutionary Wars and continues chronologically to the latest conflicts in the 2000s. It combines global coverage with thought-provoking analysis dealing not only with the military aspects of conflict but also with the social, cultural, political and economic aspects and consequences of such conflict. By placing the familiar or known alongside the largely unknown, the reader is forced to reassess the standard grand narrative of military history that rests on assumptions of Western cultural and technological superiority. It will be essential reading for students in universities worldwide whether studying modern military history, modern world history, history and international relations, or war and society.

Specially designed to be user-friendly, *Introduction to Military History* offers:

- chapter introductions and conclusions to assist study and revision
- "voices of war" sourced extracts from the field of war
- case studies in each chapter to support the narrative and provoke discussion
- vivid engravings, plans, paintings and photos to bring the conflicts alive
- a 12-page color map section plus 21 other integrated maps
- annotated references from the latest publications in the field

Jeremy Black is Professor of History at the University of Exeter. He is a leading military historian whose books include *Rethinking Military History* (Routledge 2004), *World War Two: A Military History* (Routledge 2003), *European Warfare, 1494–1660* (Routledge 2002), *European Warfare, 1660–1815* (Routledge 1994), and *Why Wars Happen*. He is editor of the Routledge Warfare and History series and has lectured extensively in North America, Europe and Australasia.

ISBN 10: 0–415–35394–7 (hbk)
ISBN 10: 0–415–35395–5 (pbk)
ISBN 13: 978–0–415–35394–6 (hbk)
ISBN 13: 978–0–415–35395–3 (pbk)